THE SECRETARY'S
PORTABLE ANSWER BOOK

Other Books by the Authors

SAVVY SECS: Street Wise and Book Smart

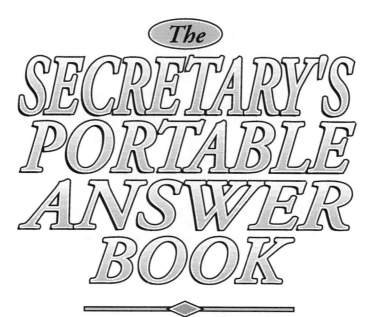

The SECRETARY'S PORTABLE ANSWER BOOK

Real-life answers to your toughest on-the-job questions in a handy Q & A format

PEGGY J. GRILLOT ◊ *LYNDA R. ABEGG*

PRENTICE HALL
Englewood Cliffs, New Jersey 07632

Prentice-Hall International (UK) Limited, *London*
Prentice-Hall of Australia Pty. Limited, *Sydney*
Prentice-Hall Canada, Inc., *Toronto*
Prentice-Hall Hispanoamericana, S.A., *Mexico*
Prentice-Hall of India Private Limited, *New Delhi*
Prentice-Hall of Japan, Inc., *Tokyo*
Simon & Schuster Asia Pte. Ltd., *Singapore*
Editora Prentice-Hall do Brasil, Ltda., *Rio de Janeiro*

10 9 8 7 6 5 4 3 2 1

Library of Congress Cataloging-in-Publication Data

Grillot, Peggy J.
    The secretary's portable answer book / by Peggy J. Grillot
and Lynda R. Abegg.
        p.   c.m.
    Includes index.
    ISBN 0-13-042466-8.—ISBN 0-13-042458-7 (pbk.)
    1. Office practice—Handbooks, manuals, etc.   2. Secretaries—
Handbooks, manuals, etc.   I. Abegg, Lynda R.   II. Title.
HF5547.5G74   1994   93-47896
651.3'74—dc20   CIP

ISBN 0-13-042466-8
       0-13-042458-7 (pbk)

PRENTICE HALL
Career and Personal Development
Englewood Cliffs, NJ 07632
Simon & Schuster, A Paramount Communications Company

Printed in the United States of America

About the Authors

PEGGY J. GRILLOT. The *Secretary's Portable Answer Book* is the second book about the uniqueness of a secretarial career Peggy and Lynda have co-authored.

Peggy began her career as a secretary in 1972 after graduating from Sawyer Business School and has held secretarial positions of varying responsibilities and duties ever since.

Peggy is currently BBS/PC Manager for the Society of Actuaries, a non-profit professional membership association. She joined the Society of Actuaries as a word processor after the birth of her son. She began working parttime in order to have more time to spend with her family, but it wasn't long until she had carved her niche and turned her part-time word-processing position into a full-time position.

Peggy lives in the northwest suburbs of Chicago with her husband, Harley, daughter, Logan, and son, Wade.

LYNDA R. ABEGG. Lynda's mother told her to "learn to type and you will always be able to find a job." Lynda took her mother's advice and, after graduating from Moser Secretarial School, discovered that secretarial work was more than just a job, it was a career.

In her twenty-five years as a secretary, she has worked for the mayor of a small southern town and the presidents of some of Chicago's best-known corporations. Currently, she is the administrative assistant to the CEO of a major real estate development company.

Lynda has served as president of a local chapter of the Business and Professional Women's club and is active in supporting women's issues. As a graduate of DePaul University in Chicago, she believes that learning is a life-long process.

Lynda and her husband, Bill, live in a Chicago suburb.

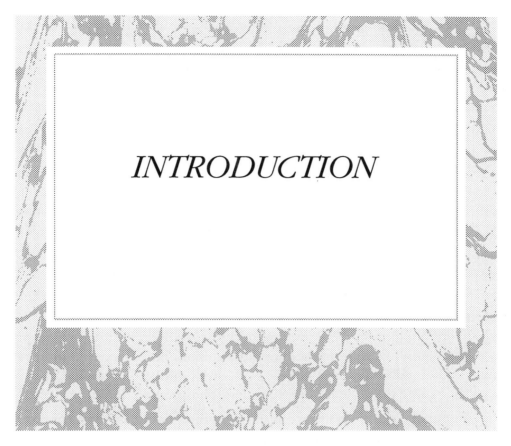

INTRODUCTION

With more than forty-five years of combined secretarial experience, we know there is a lot more to being a good secretary than typing, filing, and answering telephones. As a trained professional, you are expected to handle a wide range of tasks and responsibilities with accuracy, efficiency, and intelligence.

Computer technology has freed the secretary to take on a more administrative role than in the past. Using your word processor or computer, you can design and produce several spreadsheets in the time it used to take to type a letter. Today, your position requires you to be a highly skilled problem solver, decision maker, and communicator. Your ability to set priorities is just as important as is how fast you can type and file; your skill at managing conflicts is as important as how well you handle telephone inquiries. Your knowledge of company operations and procedures is critical as you make decisions with—and sometimes for—your boss on a regular basis.

As your boss's right arm, you are in a unique position of power. If your boss has confidence in your abilities, he or she will depend on you, respect your opinions, and even seek your advice. Your relationship will be a true partnership, based on hard work, mutual respect, and trust. Your boss will consider you an indispensable contributor to his or her success, and, in turn, can help pave the way for your own success by giving you the opportunity to take on more and more high-level responsibilities.

To be an outstanding secretary, you must first assess your own skills and talents, then you must identify your boss's strengths and weaknesses. Ask yourself these questions: What do I do best? What do I enjoy doing? What path do I want my career to take? Does my boss do some things very well, while allowing other areas to suffer? Is my boss good at closing deals, but not good at following up with the proper paperwork? By evaluating your particular situation, you will be able to tailor your job to meet your boss's needs as well as your own and create the kind of teamwork that exists in the best secretary-boss relationships.

The *Secretary's Portable Answer Book* will show you, through familiar situations and an easy-to-follow question-and-answer format, how to master every aspect of your job from creating complicated documents to planning and coordinating meetings to protecting company "secrets." The tips and techniques provided in the book will help you to strengthen your work relationships, streamline office procedures, identify opportunities, and respond to challenges with confidence. You will learn how to be an effective administrator with all the skills necessary to continually grow and succeed in your current position and beyond.

CONTENTS

CHAPTER TWO
◆
Mastering the Art of Communciation 15

CHAPTER THREE
◆
Developing Your Problem-Solving and Decision-Making Skills 43

CHAPTER FOUR

Protecting Company "Secrets" 57

CHAPTER FIVE

Winning at Office Politics 69

CHAPTER SIX

Managing Office Conflicts 85

CHAPTER SEVEN

Getting Organized for Success 107

CHAPTER EIGHT

Working Smarter 139

CHAPTER NINE

Creating the Perfect Document 155

CHAPTER TEN

◆

Sharpening Your Language and Math Skills 177

CHAPTER ELEVEN

◆

When You Are the Boss 205

CHAPTER TWELVE

◇

On-The-Job Legal Issues 221

CHAPTER THIRTEEN

◇

Business Etiquette 243

◆

CHAPTER FOURTEEN

How to Keep Your Personal Life and Your Professional Life from Colliding 257

◆

Controlling Job-Related Health Problems 271

APPENDIX

◆

Paving the Way for Success 291

INDEX

◆

323

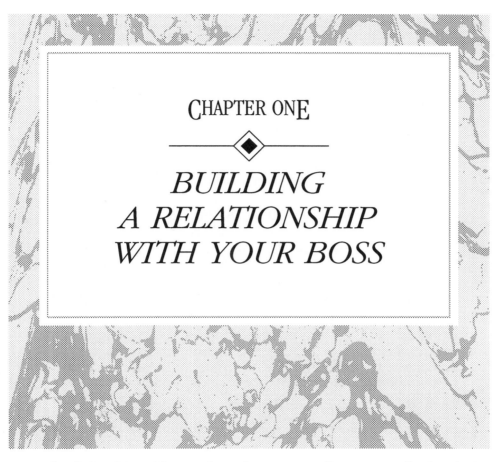

CHAPTER ONE

◆

BUILDING A RELATIONSHIP WITH YOUR BOSS

A good relationship with your boss is necessary for your professional survival. It is critical to your job satisfaction and your general happiness at work, and it often plays a major role in determining job advancement within the company

A successful relationship with your boss develops from a number of factors. You must, of course, be highly skilled and efficient at job-related tasks, but you must also be a good communicator and possess the personal traits that will enable you and your boss to develop rapport and mutual respect.

When you walk through that door every morning, you leave your personal baggage at home and become a team player, one whose primary focus is to act in unison with your boss. The energy level of two people who work in unison is much greater than two forces working in opposition.

Remember: Your boss is one of the most important people in your life. You spend at least eight hours a day with him or her, which is more waking time than you spend with your family. It is well worth your time and effort to make sure this relationship works.

1-1

WHAT YOUR BOSS EXPECTS FROM YOU

What do most bosses expect from their secretaries?

Bosses depend on their secretaries to handle office tasks with ease, to respond to correspondence, to file, to set up conferences, to supervise staff, to coordinate meetings, and to arrange travel. But most important, bosses depend on their secretaries to exercise good judgment, to remain in control under pressure, and to be a "keeper of secrets," someone who is entrusted with confidential documents, salary data, and personnel information. Today's secretaries are well educated, self-assured, and valued for their productivity, reliability, trustworthiness, and professionalism.

Secretaries, now often referred to as administrative or executive assistants, are considered professionals, on a desired career path, and their status and power are known.

My new boss demands so much more of me. My old boss was pretty easygoing and would do a lot of things for himself, such as pulling a file or calling another manager for some information. I really thought I was doing a good job before, but now I feel so incompetent. How can I get myself in sync with my boss?

You've already made progress by recognizing that with each boss comes his or her own operating style. Some are more self-reliant than others. Since your new boss expects you to handle more duties, follow the lead and take charge. This means fielding unwanted phone calls and unnecessary interruptions. Whenever possible, draft responses to letters. And don't forget to ask if there's anything else you can do to help. You'll soon find yourself thinking like your new boss.

My boss is unfriendly. His aloofness makes me uncomfortable and I am unable to do my best work. How can I encourage a more friendly relationship without seeming pushy or unprofessional?

Is your boss really unfriendly or just pressed for time and with a lot on his mind? Try to get him to open up when he seems more relaxed, maybe first thing, before the phones start ringing or late in the day, when everybody seems to be winding down. Don't try to have a chatty conversation with him when he needs to return five phone calls and is late for his ten o'clock appointment. To break the ice, ask office questions, such as, "Anything new on the schedule for today or tomorrow that I need to be aware of?" or tell him something, "I thought you'd be interested in knowing that the marketing managers' meeting scheduled for Thursday has been moved to Wednesday at ten o'clock." It's through communication that your boss will open up.

I work for two very busy people and I often have difficulty dividing my time so I can meet the needs of each one. I want to maintain a good relationship with both of my bosses, but one or the other is usually annoyed at me for not spending enough time on his or her work. What can I do to make myself available to both of them when they need me?

Devise a system to evenly divide your time. For example, you might plan to work mornings on Ms. Robert's correspondence and afternoons on Mr. Walter's projects. Also explain that the schedule needs to be flexible enough to accommodate hot projects for either of them. Then keep a log of your time. It's hard for your bosses to argue with numbers. If one seems annoyed that you're working on a hot project for the other one, you can politely remind her that you shifted gears last week to work on her marketing plan (or vice versa). And you'll have your log to back it up.

My new boss doesn't tell me anything. Since my old boss was quick to share information with me, I'm having a hard time adjusting. I really don't understand Mr. Williams at all.

Maybe he's in a learning phase and doesn't have all the answers, in which case you need to learn with him. The other side of the coin is that to some, knowledge is power. In order to protect their power base, they must safeguard all information. Try sharing your information with him. If he recognizes that you are both working on the same team, with each other and not against each other, he may open up. In the meantime, to stay current, ask your friends to keep you informed of any departmental memos or office workings.

How can I make the most of my new position? I just started working for the vice president of marketing and want to make sure we start off on the right foot.

As you get to know your boss better, analyze her strengths and weaknesses to see where you can complement her. Take charge of those areas where your strengths lie. Mentally note any areas in which you both are weak, such as making follow-up calls on a timely basis. Then devise a system to minimize any weaknesses, such as setting aside a certain time to make return phone calls. Building a good working relationship with your boss requires team work.

1-2
PRESCRIPTIONS FOR YOUR BOSS'S "LASTMINUTEITIS"

Many bosses suffer from a disease called "lastminuteitis," and it quickly becomes your problem. While you probably can't change the situation completely, you can control it more effectively by planning ahead.

My boss never decides whether he will take a business trip until the day before he is to leave. I have to make plane reservations at the last minute, which makes the tickets more costly than if the reservations were made in advance. Often I cannot get reservations at the preferred hotel and spend time trying to locate one close to the meeting site. My boss leaves with a bad attitude and I feel somehow to blame. What can I do?

The first step is to prepare a four-week rolling planner for your boss. Place the four-week planner on a hot-spot on his desk—near the telephone, perhaps. It should list all meetings and appointments for the next four weeks. You can also add conventions, committee meetings, any possible trips in bold lettering. Some computer-generated calendar programs will even print a small picture of a plane in the square, indicating travel.

Plan ahead by asking your boss, for example, if he plans to attend the committee meeting in Chicago. If he isn't sure, go ahead and make hotel and plane reservations. Just don't order any nonrefundable tickets. You can always cancel them later. In the long run, it will save you time and your company money. Your boss will get preferred hotel accommodations and flight times. See Chapter 7, Getting Organized for Success, for more planning tips.

Four-Week Rolling Planner

	SUNDAY	MONDAY	TUESDAY	WEDNESDAY	THURSDAY	FRIDAY	SATURDAY
WEEK 1			Quarterly meeting—Denver		Lunch with Mr. Smith 12:30		
WEEK 2							
WEEK 3	Board meeting		Conference call with Allied Corp. 2:30		Committee meeting, Chicago		
WEEK 4				Staff meeting 10:00			

My boss waited until the last minute to invite Ms. Petry to her meeting. I'm sure she was secretly hoping she couldn't attend. Ms. Petry's secretary then chewed me out, but it really wasn't my fault. Should I say anything?

Tell your boss what happened. Make a note of the type of meeting she was invited to. If in the future your boss calls another such meeting, ask her upfront if Ms. Petry should be invited.

My boss always calls meetings at the last minute. She serves on several different committees, and trying to get everyone together for a meeting can consume an entire morning. Some days I feel as if I am just spinning my wheels. Is there any way I can streamline scheduling meetings?

Prepare a meeting sheet for each committee or board meeting on which your boss serves. List each attendee's name, phone or pager number, fax number, secretary's name, and a column for a preferred date and an alternate date for a particular meeting. One secretary saves time by faxing the sheet to all attendees and waiting for the responses. Another secretary has found that with the meeting sheet, she can delegate the actual calling to a junior secretary, a temporary, or even the receptionist.

Task Force Committee

MEMBERS	PHONE	FAX	PREFERRED DATE	ALTERNATE DATE	NOTES
JOHN SMITH	555-8970	555-8971	5-2 morning	5-4 afternoon	Must know meeting date asap
EVA MURRAY	(708)xxx-xxxx	(708)xxx-xxxx	5-2 all day	5-3 all day	Rest of week is bad
DOLLY NELSON	(312)xxx-xxxx Pager (312)xxx-xxxx	(312)xxx-xxxx	5-4 afternoon		May not be able to reschedule 5/2 travel; out of office 5/1; use pager no.
LARRY SUMMERS	555-xxxx	555-xxxx	not available		On vacation; back the following Monday

My boss is habitually late preparing materials for meetings. I can sit all morning with little to do and suddenly at 2:30 P.M. she expects me to type a report with spreadsheets for a 3:30 meeting. Because of the time crunch, my work is sometimes sloppy and contains typos, which makes me look bad. Is there anything I can do to change her behavior?

Obviously your boss has come to depend on your skills and ability to work under pressure. Even though the job is getting done, you should tell her that it could be done much better if you had more lead time. From now on, the two of you should go over her daily schedule each morning so that you can determine what materials and information she needs for any newly scheduled meeting. Then prepare a project list with due dates to ensure that you will get the information in time to prepare it properly.

Daily Schedule

TUESDAY, MARCH 12

10:00 A.M.   Sales meeting with regional managers

Information needed:

- Sales figures for week/month/year-to-date

- Sales by unit for each region

- Dollar sales by unit for each region

Note: Possibility meeting will begin at 9:30 A.M.

Now that you know what your boss needs:

- ◆ Contact the person in the finance department responsible for gathering this information and work with her to get it at least three days prior to the meeting date.

- ◆ Since your boss has to prepare a summary of this information detailing strengths and weaknesses, along with projections for sales for the next quarter, ask her to dictate or write out some notes so that you can begin inputting the information in your word processor.

My boss can't seem to get caught up and is currently running about a month behind schedule on some projects. Because of this, she doesn't want to know about current due dates until they're past. She closes her door and I catch all the heat. I'm ready to ask for a transfer.

You could try talking to your boss. Offer your services to get her caught up. This may involve coming in early, staying late, or working on the weekends. Discuss the fact that the stress level is too high for you. However, you might be working for a person who thrives on adrenaline, one who is not motivated to act until the situation is in a crisis mode. If that's the case, she probably will not accept your offer to get her on track. If the situation continues or deteriorates, the job transfer you initially considered may be the answer.

1-3

1-3
TIPS FOR RELIEVING "UNDER THE GUN" STRESS

When your boss is under the gun, so are you. There are effective ways to deal with this kind of pressure so that it doesn't affect your productivity or your boss's.

My job often requires last-minute revisions to documents. I understood this when I took the job and that is not the problem. However, my boss stands over my shoulder watching me make each change, or she will pace up and down very nervously while I input the changes. This makes me more nervous. I told her, jokingly, that she made me nervous but nothing's changed. How can I make her understand that if she will leave or go back into her office, I can make the changes much more quickly and accurately?

Tell your boss that she makes you nervous and that you will bring the revisions in as soon as they are completed. If she still hangs around and paces, tell her now is a good time to return someone's call (then get them on the line so you can work in peace). Give her an assignment, such as asking her to go through today's mail. Or send her on an errand to run some copies or get a cup of coffee. Be inventive.

My boss has to make a presentation to the board of directors in two days. He's been gathering data and working on the presentation for months. He is nervous and frazzled. I feel there *must* be something I can do to relieve some of his tension.

There are several ways you can reduce tension and help your frazzled boss.

- ◆ Close his door.

- ◆ Hold his phone calls unless urgent, so he can rehearse his presentation without interruption.

- ◆ Take messages from people who need to see or talk to him and let him return their calls or answer their questions when it is convenient for him.

- ◆ Ask him if there are any last-minute materials he needs, such as presentation folders which will be distributed, etc., and make sure they're available. Check your supplies and make sure you have all the items you need, even if it means placing an additional office-supply order with rush delivery.

◆ Gather sufficient copies of any brochures, information packets, or single handouts to be distributed during your boss's presentation. Photocopy all materials in advance and always be sure to have a few extras for last-minute attendees.

◆ Encourage your boss to give you any notes or information you can input into your word processor. He may find it easier to fine-tune his presentation by working from typed copy.

◆ Ask him if he would like you to order lunch so that he can eat in the privacy of his office while he prepares the presentation.

1-4

KEEPING TRACK OF YOUR BOSS'S DEADLINES AND SCHEDULES

One of the most important parts of your job is keeping on top of your boss's deadlines and schedules. She needs to know that you will remind her of upcoming meetings and deadlines and that you will make sure she has all the information and materials needed to do her job efficiently and effectively. Remember: A good secretary is her boss's "right arm" and will anticipate her needs and try to avoid potential problems.

My boss knew the sales report would be used as a handout at the board meeting, but he forgot to tell me, so the report had not been updated. At the last minute, I was able to update the figures and photocopy the report. Now I'm keeping my fingers crossed that I didn't transpose any numbers. How can I make sure this doesn't happen again?

Give your boss's memory a gentle nudge. If possible, on a weekly basis, question him about what will be needed at upcoming meetings and if he has heard about any changes in meeting dates. Suggest that he carry a pocket calendar or notebook with him *at all times*. Have him log any verbal deadlines. For example, he might be talking with the vice president who mentions that all sales figures will be needed by next Friday to prepare an interim marketing report. If the notebook just doesn't seem to work, perhaps a quick phone call from your boss asking you to jot this date or deadline on the departmental calendar would be more effective. Your boss could also use voice mail to leave you a message regarding a schedule change.

If you have to keep track of a large number of deadlines, a more sophisticated process might be needed. Read on for additional suggestions.

My boss just missed another deadline. His boss is not happy with him and he is not happy with me. There are so many deadlines that it's hard for me to keep track of them all. Are there any simple techniques for making sure that I don't miss any more of my boss's deadlines?

Set up a tickler file. You can either do it manually using index cards or expanding file folders, or you can use computer-generated tickler programs.

The *index card file* is simple to set up and use; just follow these steps:

- ◆ On a 3" x 5" card, type the deadline date in one corner. The cards will be filed by date. List the information due or the name or title of the file your boss needs to respond to on the card, as shown.

- ◆ You will need two sets of card-file dividers. One set should be numbered from 1 to 31. The second set should be organized by month. The numbered files are in front and always represent the current month. Simply drop the information card under the date it is due. For example, on the morning of the tenth, you look under "10" and pull out the card. It will tell you what is due. You can remind your boss or get the information necessary.

- ◆ Sometimes the tickler is just a reminder to write a letter that goes out quarterly or it may be that you are expecting a reply to a letter and if you have not received it, you can give the appropriate person a call.

If you have information that is not due for several months, you can file that card in the back under the month in which it is due. Each month you file the current cards under the appropriate date.

An *expanding file folder* also makes an excellent tickler file. If you prefer to use this system, follow these steps:

- ◆ Get a numerical expanding file folder. Make a copy of the original letter or request you're filing and put it under the date on which it is due. If you're dealing with a large document, just put a copy of the cover

---

Sample Card for Current Month

10

- ◆ sales information by region due to accounting by the 13th
- ◆ response written to Gordon proposal regarding opening up two new branch offices? due the 15th
- ◆ make travel plans for board meeting on the 20th

---

letter in the tickler file. Make sure all original material is filed in its proper place after you've put your copies in the tickler.

- ◆ If you have material that may not be due for several months, you can file it in the back of the folder, and at the beginning of each month you can sort through that material and place it under the proper deadline date.

Software calendar programs for your computer can be set up as ticklers. Here's how they work:

First, select a date. Second, decide whether an automatic alarm is needed. If this option is activated, your computer when turned on will trigger an automatic reminder. This will be in the form of an alarm that sounds when you boot up, or a message that flashes across your screen. You can also set the time for the alarm. If you've selected a time for a meeting, for example, the alarm won't sound until then rather than when the computer boots up. Think of it as your office alarm clock.

Calendar programs work even if the alarm feature is not activated. Just use it as your computerized appointment book, logging in meetings, conference calls, report deadlines, luncheon engagements, or vacation dates. Schedules can be checked and updated daily, weekly, or monthly. A hard copy can be printed and posted in a prominent place.

When selecting a calendar program, be sure to check all the features provided against what you need, as well as compatibility with your current word processing software. Use our software checklist in Chapter 9, Creating the Perfect Document. Read on for more information about software calendar programs.

I have set up a great tickler system. The only problem is that I forget to check it. Sometimes when I come in, the phones are ringing, my boss wants a file, and before I know it, the whole day has passed and I missed a deadline because I didn't check it. Help!

Ticklers are very simple systems, but in order for them to work, you must faithfully check your tickler file every morning. Keep it in a prominent place on top of your desk. Then make checking the tickler file a part of your daily routine. When you come in, take off your coat, turn on your computer, get that cup of coffee, and check your tickler.

My boss has a heavy meeting and appointment schedule and I often have to switch dates and times. My calendar is a mess from all the erasures. Sometimes I get confused as to which meetings I have changed on my boss's calendar, and he recently missed an appointment because I forgot to make one of the changes. How can I get this scheduling problem under control?

Purchase a calendar program for your computer. You can make changes easily. Instead of erasing your boss's calendar, you can substitute a whole day, week, or month. It's easy to tell which calendar is the latest version as the date the document is printed appears on the bottom of the page.

If your boss attends a meeting every Monday at 10:00 A.M., for example, the calendar can be programmed to automatically enter that meeting for the whole year, with the touch of just one key. Special dates, such as birthdays or anniversaries, will appear automatically on subsequent years. Graphics add a nice touch. Tiny airplanes indicate travel. Gavels indicate board meetings.

I work for three salespeople, and keeping up with their travel schedules and appointments is time consuming. Will a computer calendar program help me?

Sure. You can enter any number of calendars into the program. Just name them Salesperson #1, Salesperson #2, and Salesperson #3. It's easy to access each calendar to enter appointments and deadlines. Each calendar can carry a personalized header, so there won't be any confusion as to which calendar belongs to whom. Color code each calendar so that they will be easily recognizable in a sea of white paper. Computers are great organizers, and calendar programs will make you a model of efficiency.

```
┌─────────────────────────────────────────────────────────┐
│░░░░░░░░░░░░░░░░░░░░░░░░░░░░░░░░░░░░░░░░░░░░░░░░░░░░░░░░░░░░░│
│            Letter Marked for the Tickler File            │
│░░░░░░░░░░░░░░░░░░░░░░░░░░░░░░░░░░░░░░░░░░░░░░░░░░░░░░░░░░░░░│
│                                                          │
│                                         12  T  10        │
│                                                          │
│       ───────────                                        │
│       ───────────                                        │
│                                                          │
│                                                          │
│       ──────────────────────────                        │
│       ──────────────────────────                        │
│       ──────────────────────────                        │
│       ──────────────────────────                        │
│                                                          │
│                                                          │
│       ───────────                                        │
│       ───────────                                        │
│                                                          │
└─────────────────────────────────────────────────────────┘
```

When my boss gets a letter requesting information by a certain date, I want to let him know that I have noted when the information is due or the date of the meeting. How can I let him know I am on top of things?

Whenever a letter comes in with a deadline or a meeting your boss needs to attend, simply put a *T* for "tickler" in the corner with the date, as shown in the illustration—month on the left, day on the right—and your boss will know you have tickled it for that date. He'll be pleased that you are on top of everything and he won't have to take the time to tell you what to do. It's already done.

1-5

HOW TO DEAL WITH A CHANGE IN YOUR BOSS'S BEHAVIOR

My boss has changed. He is no longer friendly to me and often appears curt and frustrated. I try to ignore his moodiness, but now my self-confidence is beginning to erode. Should I talk to him? And if so, what should I say?

If his moodiness has just appeared, you might want to wait it out. It could be caused by additional work or home pressures. However, if his moodiness has been going on for a while, confront him. Tell him you noticed that he has not been his usual self. Ask him if there is something you are doing that perhaps he would like done differently. Give him a chance to open up. If he chooses, he will tell you what's going on. If not, assume it is personal, perhaps some type of family problem, and let it go. Don't let his mood further erode your self-confidence.

I have a boss who's married and has children. In the past, she's been very sympathetic when I've had to take off because my children were sick. However, last week when my children had a day off from school, I called in to take a vacation day. The next day, she was rather cool and let me know that she was less than pleased with my behavior. I thought a woman would be more understanding of the plight of a working mother. Why did she react this way?

The lack of advance notice probably upset her day's schedule. School holidays are known in advance, published and listed on the school calendar. Unless you had a legitimate excuse for waiting until the last minute to take a vacation day, you showed poor judgment. To get yourself back in her good graces, apologize to her, then take a few minutes out to plan ahead for school holidays, spring break, or summer vacation. Put any days you plan to take off on your boss's calendar so she knows you will be out.

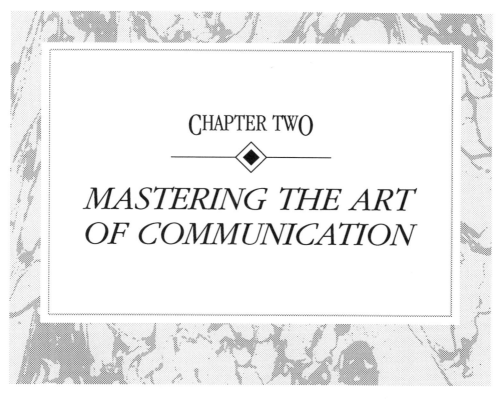

CHAPTER TWO

◆

MASTERING THE ART OF COMMUNICATION

Successful secretaries have exceptional communication skills. A top-notch secretary is expected to represent the boss in various capacities and situations: in writing, on the telephone, in person, on a one-to-one basis, in both small and large groups. In order to meet your boss's needs, you must be able to effectively communicate with people at all levels, at all times, in all ways.

Good communications skills are also critical to your own professional development. They convey confidence, intelligence, leadership, and professionalism. If you can convey your thoughts, ideas, plans, and wishes in both written and verbal communication to your boss, coworkers, and customers, you will become a respected member of the team.

2-1
HOW TO ASK FOR A RAISE

My boss keeps giving me more and more work. I'm flattered that he thinks I can handle it, but on the other hand, I think I deserve a raise. I tried to bring up the subject, but I could tell he was uncomfortable. How can I get him to listen to me?

Some bosses have trouble discussing personnel issues, whether performance related or money related. The first thing to do is to make your boss comfortable discussing the subject; don't surprise him with an announcement a half hour before he leaves for lunch. Write a memo to let him know you want to discuss your performance. Then, rewrite your position description to more accurately describe the work you are actually performing.

Add any new duties or achievements to the job description in italics so that your boss can easily see exactly what you have accomplished.

Once your boss has a chance to review the material, he will be more comfortable discussing it. Keep it businesslike and professional. Don't discuss what other secretaries are being paid; keep focused on your accomplishments. This might also be a good time to set some goals. If you want to take on more responsibility, for instance, add another paragraph to the letter detailing additional work you could do or improvements you could make.

Job Description Update Request

DATE   Month/Day/Year

TO: Bill

RE: Job Description

Because my position has grown and diversified over the past few years and my duties have expanded, I have drafted a job description for my current position. I feel this job description better identifies my contributions to your office as well as to XYZ Corporation.

I have continued to improve my knowledge of business issues by taking continuing education classes at (name of school).

Please review the attached so that we may discuss next week.

Updated Job Description

EXECUTIVE SECRETARY TO PRESIDENT

QUALIFICATIONS

- Five or more years of administrative secretarial experience.
- Strong communication skills.
- Secretarial or Associate's degree preferred.
- Ability to communicate effectively with all levels of personnel.
- Professional attitude and appearance required.

DESCRIPTION

Provide administrative support to the president to insure a smooth-running efficient office environment. Assure effective communication between the president's office and the operating groups.

SKILLS

Proficient in word-processing software.
Efficient operation of spreadsheet program.

DUTIES

- Prepare correspondence for president's signature.
- Prioritize and monitor multiple tasks.
- Coordinate board meetings, staff meetings, and outside business meetings to prevent scheduling conflicts.
- Arrange business travel, off-site meetings. Make scheduling/meeting decisions.
- *Arranged Asset Management meeting (250 attendees).*
- Work independently, with little supervision.
- *Supervise and coordinate secretarial staff, receptionist, and facilities personnel on 31st floor.*
- Maintain confidential material/files/correspondence.
- Create spreadsheets/financial reports.
- *Set up new subsidiary accounting records.*

HANDLING YOUR BOSS'S CORRESPONDENCE

My boss said she wants me to handle more of her correspondence on my own. I'm flattered but confused. I don't know how she would answer some of her correspondence. What should I do?

After you open the mail, go into her office and let her give you some quick guidelines. For instance, you have a letter requesting a bulk discount on a new product. Ask your boss if she wants to give the discount and if so, how much. This way you can draft a letter using her guidelines.

If you are unsure of how to reply to a letter or memo asking your boss to attend a meeting or speak at a seminar, write the words "accept or regret?" across the top of the letter. Your boss can then indicate how you should reply.

If your boss is not available and you are not sure how she would reply, prepare two responses and see which one she signs. This is a great opportunity to learn how your boss thinks. Don't be afraid to discuss certain requests with her and ask her why she was interested in one, but not the other.

My boss gets a lot of letters from salespeople. Can I just write them and say "No, we're not interested"? That is his standard answer anyway.

If your boss gets a lot of requests from companies trying to interest him in purchasing from them, prepare a standard rejection letter. When a request comes in, type the rejection letter and put it in your boss's signature folder with the original request. He can read the request and sign the letter or he may ask you to write a letter indicating his interest.

My boss has asked me to type a memo to all employees stating that no one can leave early the day before a holiday unless they take vacation time. How can I write a memo that will not get everyone in the office upset? Last month she asked me to type a memo stating that we cannot smoke in the lunchroom anymore. People are still mad about that one.

Delivering negative news requires a certain finesse. The example on page 19 is straightforward without being overtly negative.

This letter makes no demands but explains the reason it is necessary that the office be properly staffed during the holiday season. It also states that management understands that people want to leave early because they are having guests, etc., but requests that employees cooperate by planning ahead and requesting vacation time for absences.

Holiday Leave Memo

Date: Month/Day/Year

To: Office Staff

Re: Holiday Leave

In order to staff our office adequately during holidays, employees will no longer be allowed to leave early before a holiday. We understand that many people are expecting guests or planning travel during this time and would like to leave early. Please check with your supervisor to see whether it is possible to schedule vacation time either before or after the holiday. This will allow for proper scheduling and planning so that our company will be able to function in an effective manner.

Judith Lentz
Vice President, Human Resources

I have a problem getting the Accounting Department to cooperate whenever I request financial information. My boss is friends with the person in charge of the Accounting Department and I don't want it to look as if I am bad-mouthing his friend or trying to discredit him. What is the best way to handle this problem?

When discussing problems with your boss, the first rule is to keep it impersonal. Choose a good time, not when your boss is busy with other issues. Plan what you want to say and state your intention, "I am concerned about some problems I've encountered with Accounting and would like to discuss them with you." Don't whine, evade, or beat around the bush. Be straightforward, calm, and stay focused on the problem (not personalities). Communicate the successful aspects of working with Accounting, and ask how your boss would like you to proceed.

2-3

WRITING MEMOS AND REPORTS

My job requires that I gather operating information from my boss's staff each month. Certain staff members never seem to have the information

---

Reminder Notice

REMINDER—

Agenda items for the monthly management committee meeting should be received by Nancy no later than the tenth of the month.

Carol Wright

---

ready on time and keep putting me off. I finally receive the information at the last minute and end up working late to finish my report on time. What can I do to make the staff more responsive to my requests?

Put your request in writing. Send a reminder notice, signed by your boss, to each staff member approximately five days before the information is due.

I've sent out reminder notices until I'm blue in the face, but nobody ever pays them any attention. At the last minute I still end up phoning people to get the data. It just seems no one wants to cooperate with me. What can I do to get coworkers to respond?

A reminder notice confirming the deadline will not always make the information magically appear on your desk, but it does establish expectations. If you are still experiencing difficulties, try the following:

Highlight the date or any important change from the last meeting. When people receive mail on a routine basis, they often neglect to read it.

Use a different color paper, green or blue, for instance, to make it stand out.

Use humor, perhaps a graphic or a cartoon, to get their attention.

Ask to meet with the department head in order to outline the procedures and the requirements. Explain why you need the information by a certain date: *If you want the funding approved, I have to get the project data assembled for review by the committee by March 15, otherwise, it won't get funded for another month.*

If the staff member travels a lot or is often unavailable, ask for the name of a designated backup to be responsible for gathering the data. Then develop a working relationship with this person.

If your company has electronic mail, send the reminder via computer.

Frequently, I send a written request asking someone to approve an expense or the purchase of an item. He or she will give my boss verbal approval, ignoring my memo. When the expense comes in I have no record and have to resend my original memo to get the approval signature. I feel as if I'm just spinning my wheels and wasting a lot of time. Is there a way I can get this approval the first time?

When you write the original request asking for an approval, place a signature line and date approved at the bottom of the letter. Not only are you more likely to get a quick return but everything is on one piece of paper. For simple requests, this type of memo works well.

My boss wants me to draft reports on projects for his review. I have an idea of what he wants me to do, but I am unsure of how to express it or how to begin. Is there an outline I could follow?

When preparing to write a letter or memo, first identify the reader or the person who will take action upon reading the memo. Then state the subject

Approval Request

Date: Month/Day/Year

To: Martin Bradley

From: Linda Murray

Re: Approval for Mobile Phone

Please approve the purchase of a mobile phone for Janet Grillot who has just been promoted to handle the Midwest Regional Sales Office. She will travel between Chicago and our field offices in the Midwest and a mobile phone is necessary so that she can be in touch with the office at all times.

Thank you.

LM/la

Approved:

_____   Date: _____
Martin Bradley, CFO

of the memo on one line, as shown, or in the first paragraph at the beginning of the document. Remember to include any costs involved and, most
important, the benefits.

**My boss gives me handwritten reports on yellow legal paper. He doesn't
underline or use bullets or any of the markings I think make a letter or
report attractive and easy to read. Is it all right if I add some graphics?**

Report Outline

Date: Month/Day/Year

To: List names of people who should get the report.

From: Rosemary Gregory

Re: State the subject of the report.

FIRST PARAGRAPH

A brief description or summary.

SECOND PARAGRAPH

Historical background or statement of how the problem

is affecting the company, e.g., finances.

THIRD PARAGRAPH

Your findings or assumptions.

FOURTH PARAGRAPH

Your recommendations.

FIFTH PARAGRAPH

Request for approval of the plan or project.

It is important to send copies of this document to appropriate people or departments
so they are aware of your recommendations and can respond with any questions
and/or objections.

Most bosses will appreciate if you take the time to make their memos and reports visually appealing. Using stylistic devices such as bullets, underlines, headings, and capitals also helps to focus the reader's attention. Add the graphics and make editing changes if you feel they are necessary. He may be the expert in his field, but you are the expert in document preparation.

2-4

TAKING MINUTES AT A MEETING

Next month I'm required to take minutes at a meeting. I'm not sure just what is expected of me.

Find out what being the recorder entails. Does your boss expect a synopsis of the entire meeting, with only a brief sentence or two on certain areas? Or will your boss be looking for background discussion leading up to the final resolution?

If she is looking for the entire discussion to be transcribed, be fore-warned that the dialogue will be fast. Have a tape recorder available to catch all the discussion and eliminate any arguments about who said what. Use your shorthand to jot down important notes.

Familiarize yourself with *Robert's Rules of Order* (available in bookstores). Whenever a motion is made, get the exact wording, even if you have to ask the person to repeat a word or phrase. Note who made the motion, who seconded it, and the exact vote.

If a person wants to make a statement "off the record" it is not to be recorded as part of the minutes. Stop taking notes or turn off the recorder while that person is speaking.

2-5

PRESENTING A GOOD IDEA TO MANAGEMENT

I came across a great idea in a magazine that, with a few changes, would save our company money. But all I get is a few patronizing nods from upper management. No one takes me seriously. How can I get people to take me and my ideas seriously?

Did you run up to a vice president and blurt out your idea? Did you preface it with, "I read about this great idea in a magazine"? Your problem may be the way your idea was presented rather than the idea itself. If you have a good idea you want to communicate to management, prepare a memo to the person in charge of that area and copy your boss and any others who may be interested or affected by this idea or change. Whether your idea will save the company money or increase morale, it must be presented to the right people in the proper manner. Follow these steps:

- ◆ When writing the memo, remember to include the five W's: who, what, when, where, and why.

- ◆ Quote your sources or provide information that shows this idea was successful in similar companies under similar circumstances.

- ◆ State why you think it would work at your company.

- ◆ Attach any exhibits or charts that support your recommendation.

2-6

COMMUNICATING YOUR NEEDS
WITHOUT ALIENATING OTHERS

A good communicator is able to be assertive and take control of a situation without offending others. As a secretary with little time to waste, you must be able to make requests of your boss and coworkers when they are interfering with your work, without causing hard feelings.

I work for several individuals and manage to get all the work done and keep everyone relatively happy. However, there is one individual who always asks me if I can type "just one little letter" before I go to lunch. Then she hands me eight handwritten pages that are a nightmare to read. It means I am either late for lunch or miss it entirely and all my other work falls behind. What can I do to prevent this from happening?

The best way to handle such a request is to say "Sure, I'll be glad to type the letter as long as it doesn't upset my schedule." If it is something you can type quickly before leaving for lunch, then, of course, do it. If it turns out to be a nightmare project that will take some time, simply tell the person, "Oh, I didn't realize it would be this complicated. I'll type it as soon as I return from lunch." If you allow interruptions, the work on your desk on Monday will still be there on Friday. You will not meet your deadlines, which will make you look inefficient and disorganized.

When you work for several people, you must set your priorities at the beginning of each day. Of course, if there is an emergency, you can certainly rearrange your schedule.

I work for several people and they all want to explain their typing projects to me in detail. Most projects are pretty straightforward, and this wastes a lot of time. I could have typed half the project while they were explaining it. How can I tell them that they don't need to go into such detail? I know how to do my job.

Use a two-tiered mail box. Ask the people in your department to drop their projects in the box and if you have questions you will ask them when you begin working on the project. Put the finished projects in the second bin. It will help if you place them in folders with the name of the person on the front. This way, they can pick up their finished projects without interrupting your work flow.

My boss sometimes takes work off my desk without telling me. I spent two panicky hours trying to locate a report only to find he had removed it from my desk and taken it to a meeting. This is not the first time he has taken something from my desk without telling me. How do I let him know I do not appreciate people removing things without letting me know?

You have to communicate your feelings to your boss. Tell him of the time you spent rummaging through file cabinets and searching for the document. Ask him to leave a note when he removes a file or report from your desk. Tell him you always keep a pencil and sticky note next to your phone so he can just jot down "sales report" and sign his initials.

One person in our office is a notorious chitchatterer. I work for several people and have a heavy workload. She constantly interrupts me to tell me what her weekend was like and what color her new outfit is and just goes on and on. How can I tell her I don't really care without being rude?

It is not always politically smart to alienate coworkers. The easiest solution is to say, "Gosh that sounds exciting, but I really must complete this project. Could you fill me in later?" If that doesn't work, try some of these techniques:

◆ Shuffle papers on your desk as if you are preparing to take them into your boss or to another department.

◆ Get up from your desk and open a file cabinet and pretend to search for a file your boss needs right away.

◆ Tell her it is imperative that you make a phone call and pick up the phone and start dialing.

◆ Grab your "copies to be made" folder and head for the copier.

The secretaries in one company handled the problem by banding together—whenever the chitchatterer was at one desk for more than three minutes, one of the other secretaries would call and the secretary would pretend to be taking a long, involved message. The chitchatterer would then walk away and no feelings were hurt.

<hr>

2-7

COMMUNICATING EFFECTIVELY BY TELEPHONE

What's the proper way to answer the telephone and take phone messages?

When answering the telephone, keep your voice well-modulated and speak clearly. If your voice is high-pitched, speak an octave lower; you will sound more businesslike.

When taking a message, you need to take down enough information so your boss can see at a glance who called, why they called, when they called, and how to call them back. The date may not seem initially important; however, some bosses are never able to respond immediately to phone inquiries and the date will let your boss know if this is a new call or an old one that has been handled.

When your boss is traveling, you may want to consolidate all his phone messages onto one piece of paper. Simply keep a running log in your computer and add to it as phone calls are received. When your boss returns to the office, he won't have ten sheets of telephone message paper scattered over his desk. Instead he has one sheet of paper with all his messages. As he begins to return them, he can check them off.

My boss gets upset when I forget to put the date on his phone messages. What's the big deal?

Did Joe call again this morning or is that an old message from yesterday? Putting the date and time on phone messages eliminates returning calls that have already been handled.

People call my boss all the time but don't want to leave complete information; they say they'll just call back later. Other people act as if they know my boss when they don't. For this reason my boss likes all his calls screened. How can I get people to tell me who they are and what they want to talk to my boss about without sounding rude?

Remember that your job is to assist your boss and save time. Develop a standard questioning technique. Remember the five W's:

- Ask the caller to identify himself or herself—"*Who's* calling, please?" or "May I ask who's calling?"

- Ask what company he or she represents—"*What* company do you represent?" or the less formal "and the name of the company, please?"

- Ask "*When* is the best time to return the call?" or "*When* will the caller be in?"

- Ask "*Where* may the caller be reached?" or "Please leave the number *where* we can return the call," or the less formal "What is your number, please."

- Ask "*Why* are you calling?" Don't be shy; you need to know the purpose of the call. Ask, "May I tell Mr. Smith the purpose of your call?" or "May I ask why you need to speak to Mr. Smith?" If the person balks and doesn't want to tell you, don't push but do write that the person did not wish to state the purpose of the call so your boss will know you asked.

2-8

WHAT TO DO ABOUT PROBLEM CALLERS

My boss gets a lot of calls from stockbrokers and salespeople who want to talk to him. When you tell them your boss already has a stockbroker or that we're not interested in purchasing the product, they say they need to talk to my boss, he'll understand what they're talking about (I understand that

my boss does not want to take these calls). I finally hung up on one person, but don't feel that was really professional or appropriate behavior. What can I do about obstinate callers who just won't give up?

Stockbrokers and salespeople are paid to be persistent. They all seem to have attended the same seminar on how to get around the secretary. One tactic they are taught is to try to build a relationship so that the secretary will feel they know and have talked to your boss before. They do this by asking for your boss by his first name. If you say he's not available they will say, "I've got another call holding. I'll get back to him." Then they will call back and say "Hey, is Mike free yet?" They are trying to get you to believe they know Mike or are a friend of his, so you will put the call through.

Another tactic used by stockbrokers and salespeople is to sound authoritative and important to scare you into putting the call through. Stand your ground and put them through the "five W's" routine. Ask who is calling, etc. When you ask the purpose of their call and they say "a personal financial proposal" ask them to send the information in the mail and end the conversation by saying, "If Mr. Smith is interested in your proposal (or product) he will contact you."

When you ask for the purpose of the call, some stockbrokers and salespeople will state the purpose in such a manner that you cannot understand what they are talking about. One caller said, "It's a financial proposal dealing with fluctuating income and customary escrow and investment criteria that will save your company thousands of dollars." This is business-babble.

- They hope you will feel intimidated by their superior intelligence and put the call through.
- They hope you are lazy and won't feel like writing all that out, and will put the call through. However, one secretary very painstakingly had the caller repeat each word while she wrote the message out in its entirety and read it back to him.

I work for the vice president of a large retail chain, and I get a lot of calls from irate customers. When I tell them my boss is not in, they start screaming at me and insist on being put through to my boss immediately. What is the best way to handle these people?

Identify yourself to the caller. Explain that you are the assistant to the vice president and will see that this problem is given priority. Try not to aggravate the caller, but be firm in gathering the information needed—name, phone number, and a description of the problem.

Listen to the problem. Let the caller finish speaking before you ask another question. Try to get as much information as possible—the model number, what exactly went wrong, etc. Repeat the information back to the person, for example, "you purchased a Model 23J at the store in Greenville and the automatic timer is not working." The more information you can supply, the quicker the response time.

A good closing statement is, "If Ms. McKinney does not help you to your satisfaction, please call me. My name is Sue Johnson and I can be reached at 555-5126." This reassures the caller that her problem will get attention. If you refer the problem to another department, follow up in a few days to check the status. After two weeks or so, call each person who complained and ask if the problem has been handled to his or her satisfaction.

I get calls from people who get mad at me because they don't have the latest catalog and give me a hard time when I tell them prices have changed. It's not my fault they didn't receive the new catalog with the current prices. The catalog mailings are done by the marketing department, but customers still yell at me. What can I do to convince them it is not my fault?

This is a great opportunity for you to use your communications skills. Instead of saying, "It's not my fault," or trying to blame the marketing department, take control of the situation. Try these responses:

◆ "Do you have a copy of our latest catalog? Please give me your address and I'll have one sent out today."

◆ "You wanted to order 200 widgets in green, is that correct? The new price is now $1.75 each, for a total cost of $350. They are in stock and will be shipped this afternoon. Do I have the correct address?" Repeat the shipping address to the caller.

But don't stop there. This is where you can make some points. Write a memo to marketing stating that you have sent a current catalog to Amalgamated Institutions, for example, and to please check and make sure they are on the list to receive new catalogs in the future. Copy your boss on the memo. At the end of six months, take copies of the memos you have written requesting catalogs to your boss and tell her that your company needs to work out a solution to the catalog mailing problem.

My boss has a friend who calls very often and he is always rude to me. Whenever he calls, it takes all the control I have to be polite to him. He

always has an offensive remark to make. Should I tell my boss this guy is a real jerk?

Exactly what kind of remarks does he make? Would they be classified as sexual harassment or do you mean he is just irritating and obnoxious to deal with? If he is making sexually explicit remarks, tell him to cease immediately in no uncertain terms. If he is just one of those irritating, obnoxious people, use your most professional voice to say, "Mr. Mendez will be with you shortly," and put him on hold. Your job is to be polite to all callers, even the obnoxious, irritating ones.

2-9

WHEN TO INTERRUPT YOUR BOSS
FOR A PHONE CALL

My boss frequently gets a call from someone who says it is "urgent." However, if my boss is in a meeting, I hate to interrupt. While the problem may seem urgent to the caller, it may not be urgent to my boss. How can one identify a truly urgent call from one that is not?

There are no standard answers to a lot of the problems secretaries face. This is where it pays to know and understand your boss. Through working with him, answering correspondence, and knowing what is going on in the company, most secretaries are able to determine whether a call is truly urgent and whether the boss should be called to the phone. If you are in doubt, check quickly with someone knowledgeable on your boss's staff. Then if you feel the call may truly be urgent, take a note to your boss. Phrase the note so that he can nod a *yes* or *no* answer. Let him make the decision.

My boss's husband calls and demands to speak to her. He even insists that I interrupt her if she is in an important meeting. How can I handle this tactfully?

What you are asking is how you can tell the husband his wife should not be interrupted at the moment, and ask if she could return the call later. Unless your boss has specifically told you she does not wish to take his calls, put them through, interrupting the meeting. The last thing you want is to get caught up in a domestic squabble.

My boss gets a lot of telephone calls from different people. Some are more important than others. He has so many messages that sometimes an important or urgent message gets lost or stuck in the middle of the pile and he doesn't notice it right away. What can I do to make him notice his important messages?

All important or urgent messages should be kept on the top of the stack. Important or urgent phone calls that should be returned right away should be written on a different color paper or perhaps on an index card so that they are noticeably different from the regular messages.

2-10

WHEN A COWORKER ANSWERS YOUR PHONE

There is a secretary in our office who hates taking phone messages. She will say something like "Oh, I don't work in that department. Why don't you call back in fifteen minutes?" When she does take a message, it is incomplete or the message is garbled. The other day she gave my boss a message to call "Tom" right away. He knows three "Toms" and had no idea which one to call. What can I do to get her to improve her telephone manners?

She needs to be told to project a positive, efficient image when she answers the phone. Say, "Maria, we need the full name of the caller, the name of his or her company, the telephone number of the caller, and a short message as to why they are calling or when is a good time to return the call."

2-11

MINIMIZING PROBLEMS WITH VOICE MAIL

We have voice mail at our company. Recently, I had to call the vice presidents to inform them that a special meeting of the Management Committee would be held that afternoon. Two people were either not at their desk or on their phone, so I left the message on their voice mail. Later I was reprimanded because one person did not get the message until after the meeting. Is it my fault that he didn't check his voice mail?

Your job was to inform people that a special meeting was being held on short notice. Do you feel that you did everything you could to inform the participants of that meeting? Sometimes leaving a voice mail message is not enough. Maybe the person is out of the office and will not be back until the afternoon. To perform your job, you needed to inform that person's secretary that you left a message on voice mail regarding the special meeting. The secretary could then contact her boss at the meeting site to give him the information. This will also offer you more protection—you not only left the voice mail message but alerted the attendee's secretary.

Our company recently installed voice mail on all our telephones. The secretaries believe they no longer have to answer the phones and can let whoever is calling leave a voice mail message. They leave their desks and the phones unattended. When I was home ill, the president of the company called my boss and got his voice mail. Then he dialed my number and got my voice mail. Needless to say, he was quite angry. How can I get the secretaries to understand that voice mail was not installed for their convenience?

You are right. Many people think voice mail is a personal answering service or use it to screen their calls. Has anyone provided instructions for the correct use of voice mail? Draft a memo, for your boss's signature, that sets forth the voice mail rules. State that it is not to be used as a personal answering service or to screen calls. Perhaps you should reiterate some basic telephone courtesies. Insist that all phones be answered by a secretary on the third ring, no matter whose phone it is.

2-12

TIPS FOR USING THE FAX MACHINE

My boss will have me fax a twenty-page report to someone, and then overnight the same report to them. I feel we should do one or the other, but not both. How can I convince my boss we don't need this duplication of effort?

You need to ask your boss that very question. This is why it is so important for secretaries and bosses to communicate with each other. There could be a very good reason to fax it and then overnight it. The material may need to be reviewed before signatures are obtained on the original document.

Maybe your boss is not aware of the expense and time involved. If you don't get a monthly printout of your expenses, telephone charges, fax charges, overnight expenses, etc., then call your facilities department and ask if they can provide you with this information for one month or, if possible, for the last three months. Then, you can show your boss exactly how much could be saved by eliminating either the charges for overnight mail or the fax charges.

It could be that your boss needs to be reassured that her report was received. Attach the fax printout, which shows the fax was received, to her file copy, or you could call the receiver to make sure the fax was received in its entirety. Whatever the reasons, they need to be discussed so they can be understood.

My boss received a fax earlier this morning. Unfortunately, it wasn't until this afternoon when he was going through it that he noticed a page was missing. The person who sent the fax is located in a different time zone. Because I wasn't able to have them resend the page, my boss was not able to work on his portion of an important report. He's mad at me, but it's not my fault the fax machine malfunctioned. Was it?

Always check the page count when you receive a fax. Never assume the person who collects and delivers faxes will catch errors of this nature. That's your job. If the fax was delivered directly to your boss (bypassing you), then you're off the hook; otherwise, it was your responsibility to check the page count.

My boss gets a lot of faxes and they are always getting lost on her desk. Is there some way you can spot a fax either on your desk or in your mail?

Fax paper is white. If you have a plain-paper fax machine, load it with colored paper. Yellow seems to work well. That way, a fax is easy to spot and doesn't get lost on a cluttered desk. If your fax machine uses heat-sensitive paper, which tends to curl and is difficult to handle because the pages tend to stick together, you may want to run a copy on colored paper.

2-13

HOW TO COMMUNICATE WITH AUTHORITY AND LEADERSHIP

My boss will often ask me to tell someone on her staff to do something. However, some people on her staff resent taking orders from me. How do you tell a person who outranks you to do something without causing hard feelings?

What your boss is really doing is delegating some of her power to you. Giving orders is a tricky form of communication. Some people will understand that you are relaying your boss's instructions and will cooperate. Some may resent a secretary telling them what to do or how to do it. Whether you are giving orders to a subordinate, a peer, or a vice president:

- Be firm but don't demand—you may get the message across but you have alienated the person who has to respond to your request.

- If possible, put it in the form of a memo, which you sign. This will eliminate the possibility of someone saying they did not receive the message or it was misunderstood.

- Don't give incomplete instructions. Remember the five W's—who, what, when, where, and why. For example:

  Susan [who] *would like the comparable sales report* [what] *today before 5:00 P.M.* [when] *because the staff meeting has been moved back* [why]. The *where* is understood to be on Susan's desk or in her office.

I find myself smiling and agreeing with other people, even when I don't really want to agree with them; I just don't want to offend them. I want to speak up but I'm afraid people won't like me. Then I get mad at myself because I'm such a wimp. How can I overcome the smiling and nodding syndrome?

It is most important that you like yourself. You have opinions and you should express them. Practice communicating your message in a direct manner (this means looking the person right in the eye and not allowing interruptions until you have finished what you want to say). Should someone try to interrupt, look them in the eye and say, "Excuse me please, but I'd like to continue," and then pick up where you left off. Practice your message over and over. It will keep you from getting flustered and you can hold the line and project a confident image.

My boss never asks me to do something; he demands it. He is always issuing orders, and it really irritates me sometimes. What can I do to handle this professionally?

Bosses have different styles of communication. Some like to get to the point quickly and use declarative sentences:

Get me the report. Take care of this invoice. Tell John I want his summary before 5:00 P.M.

Others use questioning sentences:

Will you please get me the report? Did you take care of this invoice? Does John understand that I need his summary before 5:00 P.M.?

While your communication problem could be just a difference in speaking style, there are some who communicate power by making demands and issuing orders. This type of person leads by domination. Understand that you are dealing with a dominating personality type and there's probably nothing you can do to change his behavior. Be polite, but firm, and learn to use more assertive types of speech when dealing with this person.

I want to be a good leader, but sometimes it seems that screaming is the only way to get people to listen to you. If I ask nicely, everyone ignores me. What should I do?

If you can't get people to listen to you without screaming, then you are not leading. Your problem may be that when you ask nicely, you are really asking passively. Don't make a request in an indirect way. Like it or not, the short, to the point, declarative style of communication is still the accepted standard.

Don't say:

I would appreciate it if you would all cooperate so that we can have the new secretarial newsletter published before the first quarter session.

Say:

We need to have the secretarial newsletter completed before the first quarter.

Don't say:

We have been given the opportunity to set up a program to review the current file system and make any changes we find necessary. Please arrange to attend the filing meeting in Conference Room A on Wednesday afternoon.

Say:

We will be meeting in Conference Room A on Wednesday afternoon to discuss methods to resolve the problems in our filing system.

◆ Speak in a firm, confident voice.

◆ Use strong words to convey authority: management focus; corporate action; provide structure.

◆ Emphasize intent: We have determined; we propose; we constructed; we oppose.

◆ Set deadlines.

<hr>

2-14
COMMUNICATING EFFECTIVELY TO A GROUP

I have to give a presentation to all our field units on our new insurance plan. I'm really nervous and am afraid my voice will crack. Is there anything I can do so I won't appear so nervous?

You're not alone. Even professional speakers get the jitters before a presentation. Here are a few things you can do to stay calm:

◆ Take a couple of deep breaths to calm yourself before you begin.

◆ Look directly into the eyes of someone in the audience; try to lock in on someone about halfway in the room. Do not stare at the back wall or you will be talking "over" your audience and may appear wooden. If you make eye contact with your audience, you will relax a little and fall into a more natural speaking rhythm.

◆ Most important—practice, practice, practice.

I have to give a presentation on our new word-processing software to several groups of people in our company. Some of these people are against this change and are belligerent. How do you handle this type of presentation?

First of all, know what you're talking about. Research thoroughly so you will feel confident that you can answer any possible question that may come up. Make sure you have all your facts straight and any backup material or information at your fingertips. Prepare an agenda of the items you will be covering. Practice, practice, practice your presentation so you will not stumble over any items. This will give you a more authoritative attitude and will also boost your self-confidence.

I've been asked to make a presentation to all our employees on our new ordering system. I've never done anything like this before and am really nervous. Do you have any suggestions?

Make sure you prepare an agenda for your presentation and then follow it. Learn as much as you can about the new system. Anticipate what questions may be asked and be prepared to answer them. Use visual aids or a mock-up of the new system so you can demonstrate exactly how to process an order.

There are a few people in our company who want to monopolize every presentation by questioning everything you say. Most of the people understand the information and have a few questions, but these off-the-wall questions throw me. How do you handle this type of person?

Some people want to appear as smart, or smarter, than the person giving the presentation. Others like the attention they get when they present off-beat scenarios. If a person asks a legitimate question, answer it to the best of your ability. If it is a question that is "offbeat" or out of context, or perhaps a question for which you have no legitimate answer, then say, "See me after the meeting and we will address that issue in detail," or "I'll contact our representative and get an answer to that question." This will allow the meeting to continue or end without argument.

I don't want my presentation to be boring, but it does contain a lot of facts and figures. It is a serious subject so I don't want any funny, cutesy stuff, either. How can I keep my audience from falling asleep?

Speak louder than usual. You need to be heard clearly and distinctly. By speaking a little louder than you normally would, you can capture and maintain your audience's attention. Remember, too, that when you give a speech or presentation "word pictures" are very effective. For example, if you say, "We need to control costs on this project and the Accounting Department will act as our controller or policeman, directing costs to the proper accounts," it will trigger an image people can relate to. Instead of numbers, statistics, and trend lines, try using analogies. For instance, "We produced 12,000 widgets last year. If they had been pizzas, it would mean that each person in the Widget Department could have a pizza for lunch for the next six years."

2-15

GENDER-NEUTRAL COMMUNICATION

Good communicators must avoid stereotyping and make sure that all male-female references are "gender-neutral." When you omit words or reword sentences that might be offensive to a group of people, you are demonstrating sensitivity to their needs. Today, gender-neutral communication is standard in most professions and industries.

I know you are not supposed to use "male" terminology such as "his" or "he" as a general reference point, but this can be very confusing and writing "his/her" or "his or her" in reports sounds awkward after a while. Is there another word I could substitute?

Business writing often sets new trends. Technology in the work place has changed the way we use words as well as the way we write them. People who want to be "gender-correct" have found it less awkward (though not technically correct) to substitute "their" as a way to avoid any gender reference at all. Even though you may have a singular subject, it is one of the ways grammar rules are accommodating our new awareness of what is appropriate in our language. The sentence, *Each accountant must choose **their*** (instead of "his" or "his or her") *specialty*, is now considered acceptable in business writing.

Take a little time to think through your sentence structure and you can prepare gender-neutral phrasing that will not call attention to the fact that you are trying so hard to be gender-neutral. For instance, simply state "all sales reports must be in by the fifth of the month." Instead of saying "If anyone needs more time to complete the project, he/she should contact the regional office" say, "Anyone needing more time to complete the project should contact the regional office."

Using Messrs. and Mmes. seems so formal and old-fashioned when writing letters today. However, if I am writing a letter to a company and do not know whether I am addressing men or women, what should I do?

A developing trend in business letter writing is to simply drop the salutation when writing to a company and/or people you do not know. The old standby "Dear Sir" or "Gentlemen" is no longer gender-correct.

Non-sexist salutations:

◆ Direct the letter to a department:

TO: The Order Department
TO: The Purchasing Department
TO: The Marketing Department

◆ Direct the letter to a department head:

TO: Customer Service Manager
TO: Specialty Leasing Manager
TO: Corporate Communications Director

◆ Use a reference line

RE: Account No. 264562045
RE: Sales and Leasing Meeting
RE: Fire Insurance Claim

For more formal correspondence address the person being written to as either Ms. or Mr.

Streamlined Correspondence for the Nineties

Acme Credit Card Co.
620 Wade St.
Chicago, IL 60601

Re: Account No. 5478-21

I believe an error has been made in posting to my account. On July 22, my account was credited $57.89 for a purchase made at Exquisite Boutique in Dallas. I have never been to Dallas and have never shopped at a store by that name. Will you please check your records and let me know if an error was made?

I look forward to hearing from you shortly.

MKJ/la

We have a large sales force in our office made up of both men and women, and I am at a loss as to how to address them or refer to them in reports without sounding as if I am trying to make gender an issue. Do you have a "neutral" word for addressing large groups of men and women?

Address memos to "Sales Staff," which is gender neutral. When writing, use asexual words such as "salesperson" or "sales representative" instead of salesman. Instead of the word "businessman," you can use executive, industrialist, entrepreneur, capitalist, or manager. Use the field of business to describe the person: broker, accountant, designer, retailer, architect, technician, or banker.

How can I avoid using gender-related pronouns. How can I improve the sentences: "The doctor studied the X-ray and *he* said the bone was broken," and "Each secretary should learn to program *her* computer."

Remove the pronoun entirely.

> *The doctor studied the X-ray and said the bone was broken.*

> *Each secretary should learn to program a computer.*

Restructure the sentence:

> *After studying the X-ray, the doctor concluded the bone was broken.*

> *Computer programming should be a part of every secretary's training.*

Repeat the noun:

> *The doctor studied the X-ray and the doctor said the bone was broken.*

> *A secretary should be able to learn to program a secretary's computer.*

By using one of these three strategies: eliminating the pronoun, restructuring the sentence, or repeating the noun, you should be able to produce a gender-neutral sentence that does not sound awkward.

I frequently send out letters to a list of people that is quite long. I attach a distribution list to the front of the letter that lists each person's name and location. Should I put "Mr." or "Ms." in front of each name?

When you send a letter to a group of both men and women, the salutation can vary. Sales Department, Committee Members, Special Management Team may all work. Old-fashioned or archaic words are not always appropriate for business writing, which should be crisp, concise, gender-neutral, and "businesslike." For a long distribution list that contains individual names, you might try listing by the first initial followed by the surname.

Distribution List	
C. Chinn	Headquarters—21st Floor
J. Johnson	Atlanta Office
S. Miles	Midwest Regional
P. Morales	Headquarters—22nd Floor
W. Rozenski	Midwest Regional

Whenever I type "Yours truly" I almost get the giggles. It sounds more like an old-fashioned love letter than a business letter. Are there any new or more appropriate closings for letters?

Since we have such a wide choice of salutations it would be foolish to use an old-fashioned closing, so many businesses have simply eliminated it. A signature block follows the letter. Drop three or four spaces and type the name of the person. He or she can sign above the name. You omit the "Sincerely yours" or "Yours truly." If you feel your letter must have a closing, a simple "Sincerely" is always appropriate.

Our company was recently sold and the new CEO visited our office for a week to see how we operated. He had his assistant with him and she took notes and also talked to different people about our shipping operations. My boss wrote a letter to the new CEO and said "It was a pleasure meeting you and your lovely assistant." Word got back to me that she was upset because that sentence was demeaning. My boss thought he was being nice. Frankly, I don't see anything wrong with it. Why would it upset someone to be called "lovely"?

I'm sure your boss meant well, but the sentence is demeaning. It sounds as if he didn't really take the CEO's assistant's position seriously, that she was just a "lovely" traveling companion. Professional women work very hard and resent it when they are not taken seriously. What if the situation were reversed? What if the CEO had sent your boss a letter that said, "I enjoyed meeting you, John, and your handsome assistant"? It doesn't sound very professional. The proper way to have responded is, "It was a pleasure meeting you, John, and your executive assistant, Eva Murray."

We have a large planning meeting each year and the wives are invited. We always have activities for the wives while their husbands are in meetings. Each evening we have a dinner, and the wives are invited. However, we have a new woman vice president and her husband will attend. How do I address him? Do I group him in with the wives and their activities?

Do not refer to the meeting attendees as husbands and wives. Refer to them as the "meeting attendees" and their "spouses." Planned activities should also be generic. You can still plan a fashion show or makeup makeover for those who are interested in those activities. However, also offer an alternative, perhaps golf or tennis.

We have a vice president who was recently divorced and is bringing a woman he is currently dating to the planning meeting. How should I refer to her?

Obviously, it would not be correct to refer to her as a spouse. Simply refer to anyone who is not an employee as a "guest." This is an asexual word that covers husband, wife, male, female and "significant other."

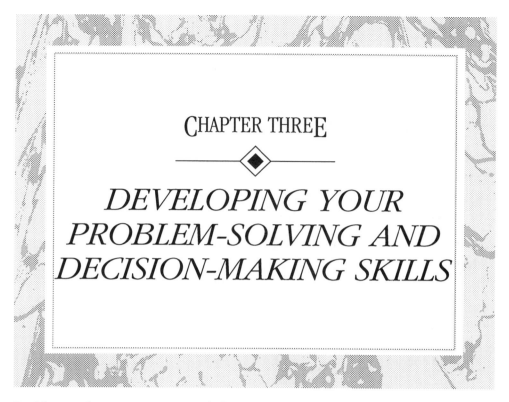

CHAPTER THREE

◆

DEVELOPING YOUR PROBLEM-SOLVING AND DECISION-MAKING SKILLS

Problem solving requires good decision-making skills; similarly, if you can make good decisions, you can solve most problems. Problem solving and decision making involve risk. If you make the wrong decision, the problem may become bigger and more unmanageable. It is a logical process. Using an analytical thought process to solve problems will eliminate most of the risk by forcing the use of logical thought instead of emotional thought. Basically, there are two types of decisions: informed decisions based on a logical thought process, and intuitive (or gut) decisions based on a feeling or "hunch." Making decisions is a part of every secretary's job. Making the *right* decisions will earn the valuable respect of your boss and coworkers.

3-1

LEARN TO MAKE THE RIGHT DECISIONS

I hate making decisions. When I do make a decision, it always seems as if it is the wrong one. Why is it so hard to make a decision?

Fear of failure and the possibility of embarrassment causes most indecision. Let's face it, if you do nothing you don't run the risk of failure. Don't make a decision until you have all the facts. For instance, a junior secretary has been asked to clean out the files. You tell him that he can dispose of anything that is more than five years old. Before you made that decision did you ask yourself the following questions:

Are these all general correspondence files?
Were any of these projects involved in litigation?
Do they contain financial data?

Even the simplest decisions require an analytical thought process. Don't make a decision until you have considered all the options.

Is there a checklist or formula I could follow that will help me make the right decisions?

Think of problem solving and decision making as a four-step process:

- ◆ Identify the problem

- ◆ Accumulate the information

- ◆ Evaluate the options

- ◆ Make the decision

Identify, accumulate, evaluate, and decide!

How can I evaluate a problem?

Begin by writing the problem out on paper. Then list your options and alternatives and what can be expected from each approach. Most people cannot figure complex mathematical equations in their heads; they need to write them out. Writing out a problem allows you to define it in specific terms. Once the problem is identified, begin searching for the solution:

Learn from others. Ask for help. How have others in your company approached a similar problem? What were their findings? Profit from the successes and failures of other people.

Don't procrastinate. Get started now. Forcing yourself to get started to find a solution or make a decision will increase your confidence level. Don't wait for inspiration to strike.

Establish deadlines. Make sure your deadlines are realistic and that you can stick to them.

I have been asked to locate the best software program for our accounting department. I have talked to several software companies and have received all kinds of literature, but how can I tell which one is the best one?

You have to make a decision and solve a problem. The problem is to determine which software is the best for the accounting department so you can make an informed decision.

Evaluate the information you have accumulated. Begin by studying the literature received on the software packages. Prepare a spreadsheet that lists the software applications for each program. (Information to help you prepare a spreadsheet can be found in Chapter 9, Creating the Perfect Document.) Take into consideration whether these programs are compatible with other systems used throughout the company. Cost is an important consideration so list the cost of each package. Also, find out how much has been budgeted for the computer program, or ask how much the accounting department expects to spend. Do all the software programs offer adequate training or support? Have you taken everything into consideration? Have you talked to some of the accounting people who will actually use this system? Interview some of the accounting people; ask questions:

What program do you use now?
What applications would you like the system to do?
Are the people in the accounting department computer-literate?

Now that you have assessed or accumulated all the information, the next step is to evaluate it.

- Look at the spreadsheet—which system will provide most of the items on your checklist?
- What is the second-best software program?
- Compare them. Where are the differences?
- Is one system more expensive than the other? You cannot always make a decision based on price alone. Is the reason for the cost difference valid? Learning to properly evaluate the information you have accumulated is often the real key to making an informed decision.

My boss travels frequently, and I end up making decisions because a lot of the work we do is on deadline. The decisions I've made have been inconsistent. Usually I don't have time to think out the problem and I just rely on a

"feeling" or "hunch." It makes me uneasy to rely on a "feeling." Is there a quick way to work out a problem in order to make a fast decision?

Decisions based on a "feeling" or "hunch" have a logical basis. In the course of your schooling, work, and general life experience, you accumulate a large amount of data that are absorbed and stored in your brain. Along with this information, you have also stored a set of rules for processing and evaluating the information. When you are working under a deadline and need a quick decision, your subconscious sorts and evaluates this information. Thus, you make a quick decision based on a "feeling" or "hunch." Your decision-making skills are only as good as the information you have stored in your brain.

In order to make good decisions under pressure, learn as much about the project as possible. Make it a point to know what the customer is looking for in a final product, what the cost should be, how important it is, where it is to be shipped, etc. Based on this knowledge, you should be able to make more consistent and accurate decisions.

Although I've worked for my boss for over a year now, I still don't feel comfortable making decisions without his input. How can I change my behavior and take charge of the situation?

Start with little decisions. Write responses to letters. Respond to telephone inquiries yourself and write your boss a short note or let him know how you handled the problem or what decision you made.

When you do make a decision, make sure your boss is aware of it. Jot down little notes "I approved the wording in the new policy book," or "I told accounting to proceed with the changes to the expense reports." It not only makes your boss aware of the decisions you are making but makes you more aware of just how many decisions you are making on a routine basis. This will also increase your decision-making confidence.

We have been having a problem getting our invoices paid on time. Nobody will do anything about it and everybody blames the problem on somebody else. My boss said he wants more teamwork and has asked me to meet with the accounting department and the secretaries in marketing, communications, and finance to brainstorm until we work out a solution. I have heard the term "brainstorm" before and know what it means, but how do you do it?

Brainstorming is a good way to generate ideas. In a typical brainstorming session, you would all gather in a conference room for about one hour. Write the question on an easel. The idea is to encourage the people in the group to generate suggestions for solving the problem. Every idea should be written on the board or easel, no matter how wild. The greater the number of suggestions the more likely that a combination of ideas or improvements will solve the problem. No judgment or criticism of any idea is allowed, no matter how wild or absurd the suggestion.

3-2
MAKING DECISIONS BY COMMITTEE

I have just been asked to serve on a committee to revamp our company newsletter. I have never served on a committee before and feel a little out of my element. The committee recently decided to change the name of the newsletter and everyone agreed on the new name. I didn't really like it, but I went along with the group. Should I have said something?

Committees are notorious for making poor decisions for the very reason you just expressed. Was the reason you did not speak up because you didn't want to antagonize others in the group? Usually one person is the group leader (or one person will take control) and because the other committee members either don't really care or are anxious to return to their offices, they will go along with whatever is suggested. You should tell the other committee members how you feel about the name and why. A good way to reopen the discussion is to say something like, "I've been thinking about the name we chose and feel we should give it more consideration. The reason I feel this way is . . . ."

If you are on a committee and it makes a poor decision, who is responsible, the committee leader?

Stop looking for someone to blame for a poor decision. Instead focus on what went wrong. Did the committee members secretly feel the decision was a poor one but did not want to be thought of as antagonistic? Did one or two people think it was a poor decision but did not speak up because they thought they would be outvoted anyway? Was it because the committee members failed to communicate honestly with one another? Look for a solution, not a scapegoat.

I am on a committee that is supposed to review our office forms and bring them up-to-date, making them computer compatible. Now we have been

formed into subcommittees to study particular forms; for instance, one group is looking at the expense-report form and one group is looking at the accounts-payable request form, etc. The problem is that two people on the committee want things decided their way for political reasons. Meanwhile, we are not making any progress. How can I get the committee to override the few who are holding us up?

Members of a committee can experience frustration, anger, and irritation when it appears they are not accomplishing their objective, which is to find a solution to a particular problem. Forming subcommittees won't always solve the problem unless the subcommittee has a specific goal. All too often, people in the subcommittees break off into their own groups and may express doubts or concerns to trusted individuals or the small subgroups when the entire committee should be aware of any and all concerns. But, if each subcommittee has a specific piece of the puzzle to solve without taking other aspects of the problem into consideration, it will be able to define its focus. Then the committee leader will be able to put the "pieces" together and the committee can see the whole picture. It is not unusual for people to want to twist information in order for the decision to go a particular way for political reasons.

Take the logical approach. Identify the problem you are trying to solve. Accumulate the information necessary to come to a decision. Once again, a spreadsheet will compare the different forms in an analytical manner, that is, how the form will interface with the computers already in place, the cost involved, etc. The entire committee can then help evaluate the information accumulated. Each subcommittee can then put its form to the "spreadsheet test" to see how it compares. This will help the committee make an informed decision.

I was on a committee to purchase new software for the secretaries. We reviewed different types of software, and several sales representatives spoke to our committee and dropped off literature. We decided to purchase one particular type of software and everyone agreed to the purchase. Now, however, the people on the committee aren't happy with it, saying the software won't do enough and it's too expensive.

No one on the committee wants to be perceived as unwilling to cooperate or viewed as obstructing or holding up the purchase, therefore poor decisions are made. Committee members may think the committee is making a poor choice, but won't speak up for fear of antagonizing the others. If you have doubts, speak up—that is why you are on the committee in the first place. If people on the committee become argumentative and debate the merits of your choice, it is a good way to explore alternatives to make sure nothing has been overlooked. Honest discussion in an open atmosphere should be the goal of every committee.

Identify the problem. In this case, the problem is that the committee has made a poor choice.

Since the information has already been accumulated by the committee, evaluate it again and compare it to the complaints received about the software package. Was enough information collected to make a proper decision? Was the information evaluated properly? Was something missing from the information? What was it? The only way to correct a poor decision is to determine what went wrong and why. It will also help to improve decision-making abilities in the future.

Where did the decision-making process fail? Can the problem be corrected?

3-3
ADMITTING MISTAKES AND RESOLVING DILEMMAS

Did you ever find yourself in a dilemma? A dilemma is a situation requiring a choice between equally objectionable alternatives, an embarrassing situation incapable of being resolved satisfactorily. To escape or survive a dilemma usually requires an "ethical" decision. Good problem-solving skills, coupled with a strong moral attitude, encourages ethical decisions in the work place. Should I tell the truth? Should I lie? Why risk my job? Who cares, anyway?

I have made a rather serious mistake. I forgot to incorporate the final changes into a contract I mailed out. I'm afraid to tell my boss. I know when the contract comes back without the changes, I'll be fired. I'm hoping the other party will demand more changes and then I can also put in the changes I missed and maybe nobody will ever know. Should I tell my boss and get it over with or keep hoping it will work itself out?

First, analyze why you neglected to put the changes in the contract. Were you working on several projects or did someone else want something finished right away? Were you simply not concentrating on your job, talking with friends, etc., and it just slipped your mind? Unfortunately, the reason something happens is inconsequential to the results. For whatever reason, the result is that a contract was mailed without the final changes. However, if you analyze and can pinpoint why it happened, you can prevent it from happening again.

Begin by setting up your own checkpoint system to make sure you have the most current contract with all the changes. Do you need to reorganize your desk, your "in" box, the way you process a contract? If you had enlisted the help of others in the department to answer phones or run copies, would it have prevented some interruptions? Some people who work under pressure try to go on as if nothing were unusual—this can be a mistake. People under pressure are more likely to make errors and interruptions (whether a phone call from a friend or someone stopping by to ask you to lunch) translate into errors.

Tell your boss what happened. Be honest and specific. Tell him what you are doing to prevent such occurrences in the future. Ask him if you can contact the person to whom the contract was sent, explain your error and overnight a new contract. Perhaps your boss will want to contact the person receiving the contract and explain what happened.

While your boss may be disappointed in your performance, if you seldom make errors, he probably will not fire you. However, if your performance has been slipping and you have made other similar errors, expect a more severe reprimand. Take responsibility for your mistakes.

I've made a costly error. The price quotes I received for a print job were based on single-sided copy, but the project was to be double-sided. I made the decision to go ahead before I had all the information about the job. Unfortunately, the printer has already begun to run the job. I hate to tell my boss I did something so careless. I'm afraid I'll start to cry and he'll fire me.

Don't let the fact that you might cry deter you from telling your boss; just take some tissues with you. Try writing out what you want to say and practice saying it in an unemotional tone of voice. If you have prepared what you need to say, you may be less inclined to start crying. Remember to tell your boss what you will do to prevent this from happening again, such as how you will devise a checklist or program so that all job requirements are known before making a decision.

I blew it! I worked long and hard compiling figures and tables for a project, but somehow I picked up an incorrect number. I used the June figures

instead of July because I wasn't working from the latest copy of the sales report. It doesn't make a big difference in the final analysis. Should I let it go and pretend I don't know it is a wrong number or should I take a deep breath and go in and tell my boss?

Don't bury your mistake. You will never be happy knowing that this error exists. Besides, you don't want your boss to be sitting in a high-level meeting and have a financial analyst point out that he used the June figures instead of July. Not only would it embarrass him but it would make the entire report suspect. Your boss would also lose faith in your ability to compile data. If he found out you knew the report had incorrect figures, he would certainly lose all confidence in any future work. Tell him what happened and ask if you can issue a revised report immediately.

I scheduled a meeting at a local hotel. Later I learned the meeting room was too cramped and several people, including the chairman of the company, made comments about the poor service. I explained to the chairman's secretary that I had actually reserved a different room but the room I reserved had a water leak and so the meeting was moved to the only other available meeting room. Also, several of the hotel's wait staff did not show up for work and they were extremely shorthanded. The hotel did not charge us for the meeting room. Later on, my boss called me into his office and told me I hadn't handled the situation very well. What should I have done?

First of all, you used a third person (the chairman's secretary) to deliver the apology that should have come directly from you. Second, you neglected to apologize to the other attendees. It probably sounded to your boss as if you were saying, "It's not my fault." It would also have been wise to have stopped by the hotel on your way to work to see how the meeting was progressing. The meeting was your responsibility. A memo to all attendees apologizing for any inconvenience would have shown you as a person who knows how to take responsibility for a difficult situation.

We have had a rash of office thefts lately—hand-held calculators missing from people's desks, wallets disappearing, etc. I saw one of the managers going through the coat pockets of another manager who had left his suit coat in his office while he was in a meeting. Since I'm a secretary and this person is a manager, I'm afraid I'll get fired if I tell. It will just be my word

---

Apology Memo

DATE: Month/Day/Year
TO: List names of attendees
RE: Meeting at (name of hotel)

Due to a water leak in Conference Room A, I understand that the hotel moved your meeting to Conference Room B. Conference Room B was smaller and your meeting space was cramped, but it was the only room the hotel had available. The hotel did not charge us for use of the conference room. The hotel was also shorthanded because several of their wait staff did not show up for work. The manager has apologized for the resulting poor service.

I would like to offer my apologies for any inconvenience and assure you that in the future I will personally check the meeting space before each meeting. If you have any questions or suggestions to improve our next meeting, please let me know.

Diane Burke

---

against his. On the other hand, I had $20 taken from my wallet. Should I take a chance and tell what I saw?

Accusing someone of theft is a very serious charge. You are right; it will come down to one person's word against another and you did not actually see the person take anything. There could be several legitimate reasons why one manager was going through another's coat pockets. Maybe he asked him to bring him his pen, which was in his coat pocket, into his office; maybe he asked him to look for a business card he had dropped in his coat pocket. If you are wrong, it could be very damaging to you and to the person accused. An easier way to get around this dilemma without accusing anyone is to tell the manager, "I saw John looking through your coat while you were in that meeting; did you forget something?" If the manager smiles sheepishly and says, "Oh yeah, I forgot my calculator," you have your answer. If he is upset about what you saw, then the two of you should approach Human Resources and tell them what you witnessed.

3-4

MANAGING "TICKLISH" SITUATIONS

My boss cheats on his expense account. He will give me a receipt for dinner at an expensive restaurant and say he went with some clients, but I know he went to celebrate his wife's birthday because I made the reservations. This is not the first time he's done something like this. Should I send the accounting department an anonymous note?

What you may view as cheating, he may see as a "perk." In many companies, it is part of the corporate culture to "cheat" on your expense accounts a little bit. In other companies, the slightest deviation gets you reprimanded. You are not a police officer, but neither should you be made an accomplice. Follow your boss's instructions, but make sure it's his signature (not yours) that's on the expense-account form. Sooner or later your boss will have his expense accounts audited. Let the auditing department handle it; they know what to look for and what the rules are.

My boss cheats on his wife. He leaves the office early to meet his "friend," and invariably his wife calls. I tell her he's gone to a meeting, as he's instructed me to do, but she's getting suspicious. His wife is so nice; I met her at several office functions. Should I tell her he left the office at 3:00 P.M. and I thought he went home?

What would be accomplished by telling his wife he left at 3:00 P.M. to go home? You should tell your boss that when his wife calls and asks where he is, it makes you uncomfortable. If he insists he is at a meeting and that is what he wants you to tell his wife, it is up to you to make a decision. Do you want to continue working with this person? It sounds as if you have lost all respect for your boss and that makes for a difficult working relationship. Maybe you should consider asking for a transfer to another area in the company.

My best friend at work, Marcie, just filed a sexual harassment claim against her boss. I work for human resources so the complaint is being handled through my office. Marcie asks me what is going on. I am sympathetic to her problem and tempted to tell her. However, if my boss finds out we are best friends, I am afraid I'll get in trouble. What should I do?

Immediately go into your boss's office and tell him you and Marcie are friends and that you do not feel comfortable handling the paperwork regarding her harassment claim. Tell him you would appreciate it if another secretary would work on that particular claim. He will appreciate your sensitivity to the situation. If you are not "upfront" and he finds out that you and Marcie are friends, he will no longer trust you. He may even suspect you leaked information to Marcie about how the company planned to respond and you may find yourself without a job.

One of the women in our office wears these tight black skirts cinched at the waist with a big belt. She thinks they make her look slender, but they're very unprofessional looking. I believe in being honest and straightforward, but my friends say it will hurt her feelings. However, the truth is the truth. Should I tell her to wear a different style?

Truth and honesty are admirable traits, but they should be tempered with compassion. You should be honest with your coworker, but in a tactful way that will not hurt her feelings or embarrass her. Perhaps you could go to a style show together (many department stores sponsor them) and you could point out what looks attractive, slenderizing, and professional. Perhaps you could get a salesperson to help you out. The salesperson could have your friend try on outfits more suitable for the office and make comments such as, "Isn't that lovely; just right for work."

On Fridays, some of the secretaries go out for lunch. Most of them order drinks. I am a recovering alcoholic (but no one knows). How should I handle this?

Listen to your inner voice. You can't drink alcoholic beverages. Don't jeopardize your present job and your future with the company. Order bottled water, a soft drink, or iced tea. Your coworkers may think you are health conscious. If pressed to order something alcoholic, say "I really don't like the taste of alcohol."

3-5

COPING WITH SERIOUS AFFLICTIONS

My boss has a drinking problem. Everybody in the office knows about it. As a matter of fact, they make jokes about getting any approvals or signatures before lunch. After lunch he is pretty much wasted. Sometimes he is very

mellow and happy, other times he is angry and belligerent. But everyone ignores the problem or manages to work around it. He heads the regional office. The work gets done because he has a good staff. I am tempted to let the New York office (and his boss) know what is really going on. I don't want him to get fired, but his mood swings and the constant covering for him is driving me, and the staff who is doing his work, crazy. Several of the staff members feel we shouldn't intervene at all. It is none of our business. Should I tell?

Alcohol abuse is a serious illness. The Americans with Disabilities Act states it is a disabling illness. You and your coworkers should approach your boss as a group and tell him you believe he needs help. Avoiding the problem and delaying intervention will only allow the problem to get worse. The longer his drinking goes on, the more difficult it is to treat. Also, his job performance will continue to deteriorate, which means the burden of extra work will have to be completed by his staff, causing low morale.

It appears that the staff is spending more time working around the boss's problem than seeking a solution. Avoiding the problem and delaying treatment can have serious consequences. For many years it was felt that alcoholics had to "hit bottom" before they could be helped. However, the earlier intervention occurs the better the chance for recovery.

Many companies offer Employee Assistance Programs (EAP) which provide employee counseling for drug or alcohol abuse as well as for emotional or financial problems. If your company does not have an EAP, ask your human resources department to check into one. Perhaps a note (either anonymous or signed by staff members) to Human Resources or someone in a position to take action will help. However, anonymous notes should be used as a last resort.

What if we confront our boss and he tells us his drinking is none of our business? He could even fire us. It might not be worth the risk of alienating him.

When confronted, a person who is abusing drugs or alcohol will usually become defensive and deny having a problem. You can respond by saying that maybe he doesn't have a problem, but he should see a professional or have an in-depth physical, because something seems to be wrong. If he refuses, tell him you (as a group) will talk to his boss about the situation in your office.

I think my boss is a schizophrenic. I'm serious. Some days she is fine and seems happy and productive. She will work from early morning to late at

night and never lose her enthusiasm. Other days she will sit in her office with the door closed and the lights off and will not speak to anyone. Everybody seems to ignore her behavior but it is starting to really bother me. Everyone just says she's "depressed" and she'll get over it in a few days. I can't tell her boss; she is the boss; she is the owner of the company. Is there anything I should do?

Organizations will often adapt to fit the behavior of the person in charge. Aides will protect the boss while employees have little choice but to tolerate the atmosphere. Your boss could be suffering from manic depression. People who are manic depressive have so much energy and enthusiasm they can accomplish a great deal in a short time. Manic depression is often associated with people who have high intelligence levels. The disease produces rapid mood swings. Their extraordinary drive often propels them to positions of importance. Manic depression can be controlled with medication. Whether or not your boss suffers from manic depression is a question only a doctor can answer. Talk to one of her close friends who is aware of the problem and see if the two of you can get her to see a doctor.

CHAPTER FOUR

◆

PROTECTING COMPANY "SECRETS"

The word *secretary* is derived from the Latin word *secretum*, which means secret. A secretary was originally a confidante, one entrusted with secrets, and, today, this is still an important part of the job.

Secretaries are trusted with sensitive information that must be kept confidential. You are expected to protect this information from coworkers and competitors. It is your responsibility to know how to handle this professionally.

4-1
WHAT TO SAY TO COWORKERS WHO ASK YOU FOR CONFIDENTIAL INFORMATION

Sometimes when I go out with friends after work and we have a few drinks, the conversation turns to the office. People have actually asked me how much money I think my boss makes. I need a good response.

Laugh and say "according to her, not enough." If they persist (or pretend they don't get the hint), take a firmer approach, such as, "You'll have to ask her accountant."

Because I have access to payroll information, people will occasionally ask me how much a person makes. Is there a way to respond gracefully to these questions?

You don't need to respond gracefully, but you do need to respond so that it is understood that you do not discuss confidential information. "I really can't answer that question," should get the message across. Protect your reputation as a person who can be trusted.

Friends know that I have access to payroll information and sometimes press me for details. I get a lot of questions like, "Does Harlan make more than $150,000 a year?" One of my friends said that if I just answer yes or no, I'm not really telling what the person's salary is, so I won't get into trouble. How should I respond?

Friends who ask you for privileged information are not your friends. They are merely working acquaintances who are trying to use you. If you acknowledge that a person's salary is higher or lower than a certain number, you are divulging confidential information. In many companies, breach of trust is grounds for dismissal.

I have access to confidential material. Recently, the directors have been meeting in the conference room about a proposed new organization structure. Coworkers have started asking me what's going on. I am uncomfortable telling them I don't know, when I do know what's happening, but I can't elaborate.

Of course, the easiest response is to deny that you know anything by saying, "I am not sure what they are meeting about." If you are uncomfortable admitting you do not know when, in fact, you do, say, "Yes, I'm aware of the meeting. However, I really can't discuss it."

Because of changes in our company, there are always rumors floating around. Some are true. Some are not. Some are combinations of the truth and speculation. I work for the president and am well aware of all the changes. If someone asks me if a rumor is true or false, how should I respond?

One of the easiest ways to get yourself off the line is to hook someone else. A great comeback is, "Mr. Gregory is in his office. Perhaps you would like to ask him that question." A variation would be, "Mr. Gregory has stepped away. I could have him call you back so you can ask him yourself."

Another manager is very friendly. He often stops by to chat and casually slips in the conversation, "Another closed door? Wasn't Jerome in there last week?" Because he's so subtle, I find myself answering his questions. Just what is he up to?

He's using you. A friendly manager who is able to glean a bit of information here and a memo there may be able to piece the whole picture together later on. You are much too free with your information. Don't be so quick to answer his seemingly innocent questions. You may be surprised to find out that this manager isn't so friendly after all when the information starts to dry up. Exercise reserve when talking to him.

4-2

WHEN YOU HAVE CONFIDENTIAL INFORMATION THAT WILL AFFECT A FRIEND

Our company is being downsized and I have been working on various financial plans. One of my closest friends is going to be terminated after the first of the year. Should I tell her?

No. You are not doing your friend or yourself any favors by telling her what you know. Besides, plans have been known to change. You have an obligation to your boss, who is responsible for your salary, not to divulge privileged information.

I am aware of a merger that will soon be taking place in our company. I have a friend who is a stockbroker, who is always asking me what's happening at our company. Should I tell her what I know?

What you are thinking of doing is not only unethical, it is illegal. You would be giving your friend "inside information," something the Securities Exchange Commission frowns upon. Never divulge privileged information.

A friend is being considered for a position in our department. She has no idea at all there's going to be an opening and that her name has come up. I know she'd love to work in our area. Should I tell her?

What happens if approval is not received for the new position? What happens if her name is eliminated from the list of candidates? There are too many things that can change. Don't say anything to her. When the time comes, the appropriate people will handle the situation.

If your boss knows of your relationship with your friend, she may ask what you think of her as a coworker. Be prepared to field this type of inquiry. You may choose to beg off, saying "I really shouldn't answer that. I'm afraid I would give you a purely biased viewpoint." Or you may want to answer the question. "Although I'm a friend of hers, I know that her boss has been really pleased with the new filing system she set up recently."

4-3

PROTECTING SENSITIVE DOCUMENTS AND INFORMATION

Some sensitive information is circulating around the office. I didn't leak it, but I knew about it and feel that some people think I'm the one who talked. How are people able to find out confidential information?

A few tips should help you maintain confidentiality:

1. Safeguard confidential material on your computer by protecting it with a password. You would be amazed at how freely employees can roam from department to department after hours. It is very easy to turn on someone's computer, scan the directories, and print out a copy of a sensitive document. If you are networked, just by changing directories a person will have access to your documents.

2. Shred sensitive material. Don't toss it out in the trash or recyclable bin. If you rip it up, discard half in one wastebasket and half in another. Sensitive documents carelessly discarded are open invitations for office snoops.

3. Don't leave anything in the copier. Sometimes material that has been jammed in the copier is not completely removed. This can give the next user an eyeful. Shred incomplete sets or revised copies.

4. There are individuals who can and do read upside down or over your shoulder. If you are keystroking confidential material from handwritten copy, switch the screen on your computer and cover the handwritten sheets. If photocopying confidential material, strategically place yourself between the copy machine and the person waiting to use it. Or say to the individual waiting to use the machine, "I'll be a while" (even if you won't) and "I'll call you when I'm through."

5. The walls have ears! Don't talk about sensitive matters on the phone if there's a chance someone can eavesdrop. Don't discuss confidential matters in hallways or elevators.

I recently was reprimanded for throwing away some old documents without shredding them. My boss said they contained proprietary information. Exactly what is proprietary information and why is it so important?

Proprietary information includes marketing plans, business negotiations, advertising strategies, trade secrets, labor or contract negotiations, customer lists, and computer data. This information is vital to the operation of the company and should not be read by individuals outside the firm. It is considered privileged information and should be kept confidential. Documents carelessly tossed away may end up in the hands of a competitor. Documents that you think may contain proprietary information should be shredded. What you may consider unimportant lists of numbers can be substantial to others. Learn to recognize what information is considered confidential.

A coworker has been leaking salary information. Should I tell our boss or should I tell the coworker I know she's been leaking salary information?

Caution your coworker that in some companies breach of confidentiality is grounds for dismissal. Tell her in no uncertain terms that it is not professional for her to reveal such information. If she continues to leak information and you have proof, you have an obligation to discuss her behavior with your boss.

A secretary was cleaning out her boss's files and found several others make more than she does. Now she's developed a bad attitude and has been divulging information. What should I do about this?

Salary information is confidential. This is a delicate situation between the secretary and her boss. Tell her boss what you know, then let him handle the situation.

Discussing general employee problems and annual reviews is hard when your workspace is a cubicle. There are too many interruptions and we can be overheard very easily. How can I ensure privacy in these situations?

Use a conference room for confidential employee discussions, and ask the individual to meet you there. There will be no interruptions and no worries about someone overhearing your conversation. Employee meetings also can be held off-site, at a restaurant for breakfast or lunch.

I recently had to fax a confidential document. Our fax machine is located in a high-traffic area—the mail room. Once the cover sheet has been transmitted, the document is there for all to read. How do I protect sensitive documents that I have to fax?

Fax at off hours—during lunch time, for example, or at the beginning or end of the day. When there are fewer people around, there's less chance of someone accidentally reading your document. If you must fax during peak hours, carry a blank sheet of paper or folder with you. Just hold it over the fax copy, blocking out any text. If anyone comes up behind you to fax, your document will be screened. If you continuously fax confidential material, you may want to invest in fax modem and software for your computer. This way you can fax from your terminal. However, these programs are usually dedicated, which means while faxing the computer cannot be used for anything else—a small price to pay for the security and convenience of faxing at your work station. Be sure to call the receiving party so she can be on standby for the transmission. This is particularly true if the receiving machine is located in a central place. Remember faxes are not a good way to send confidential information because they can be easily intercepted.

I was working on a confidential document at my terminal when a manager came over to ask for a file. I was certain that while I went to the file cabinet, she was trying to read the hard copy upside down. Is that possible?

Sure. Try it yourself. You'll be amazed at how easily the document can be read. In the future, turn over the document from which you are typing and be sure to change screens on your computer.

Recently, an employee was terminated from our department for just cause. Afterward, he gained entry to our office over a weekend and erased documents on several computers that were password-protected. Apparently somebody forgot to delete his password code. What can we do to see that this does not happen again?

You've learned the hard way that security codes need to be updated immediately whenever employees are terminated. When a person is terminated, Human Resources should conduct an exit interview, at which time the employee should return any keys, company identification cards, or elevator passes. Human Resources should also make certain the terminated employee's password is immediately removed from the computer system. A message should go out to all computer operators to change their passwords.

In many companies, keys have been replaced by digital security pads. During business hours, employees punch in a universal password code into a keypad security lock. At night, the keypad is deactivated and keys are needed. Passwords should be changed whenever an employee is terminated. Some companies use plastic key cards that should be returned and deactivated when an employee is terminated.

We're in the midst of a big merger. I think someone has been listening to my telephone conversations at work. How can I find out if I'm right?

Telephones should have a privacy feature so that when a person is talking, no one can pick up an extension and listen to the conversation. Ask the person in charge of your telephone system to make sure the privacy feature on your phone is activated.

If you think your phone may be bugged, a security agency can come out and check your telephone system and your offices for listening devices. If your boss is involved in some sensitive negotiations, it may be worthwhile to have the office scanned. In the meantime, sensitive meetings should be scheduled off-site, in a hotel conference room, for example.

My boss is involved in a lot of confidential meetings right now. What can I do to improve security in our working area?

If your boss handles a lot of sensitive information, a desk-top paper shredder should be placed in her office—perhaps next to her telephone—so that any confidential notes or papers may be shredded immediately. Your boss will be more inclined to use the shredder if it's convenient. A shredder also serves as a reminder of the sensitivity of certain data and information.

Adopt a clean-desk policy and clear all documents from your desk and your boss's desk. This reduces the temptation of someone casually looking at sensitive files or letters left out. Someone could easily remove sensitive documents and copy them after you have gone home.

Lock all file cabinets before you leave the office and don't hide the key under your calendar or note pad. Keep the keys with you on your key ring. Give a key to your boss in case of an emergency. If you are absent or ill, she will have access to your desk and file cabinets.

Our office is relocating to another floor. I work in the Human Resources department, so the need for confidentiality is a must. Right now my boss has been offered one of three office areas for our location. Are some areas more secure than others?

Some office areas have natural barriers, such as floor-to-ceiling walls housing an elevator bank or conference room, which insulate the department. Avoid high-traffic areas or office amenities where workers can legitimately linger, such as near a copier machine, the lunchroom, the company library, or a drinking fountain or water cooler.

Another location is faxing a sensitive document. My boss told me to wait for it in the mail room, where our fax machine is located. Isn't this a bit much? After all, the mailroom person is supposed to deliver all faxes immediately.

Here's what really happens in the mailroom. The mailroom person steps out to deliver an important fax. Mr. Wiley, the marketing manager, drops off some mail and sees an incoming fax. Mr. Wiley, under the ruse that he's been looking for a fax, reads the incoming fax for your boss. Sensitive information has now been disseminated to the marketing department. Follow your boss's instructions and stand in the mail room. If sensitive faxes are received daily, suggest that your boss purchase another fax machine for your area or a fax modem and communications software for your personal computer. You can then receive these faxes in the privacy of your work area.

Another secretary has repeated things that are confidential. I think she's been eavesdropping from her work station, which is close to my boss's office. Is that possible?

After hours, sit at her work station. Have your boss pretend to talk on his phone and see what you can hear. You might also try this from your desk as well. In some offices the acoustics are such that you can actually hear what whispering individuals are saying. If that's the case, some additional soundproofing may be in order. In the meantime, having your boss close his door whenever he's on the phone may solve the information leak.

4-4

PROTECTING COMPUTER FILES

How can I protect information on my disks?

Follow these general tips:

- ◆ Disks can be erased by any electromagnetic field. Keep them away from your telephone.

- ◆ The surface of a disk should never be touched or cleaned. Don't set heavy objects on your diskettes or use paper clips, which causes warps or crimps and can lead to track failure.

- ◆ Safeguard information on master disks with write-protect tabs.

- ◆ Don't remove diskettes from the disk drive while the drive light is on. Early removal can scratch the disk, causing sectors to be unreadable and unrecoverable.

- ◆ Lock your storage box of disks inside a file drawer at night. Left in plain view, it is easy for someone to walk off with the whole file box and go through the disks at his or her leisure.

Somebody has been using my computer at night. How do I know? My keyboard is on an adjustable stand and the height has been changed. I do have some sensitive documents on my computer. Could that be what they're after?

In today's climate, you never know. You may have one document that coupled with others could provide someone with the whole picture. Nobody ever got into trouble because they were overly protective. Be cautious. Password-protect any sensitive documents. Keep your diskettes out of sight during the day and locked up at night.

Tell your boss you suspect someone is using your computer. He may admit that he was looking for something or that a family member was working on a school project. There could be a simple explanation. Then again, he may want to discuss your suspicions with the office manager and have a lock installed on your keyboard.

Over the weekend, someone entered my computer files and read twenty-seven documents. Many of these contained highly sensitive information. The person was identified and has admitted looking at the documents. My boss told me that this person, who is a vice president, was searching for information on a project he was involved with. When I asked my boss why this person was pulling up spreadsheets with titles nothing like the information he wanted, my boss said he thought it might be something he needed. If this had been a secretary instead of a V.P., she would have been fired on the spot. Why are they letting him get away with this?

Your boss knows what happened. This vice president may be in more trouble than you are aware of. Obviously, management wants to keep the situation quiet, so you should follow their example. Talk to the computer department to find out what additional security features need to be added to the computer system so this doesn't happen again. This may include installing software that will not allow access without a password or password log on. Check with your local software dealer for the one best for your office.

I went back to work after hours to get something I had forgotten and caught a coworker going through her boss's trash. Her face got really red and she said she was looking for a letter she thought he had tossed. I feel uneasy. Should I tell her boss?

There are legitimate reasons for a secretary to go through her boss's trash. Bosses frequently toss letters they should answer. One secretary would retrieve magazines and newspapers her boss had tossed so she wouldn't have to buy them. There are also some not-so-legitimate reasons. Was she looking for salary information, a confidential letter, or some revised marketing plans? Alert her boss. You might suggest that he get a desk-top paper shredder for any confidential documents.

Our company is coming out with a hot new product. To protect the company's product, a code name was used. Unfortunately, some product information has leaked out. Just how did this happen? We thought we had all the bases covered.

Since information was leaked, your company is still at risk. In order to protect future products and projects, your company may want to have its internal security audited by a consultant. An objective approach may provide some positive suggestions to improve security.

Our company is planning to sell one of its divisions. Negotiations have been going on for about a month now. This is top secret and only a few people know what's going on. There have been rumors from time to time that the company might sell a division. A newspaper reporter called me and told me he could make it "worth my while" if I would confirm the rumors so he could scoop the other papers. I could really use the money. I'm tempted because nobody would suspect me. Why shouldn't I make a little extra money?

If money can persuade you to talk, you shouldn't be on the team. Your boss trusts you to the point that you are considered a key player, privy to the team's game plans and strategies. Leaking information will destroy that trust. Since very few people know about the negotiations, it will be easy to pinpoint the person who leaked the information. You may find yourself out of a job and facing criminal charges. Warn your boss that a reporter has been trying to buy information.

I keep hearing about computer viruses. What is a virus? How do you protect your computer from a virus?

Computer viruses are hidden programs designed to worm their way into your disk operating system or software programs. They are transmitted by diskette or modem in executable programs. Viruses, can be just nuisances or totally destructive. Destructive viruses can change all 2s to 3s in spreadsheets, which may go unnoticed for a long period of time, or multiply in size to the point that no more storage space is available. Viruses can result in lost data and can even crash your computer system.

There are programs that detect whether your computer has been infected with a virus. If you do not have such a program, get one. The later versions of DOS have virus scanning capabilities built in.

Once your system has been deemed virus free, screen any diskette received for viruses. Diskettes interchanged among locations can easily be infected by viruses.

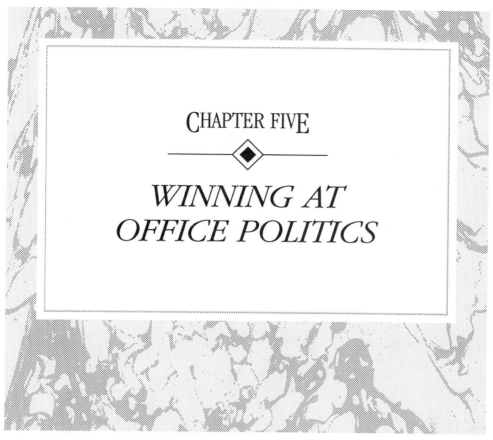

CHAPTER FIVE

◆

WINNING AT OFFICE POLITICS

Politics exists in every company in one form or another. For secretaries, office politics can be a nightmare because they're dealing with warfare on two levels, with their bosses and with their coworkers. In order to survive and succeed, you need to know how to "play the game" by understanding the dynamics of your office and by using this knowledge to your advantage. Remember, politics tend to get worse the higher you climb or whenever the job market tightens up.

Average employees often get ahead because of their political skills, while outstanding employees fall behind. Learn how to create opportunities for yourself by knowing who is in control, who has the power, how to spot the troublemakers, how to get the recognition you deserve, and how to handle a variety of political situations by avoiding common mistakes.

5-1
TIPS FOR GETTING AHEAD

I work very hard at my job, and I try to be an exceptional employee. My boss praises me constantly. I keep thinking I will get noticed and land that promotion, along with a raise, but I see people who don't work as hard as I do moving up. Why are mediocre workers being promoted, while I'm left behind?

If you have been in the business world for any length of time, you will see that you are surrounded by inequities. It is true that people who do a good job and are at their desks every day are often passed over for promotion. Secretarial jobs vary widely. To work as a legal secretary, you may need to be a fantastic typist with a legal vocabulary. To work for the CEO, your administrative skill is much more important than your word-processing speed. How do you measure up? Do you go that extra mile for everybody, not just the managers you want to impress? Are you viewed by others as extremely dependable? How innovative are you? Are you eager to try new software or implement new procedures? Probably the best compliment a CEO paid to his secretary was, "You continually amaze me. You're always trying to learn new things."

If you appear happy and content at your job, people may not think you are interested in a change. Sign up for a supervisory-skills seminar or a software class. Tell your boss you are interested in moving up. People don't know what you're thinking. You have to tell them. Also, you need to keep your coworkers informed of your accomplishments. Begin networking. Seek a mentor. You will find more information about networking and mentoring later in this chapter.

I'm accurate, but slow. I've been told by my boss that I'm doing a good job, yet the promotions never seem to come my way. How come?

Being accurate is a plus, but are you consistent? Selective bragging about the quality of your work may also help. And it's never enough just to do your job; you need to be enthusiastic about your work environment. Talk about challenges. Ask for additional assignments to prove you're ready for that long-awaited promotion. Also, image counts. Assess your professional image. Are you dressing for your present job, rather than for that future one? A selection of classic-styled suits can give you the edge to get you noticed.

Your boss and Human Resources can be great sources of information. A frank discussion with your boss might reveal that she has been leaving your name off lists because she felt you were comfortable or she was too comfortable to let you go. Human Resources might mention that senior-level positions require a skill that you are lacking. They might also be able to give you some career direction or counseling.

About once a month, my boss takes everyone in our department out for drinks after work. I don't drink and I really don't like to socialize after work. One of my friends, though, said I should go anyway as it would help my career. Does socializing after work really help you get ahead?

The fact that your boss invites everyone out for a few drinks to discuss something other than work indicates that it is important to him to get to know his staff on a social level. Yes, you should attend these sessions— maybe not every time, but often enough so he will know you are part of his team. If you don't wish to drink something alcoholic, don't. The designer bottled waters have become the trademark of the twenty-first century.

I can never think of anything clever to say in social work situations. I usually put my foot in my mouth. Are there any classes I can take for my foot-in-mouth disease?

Don't try to be the life of the party. By focusing on listening, there is less chance for a social faux pas. Keep a low profile. Let your boss or others grab the attention. It's enough that you are there. As you become more comfortable, you will be able to join more easily into the conversation. Socializing with coworkers often leads to a better understanding of them, which improves working relationships and diminishes the chance of saying something inappropriate.

I want to get ahead like everyone else, but I refuse to play the political game. As a secretary, I keep myself apart from all the manipulating, calculating "friendships." I think that by doing my job well, I will succeed. I also believe in telling the truth. During my last review, my boss said that while I did a fine job, other people in the department found me inflexible and reserved. I told my boss I was not into the political pretending that goes on in our company. He said he was surprised at my attitude. I've been feeling uncomfortable ever since. Why do I feel as if *I* did something wrong?

Politics is not all bad. Office politics, like government politics, can incorporate the good as well as the bad. Networking and mentoring are considered positive political strategies. Perhaps your concern about appearing political makes you seem inflexible and aloof to your coworkers.

Friendships formed at the workplace are not all calculating and manipulating. It is only natural that one wants to help one's friends. Perhaps people in your department feel you are not a team player—that you want only to do what is right for you, not necessarily what is right for the entire department. While doing a good job is important to anyone's success, it is difficult to win the game when you are not part of the team.

I have never been involved in office politics. It is degrading, childish, and is usually practiced by those without enough education or intelligence to get ahead on their own. However, I was recently told that I was guilty of political maneuvering in order to get some new computer equipment. Specifically, I was accused of sucking up to the boss and "pumping up" the amount of work I actually do in order to get the new equipment. The person who accused me also wants a new computer system, and I think she is the one doing the political maneuvering. What is the best way to handle this situation?

One of the unique qualities of office politics is the ability to clearly see political maneuvering in others, but not to recognize it in yourself. When someone else is currying favor with the boss for a specific reason or project, it is political. When you, perhaps, shade the truth a little, the situation becomes different. After all, you are simply being practical and straightforward to get the support you need. Managers encounter people currying their favor for a variety of reasons, and the good managers make a decision on the merit of the request. You might say to the person, "The decision to purchase equipment is not mine to make. I only presented my situation." And leave it at that.

Recently our department received several new computers and a laser printer. A close friend of mine was really upset. She has been begging for a new system, but nobody seems to feel it necessary. Of course, she's mad at me now. It's not my fault that I received the new computer equipment and she didn't. Isn't she being childish?

Since she is your friend, offer to show her how to make her request and present the facts. You might say, "I prepared a one-page summary describing what our present equipment could do, what our future projects were, and how we could best handle those tasks based on updating our equipment. I'd be happy to help you prepare a request for new equipment." She could have a legitimate need for new equipment yet not know how to convey that information to management.

I work in a large corporation in the marketing area. All the secretaries are pretty much on the same level, but one is always dropping names. She'll say that we should do something a certain way because it's the way "Charles" wants it. Charles is the senior vice president. Or she'll say "I told Charles my idea last week, and he thinks it will work in our department." Why does she feel the need to constantly tell us how "Charles" likes it?

Name dropping is probably one of the oldest political maneuvers. Insinuating that the "top" person has approved the idea is simply a way to control other people's actions and insure their cooperation. It usually works.

I told another secretary about my cost-savings idea for express-mail shipments. She wasted no time in mentioning my suggestion to the office manager, taking all the credit. She will even receive a bonus based on a percentage of the average monthly cost savings. I'm thoroughly disillusioned. I thought she was my friend.

Welcome to office politics, where anything goes if it means getting ahead. Confront your friend and explain why you resent the fact that she took all the credit. She may just try to salvage the situation by offering to straighten out the misunderstanding and sharing her bonus. If not, write off her friendship. You learned a valuable lesson. Next time you have a suggestion, keep it to yourself until you've worked out all the details or talk it over with someone outside the company. Then present your suggestion to management yourself, in writing.

A friend applied for a secretarial job in the company, but the position went to the CEO's niece. I'm upset about this blatant display of nepotism. Several secretaries have decided to ignore the niece.

It's not politically smart to alienate her. Reserve judgment until you get to know her better. She may be exceptionally sharp and bring other skills or experience to the job that your coworker didn't have. A positive networking opportunity awaits you.

5-2

UNDERSTANDING THE CORPORATE CHAIN OF COMMAND

I work for a vice president. Sometimes I get confused as to who has priority over my boss and whom my boss has priority over. How can I tell who outranks whom?

Every office has its own culture and chain of command. If you want to succeed, you must understand the power structure and learn to work effectively within that corporate organization. It starts with the president or CEO and works its way down.

Study your company's organization chart. By locating your boss's position on the organization chart, you can easily see who has authority over him, whom he reports to, who are his peers and who are his subordinates.

I work for the president of our company, and some people try to go around their boss and get approval for a project directly from my boss. My boss always sends the request back, irritated, and acts as if it's my fault. I feel that it is not my responsibility to tell a manager what he should or should not do. Am I correct?

All companies have a chain of command. Most people know the chain of command and respect it. However, there are always those people who think their situation is special or, because their boss is out of town, they try to skip a signature level. Your responsibility to your boss is to see that his time is not wasted. Simply point out to the employee that the project needs a certain approval signature before your boss will review it.

At certain companies, I can just as easily talk to the CEO as the marketing manager. At other companies, it's like pulling teeth to get to talk to a manager, let alone a vice president. Usually I am calling at the request of my manager, who is also a CEO. How can I get through?

Since your boss is a CEO, use that information to your advantage by mentioning it in all phone conversations. "Mr. Wade is returning Ms. Logan's call." Become familiar with the corporate culture of the various companies your boss deals with. If the CEO makes himself accessible, his managers will usually follow suit. Likewise, if the CEO makes himself inaccessible, his managers will probably do the same. You have an edge. Use your boss's name whenever possible.

Our office is downsizing, and we are eliminating an entire floor. Some vice presidents who had window offices are now getting interior cubicles. My boss refused a bigger office because I would be located down the hall. He took the smaller office because I would be located just outside his office. Now the other secretaries are jealous. Why? Frankly I think some of the other secretaries have nicer work areas.

Secretaries are status symbols. Since your boss placed more importance on you and your location than on himself, he demonstrated his level of respect for you and your skills. With this instant recognition comes increased political power. Give your coworkers some time to adjust to your new stature.

5-3
PROTECTING YOUR PROFESSIONAL REPUTATION

The other day I had completed all my work, so I called my friend. My boss kept giving me dirty looks and then asked me to hang up and come into her office. She told me not to make any more personal calls. Am I supposed to sit at my desk and stare into space until she gives me more work to do?

You are being paid to do a job. Once that job is completed does not mean you are necessarily finished for the day to do anything you desire. Be ambitious. Update your files or ask your coworkers if they need help. Ask your boss if there is a special project you can work on. Increase your computer knowledge. Don't develop a reputation as a person who lacks initiative and spends too much time on the phone chatting with friends.

Do you think it affects your reputation to hang around with someone who's mediocre? Evelyn was recently hired and I really like her, but her work habits are poor and she has already developed a reputation for being late.

Be careful. Your reputation is on the line, and it can be affected in two ways. If Evelyn begins showing some improvement, people will say that you're a positive influence. On the negative side, if your quality or quantity of work slips or you are absent frequently, people will say, "Oh, she must be taking lessons from Evelyn." You need to decide just how important this friendship is to you.

I was accused of saying something that I did not say. The person who accused me works in a different department, has been with the company longer, and for some reason has taken a dislike to me. There is no way I can prove I am telling the truth. What can I do in this type of situation?

Take the time to analyze your adversary. Does this person feel threatened by you? Is she jealous of you? Is there a problem or a specific situation you can remember that may have caused hostility; for example, did you embarrass her in front of her boss or peers? If so, she may be vindictive.

Once you are able to analyze her motives, you will know how to approach and deal with her.

Since you have denied the remarks attributed to you, consider the situation closed. In the future, though, don't underestimate your adversary. Be careful around this person. Put any instructions or questions to her in a written note and keep a copy for your file.

Develop your reputation for honesty and integrity:

◆ Avoid gossip. Don't start it and don't repeat it.

◆ Develop good work habits. Come in on time and don't stretch your lunch hour.

◆ Let coworkers know you can be depended upon to meet deadlines and to do a conscientious job.

Lunch has always been a gripe session. We complain about everything— our bosses, our workload, even our home life. We had no idea one of our lunch companions was telling her boss what we said. I told her I didn't appreciate her repeating our lunchtime conversations to her boss and have been giving her the cold shoulder ever since. Why would she do that?

People feel superior when they know things that others don't. The fact that she tells her boss makes her feel important and that she is not one of the gripers. At the same time, her boss is using her as a source for petty gossip. Don't say anything to her you don't want repeated to her boss.

Ms. Jones wasn't invited to my boss's meeting yesterday. My boss told me she didn't need to attend this session, but Ms. Jones didn't give me a chance to explain. She accused me of being inefficient and said I had deliberately dropped her name off the list. How should I have handled this?

Just why was Ms. Jones not invited to your boss's meeting? Was it an oversight on your boss's part or political maneuvering? An oversight needs only an apology and an indication that it won't happen again. Political maneuvering is another matter. Have your boss and Ms. Jones been feuding for some time on this issue or on previous ones? Stay out of the middle of this political battlefield. Tell your boss that Ms. Jones was quite angry because she wasn't invited and that the next time this happens, you will encourage her to speak directly to him.

Another secretary, Marilyn, has been bad-mouthing me to others, never to my face, accusing me of errors I had nothing to do with. Just how should I handle this?

Speak up. Let Marilyn know that you don't appreciate her comments about your work. Whenever the opportunity presents itself, refute her claims. For example, if approached by a coworker about a mistake, say, "You've been misinformed. That report was not my responsibility" or "Did Marilyn suggest that I worked on that? That's interesting. I was on vacation that week." The more concrete and definitive your rebuttal is, the easier it is to dispel rumors. Soon your coworkers will catch on to the fact that Marilyn is not always accurate. Also, let your boss know what's going on. He, too, may be in a position to provide some positive politicking for you.

<hr>

5-4

AVOIDING GENDER BIAS

I was just offered a promotion, but I would be working for a female boss. I have always worked for men and feel I might be uncomfortable working for a woman. Is this unusual?

Don't handicap your career with antiquated ideas about working for a female boss or with a male secretary. Decisions should be based on concrete facts, not fiction. Office bias is a sure way to slow or permanently stunt your professional growth. Always keep an open mind for growth opportunities.

It's only natural to feel apprehensive about job changes. Some secretaries resent women bosses because they make them feel inadequate by reminding them that their own career path did not lead them to the same high position. Analyze your reaction honestly. How do you know you won't like working for a woman boss until you try it? Don't let jealousy impair your judgment.

My friend is a good secretary who recently stated she prefers working for men because she can get away with more than she could if she had a woman boss. For instance, if she wants to leave early, she tells her male boss she doesn't feel well, that it is probably "that time of the month" and he gets flustered and tells her to go home. Is it true that male bosses can be manipulated this way?

To a certain extent, yes, male bosses are more susceptible to manipulation by female employees. The attraction between males and females is natural. How people use this attraction is unique. Some female secretaries adopt a flirtatious attitude to ask their male bosses for a favor, a day off, or to leave early. However, they would probably still get the day off had they asked without manipulation or flirtatious strategies.

I worked for a woman boss once and she was terrible. She constantly changed her mind about how she wanted things done, would fly into a rage if the file folders were out of alignment, and generally made my life miserable. Are most women bosses bad managers?

There are women bosses who are poor people managers. There are women bosses who feel insecure and focus on the smallest detail because they can't or won't focus on the "big picture." There are just as many men bosses who share these very same traits. What you want is a boss who recognizes your talents. You had one bad experience. Don't let bias color your judgment. It doesn't mean that all women bosses will behave in the same manner.

Our office just hired a male secretary/receptionist. He's asked me to lunch a few times, but I'm reluctant to go. I'm having a hard time understanding why he was hired. He just doesn't seem to fit in.

In all probability, he was hired because his job skills met management's requirements. On the other hand, office politics can sometimes be subtle. Management may have wanted to break up the female hierarchy or a well-entrenched clique in the office. About 12 percent of the secretaries in today's work force are males, and this segment is growing. Many males learned to type in order to keep up with today's computer technology. As traditional student summer jobs in construction and manufacturing became scarce, males found other employment. Temporary agencies recognized that typing is a skill and began placing students, whether male or female, in office positions. You may find him to be a valuable office ally. Get to know him better. You might ask a few friends to join you for lunch if it makes you feel more comfortable. He may welcome the chance to meet more people as well.

When women went into nontraditional jobs, they faced discrimination and harassment. Don't be guilty of the same gender bias. Secretarial work is challenging and rewarding. The scarcity of people with good administrative skills keeps employment high and salaries competitive. The male secretary has found a niche in the work place, working alongside his female counterparts.

We hired a male secretary in our office over the summer. People would walk through our department just to see him. It was very disruptive. The women would "oooh" and "aaah" and ask him how fast he could type. The men in our department said they liked working with him because he got the job done, as if we didn't. Why can't men stay out of places they don't belong?

The sentiments you expressed are the same ones women encountered when they entered jobs that traditionally had been held by men. Don't be guilty of fueling office bias. In a work environment, everybody belongs. The person who has the skills and ability to do the job should be able to work without harassment. Remember, too, that the "ooohs" and "aaahs" could be viewed as sexual harassment.

We hired Robert over the summer and he was great. He could type 68 words per minute. The managers loved him because he didn't get involved in cliques and wasn't seen chatting with the other secretaries. One manager said he never had to worry about what Robert would wear to the office on the day of the board meeting because he always wore suits. Another manager said Robert approached his job differently. What did he mean?

Robert obviously telegraphed the fact that he took his job seriously with his professional attitude and attire. By handling his position efficiently and effectively, Robert was guaranteed to be noticed. Don't ever discount the importance of secretarial work when climbing that corporate ladder. It all depends on where you put your career sights. For instance, Dan wants to work in corporate law and is working as a legal secretary while going to law school. He feels he is learning the job from the bottom up, making valuable contacts, while having full use of the company's law library for his studies.

Recently I lost out on a promotion to a male secretary. Frankly, I felt that I was better qualified and that he was hired because he was a male. What can I do?

Examine your thinking. If a female had landed the job, would you be so quick to cry foul? Promotions are not always based solely on skill level. Other factors are experience, education, appearance, attitude, and personality. Talk candidly to Human Resources. Find out how you compared in all aspects, not just skills. Then put your disappointments behind you. Management is already aware that you're interested in moving up. Maintaining a high level of professionalism may give you the edge the next time around.

I'm a male who has been working as a secretary for the past three years. I like the work and I'm good at it. I type 90 words per minute and took a shorthand class to increase my efficiency. The female secretaries resent me, and I feel locked out. It would be nice to talk to my peers about work-related problems, and I'm sure I could get some good tips. What can I do to make them accept me?

When you first started, perhaps you tried too hard to prove you were an equal by being self-sufficient. The result was that you created an invisible barrier that removed you from the other secretaries. Unfortunately, it can be difficult to break down barriers once they have been erected. Go slowly. Begin by asking for help. Ask someone to help you with something or ask a question relating to grammar or format. People like to help out. It makes them feel important. Work with your coworkers. Don't compete with them.

As a male secretary, I have a unique problem. I would like to get to know my coworkers better and socialize at lunch, but if I ask one of the other secretaries to join me for lunch, she thinks I am asking her for a date or trying to hit on her. How can I bridge this social gap?

Instead of trying to go out singly, ask if you can join the group. For instance, if several secretaries have lunch in the cafeteria, simply ask if you can join their table. If a group usually goes out once a week, ask if you can come along. Group settings are less formal. You will be able to get to know them, and more important, they will get to know you.

5-5
MENTORING

I hear so much about mentors. Just what is a mentor?

A mentor is a senior individual who has already achieved status in his or her career path and is willing to show you the ropes as well as the pitfalls. Think of a mentor as a coach, teacher, advocate, one who wants to give something back, to help the advancement of someone else. A mentor can also be someone outside the company, such as a priest, rabbi, or minister; a political figure in your community; a mayor, congressman or senator; a teacher you admire; or perhaps the owner of a local business. The individual receiving the advice would be the protegee—the pupil, the willing candidate.

A mentor will give you the guidance and constructive criticism you need to overcome obstacles in order to achieve your goals. Remember, mentors aren't around to solve your problems, only to guide you in making the best decisions for your career.

I can't just go up to someone and ask them to be my mentor. It sounds so hokey. How can I approach someone without appearing as if I just want to "use" them?

If you particularly admire the president's secretary, ask her to join you for lunch one day and explain how you would like her help and input. If you choose your boss as your mentor, enlist her help by explaining your goals. Start by asking your mentor how she achieved success, what the most important advice anyone gave her was, and what she would do over if she could.

If I asked my boss or someone in my company to be my mentor, she would just think I was brownnosing. What if she just laughs or doesn't take me seriously?

Most people will feel honored. However, in order not to be perceived as brownnosing, you have to listen to the advice given and act upon it. For instance, if she suggests that certain courses are needed before you can reach your goal, begin taking the courses. If you refuse to take the advice given, she will begin to suspect ulterior motives.

Someone asked me to be their mentor, but frankly, I don't feel that I am qualified. I really don't think I can help someone become successful in a career. Should I just tell the person I can't do it?

Some people are reluctant to become mentors because they don't feel particularly successful or politically savvy. Perhaps you need to reevaluate yourself. Obviously others see you as both successful and a leader. By becoming a mentor, you will be able to add another accomplishment to your career skills that will be recognized by your boss as well as your peers.

For quite some time, I have had a mentor who helped me very much. Without her support and guidance, I wouldn't have had the nerve to ask for the promotion I felt I deserved. However, I have outgrown her advice and now I feel guilty. How do you terminate your relationship with your mentor gracefully?

People tend to look up to their mentors, and that's the way it should be. You want advice from someone you admire. However, as you become more self-sufficient, you may begin to see weaknesses in your mentor and her advice. Sometimes a mentor will try to make you into a copy of herself, when you have no desire to be "made-over."

Thank your mentor for her support and advice. Casually mention that you are moving into the next phase of your career. Or you can ask her advice less and less frequently and let the relationship fade out slowly.

Recently a coworker was turned down for a job and she asked me if I had any idea why. I have a few suggestions, but I am reluctant to tell her. Should I be candid?

If you would like to help this person, this is an opportunity for you to become a mentor. A mentor would indeed tell her friend, in a compassionate manner, what suggestions might improve her chances a second time around. And make sure your comments are constructive and concrete, not critical or vague.

5-6
NETWORKING TO GET AHEAD

I keep hearing about networking and how it can help you get ahead. Exactly what is networking?

Networking is an example of positive politics. It's meeting the right people, being in the right place, and joining the right clubs. It's making important business contacts to gain access to information, business tips, and introductions to the right people.

To begin networking, join professional associations and organizations. Get active in your community. Do volunteer work for political functions. One of the best ways to network, however, comes from within your own organization. Get to know a variety of people in a variety of positions. Expand your awareness of others as well as your opportunities.

How will networking in my company help me in my career?

Networking within your company keeps upper management aware of your skills as an administrator. When an opportunity is available for advancement, your name may be right at the top of the list.

I want to get a job in the marketing department. However, nobody in marketing knows I'm alive and I heard there may be a secretarial position opening up. How can I get them to notice me?

Networking within the company means you should get to know some of the people in marketing. Ask the secretaries or others in the department to join you for lunch. Ask them what they do and respond in an interested and enthusiastic manner. Ask them to introduce you to others in the department. Let them know what you do and what you are capable of doing.

I am out of a job. You suggested networking through friends for employment, yet I really don't want my friends to know. I am afraid they will think I did something wrong and deserved to be let go. How can I keep my friends from thinking I'm a loser?

In today's job market, downsizing is synonymous with layoffs. Many people who went to work each day and did a good job are unemployed through no fault of their own. Friends recognize this and will try to help you. Tell your friends what happened and simply ask them to let you know if there are any openings where they work. Always keep several resumes with you and ask friends to distribute them to their Human Resources departments as well as to any friends in other companies. Call them on the phone to chat briefly and bring them up to date on your job search. "Well, I had a good interview yesterday, but I'm still looking. Any help will be appreciated. Keep in touch."

How can volunteer work help you get a better job?

You'll be meeting a lot of new people, which creates networking opportunities. People who do volunteer or community work are perceived as "doers." They are willing to take a stand and are considered leaders. They are willing to help those less fortunate, which shows compassion. You will be doing a service to your community as well as to yourself. You will meet other "doers" and other leaders. An unexpected opportunity may arise.

How can joining a professional organization help me get a better job?

You will meet people who work in your particular profession. Once again, this creates networking opportunities. Professional organizations also keep you informed on issues that may affect your job. They lobby for political reform; their strength is in numbers. While you, alone, may not petition for signatures or march for reform, you will have strength in the knowledge that you, as a member of a professional organization, will be represented. For a list of professional organizations of interest to secretaries, see the Appendix, Paving the Way for Success.

Is there any organization that can assist me in my job search?

Many secretarial associations provide support, information, and assistance in job searches. One of the major goals of many organizations is improving promotion opportunities. They will also keep you informed about the latest developments regarding employment and any new government regulations that may affect secretaries. Many of these professional organizations actively promote coalitions among civil rights groups, women's organizations, and labor unions to oppose federal initiatives to dismantle enforcement of equal opportunity laws. See the Appendix, Paving the Way for Success, for a list of organizations.

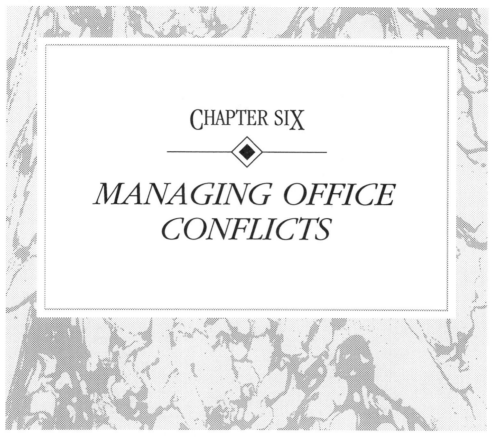

CHAPTER SIX

◆

MANAGING OFFICE CONFLICTS

As a secretary, you interact with many different people every day, from the secretary in the next cubicle to the president of the company, to the person who repairs the copy machine. You will inevitably face conflicts of one kind or another on a regular basis. You must know how to manage these conflicts— both minor and major—and how to prevent them from escalating into a crisis.

6-1

TIPS FOR DEALING WITH COMMON CONFLICTS

I work in a large office where I manage five secretaries. I realize that everyone can't get along all the time. What are the common causes of conflict in an office, and are there any general guidelines I can follow to deal with them?

85

Identifying what causes conflict is the first step to handling it.

- ◆ Communications failure is frequently a cause of conflict in offices. Incomplete directions and misunderstood commands both contribute to conflict. The reaction can range from frustration to inward anxiety to outright grumbling.

- ◆ Change is another contributor to office conflict. People have trouble adjusting to new ways of doing something, or to learning new techniques. People frequently have difficulty when the rules are changed. The safety net of familiarity is suddenly pulled out from under them. Nothing they do is good enough anymore. People feel threatened by change. Reaction is usually frustration, anger, and lowered morale.

- ◆ Rejection causes conflict. When an idea or plan is rejected, certain individuals may take it personally, feeling they are being told they are no good. Or they may feel their idea or plan was rejected for political reasons. Reactions can vary from grumbling to open hostility. Morale is affected as people take sides in the dispute.

6-2

WHEN YOUR BOSSES DON'T GET ALONG

I work for two managers who are feuding, and I am the one caught in the middle. How should I handle the situation?

Stay out of it to avoid being forced to choose sides. Don't get pulled into bickering situations. If they argue in front of you, just stand there and let them argue it out. When they decide how it (whatever they were arguing about) is to be handled, repeat your instructions back to them: "You want a list of all the customers in the Southwest region by zip code?"

6-3

HOW TO RESPOND TO INAPPROPRIATE OR UNJUST CRITICISM

My boss made me so angry I could spit! He deliberately embarrassed me in front of a group of friends by accusing me of an error that I didn't make. I

just stood there like a dummy and didn't even defend myself. What should I have done?

To be falsely accused is an injustice that should be corrected as soon as possible. Ask your boss if he has a few minutes and explain that you will accept the responsibility for errors you make, but that you did not make that one. Avoid finger pointing or saying "he did it, not me" but let your boss know you do not appreciate being accused of an error you did not make, especially in front of colleagues.

I work as a secretary-receptionist for a small firm. I was told to screen all calls. We hired a consultant to do some work, and I was told the consultant would be in one of our offices for three to six months and that it was not necessary to screen his calls. One day, I paged him, but he did not answer the page. I asked the caller if I could take a message. She said no, that she would call back. Later on, I mentioned to him that he had missed a call. He asked me who had called. I told him I didn't know, that she said she'd call back. He asked if it was his wife. Once again, I said I did not know. He walked off irritated and told my boss I was doing a poor job. My boss told me to screen all calls from now on. How can I do a good job if they keep changing what I'm supposed to be doing?

This is a classic case of communications failure. You feel frustrated and angry because they changed the rules in the middle of the game without telling you. You also feel helpless. You have now been given a new set of directions. Screen all calls from now on. Also, don't be afraid to expand the rules a little. If someone calls in, it is always appropriate for the person answering the phone to ask "who's calling" in order to inform the person who missed the call.

There's a secretary in our office who constantly finds fault with me and is quick to point out my errors to coworkers. I don't know her very well and have no idea why she is doing this. What should I do about it?

There can be any number of reasons for her behavior. She could feel threatened by you and must constantly point out your shortcomings so she can feel superior. She could be jealous of your position or she could feel that people like you and not her. Maybe you remind her of someone she never got along with in school. Whatever the motivation, she's acting like a bully. Talk to her privately and ask her what's bothering her. See if you can get her to open up. There could have been a misunderstanding that you are not even aware of. If you can't straighten it out privately, then the next time she attacks, be ready. Prepare a game plan. Don't raise your voice but firmly tell her to cease and desist.

There is a person in our department who has to have a scapegoat. He has attacked several people in my department with his cutting comments. Unfortunately, it now appears that he has chosen me. Just because I'm quiet doesn't mean I'm insensitive to his cutting remarks. I'm ready to quit. Is this my only solution?

Don't quit. What happens if you go to another company and have to work with another person who always needs a scapegoat? Solve the problem instead of running away from it. Privately confront this person and ask why he is dumping on you. Explain that you have always tried to do your work properly and you can't understand why he is constantly undermining your efforts. People who are looking for a scapegoat are no worse than bullies. By standing up to the bully, you have sent a message that he should back off and he will, most likely, go find someone else to pick on. This may be why he has used so many scapegoats in your department—when one stands up to him, he finds another.

6-4

COPING WITH COMPLAINERS

We are having a new telephone system installed in our office. I am in charge of coordinating this change, which involves removing the old phones and replacing them with the new units. I am also in charge of training people to use the new system. Some of my coworkers whine and complain about the new system. They don't like their new phone numbers. They don't like the color of the new phones. The new phones just don't "sound" right. People are also uncooperative about attending the training classes. This is so petty, but responding to all these petty complaints takes up a good part of my day. What can I do?

Change is threatening. The telephone on your desk is a familiar friend you can depend on. Suddenly, there is a different phone, a different system, new passwords for voice mail, the need to think before you transfer a call.

Change disrupts familiar patterns. What was once automatic now requires effort.

Understanding why people react the way they do will help you deal with them. Urge as many coworkers as you can to attend the training sessions. Be patient. Expect complaints, but be ready with explanations for the purchase of the new system. This is one of those occasions when you should be prepared to meet any conflicts and questions head-on. One way to do that is to prepare a handout that outlines why the change is being made, what new features will be available with the new system, and whom to call with any questions.

There is one secretary in our office who is always complaining. I get so sick of hearing about all her problems and complaints I could scream. I want to tell her I'm not interested in hearing her complaints and if she's that miserable in her job she should quit.

The constant complainer can get on your nerves, especially when she complains about things over which she has no control. This is usually a person who is used to getting her way by whining and complaining until someone else takes action to handle the problem. When she starts complaining, tell her to work out some solutions to the problem and then let you know what they are and you will be glad to discuss them with her. Or, tell her there is nothing you can do about it and change the subject to the weather (something else you cannot control).

6-5

WHAT TO DO ABOUT KNOW-IT-ALLS

There is a person in our office who seems to thrive on confrontations. If there is ever a problem, she is in the middle of it. Yet, she never seems to suffer and walks around with this know-it-all attitude. I try to avoid her. I don't understand why the company doesn't do something about her. Is there anything I can do?

In just about every office there is a person who is a troublemaker, show-off, or know-it-all. There are certain personality types who thrive on being the center of attention, even if it's unfavorable. By being in the middle of office conflicts, they get the attention they desire and make a power statement at the same time. In effect, they are saying, "See, I can take care of myself and nobody better cross me." Don't get caught up in her anger. The more you can ignore it, the more you will defuse it. However, in the event you end up in a confrontation with this type of individual you should be ready to stand your ground on issues that make a difference.

No matter what I say or do, there is one person in the office who always has to check my information. If I say the board meeting was moved to Wednesday, she'll call someone else to confirm it. If I say I ordered lunch for the marketing meeting, she will call the caterer to make sure I did. If I say someone is sick or in the hospital, she will call Human Resources to see if it's true. It's annoying that she doesn't believe me as I've given her no cause for this type of treatment. I don't notice her checking up on other people's information. How come she's singled me out?

Perhaps she was caught in an unflattering position in the past when she relied on information that later proved to be inaccurate. Trust is a very fine thread and once you have misplaced your trust in someone and the thread is broken, it can become impossible to patch the thread back together. You feel safer trusting no one, depending on no one. Some people are simply uncomfortable with information received from others. Whatever the reason, her behavior, while annoying, is harmless. Try putting information to her in writing, in the form of a memo or short note.

6-6

DEALING WITH BLAME-SHIFTERS

There is a secretary in our office who gets away with murder. Whenever anything goes wrong, it is never her fault, even when it is. She always manages to wiggle out of it.

Blame-shifters (it's not my fault, no one told me, or I couldn't help it) are found in almost every office. The blame-shifter is usually also the helpless victim (poor me, everything happens to me). The blame shifter needs to understand that she is responsible for what happens in the department whether it is her job or not. Make power statements "even if it is not your job, you know how we usually handle this report." This individual needs to be taught to think to solve problems instead of to think of ways to get around problems.

Individuals who take responsibility for their actions receive the respect of coworkers and managers. You might remind the blame-shifter that a person who is never responsible for a project can never receive credit for it either.

6-7

WHEN YOU SPEND TOO MUCH TIME COVERING FOR A COWORKER

One secretary in our office is never at her desk. She flits around all over the place, and I end up answering her phones. I work for five sales managers, and my phones are always busy. I'm fed up. Short of tying her to her chair, is there anything I can do?

Since you are covering her phones, and the messages are getting through, no-one notices that this secretary spends a lot of time away from her desk. Because there are no complaints everyone thinks everything is just fine—except you. Get a telephone message pad that makes a carbon copy of all messages. Make sure you fill in the date and time on each message. It won't be long until you will have documented evidence that she is away from her desk for long periods.

Go to your boss and tell her what is happening. But don't point the blame at the other secretary. Say something like, "Since Sherry is always running errands or making copies, I spend too much time answering her phones and my work is falling behind." Suggest solutions such as, "Perhaps we need to hire a part-time person who could come in during the afternoons and (either run the copies and/or errands) or help answer the telephones." Maybe you should simply request the addition of voice mail to your coworker's telephone. Don't go into your boss whining and complaining; state the problem without being judgmental and offer solutions.

6-8

HOW TO HANDLE NOSY COWORKERS

I work for a partner in a law firm. The office manager is always questioning what I am doing. For instance, if I come back late from lunch, she wants to

know where I was, intimating that I was shopping or dawdling. Actually, my boss asked me to drop off some documents on my lunch hour. On other occasions I arrive late for work because I am either dropping off or picking up some important legal papers or depositions. My boss knows what I am doing, but I don't quite know how I should respond to the office manager.

Don't be put on the defensive. You don't have to defend your actions to anyone in the office (except your boss, of course). But, perhaps the office manager needs to know in order to assure adequate phone coverage; maybe some of the other secretaries are jealous because they see you coming in late or leaving early and they can't. Talk to the office manager and explain briefly that your boss frequently asks you to do these errands, and if it is a problem then the three of you need to sit down and discuss other ways to handle it.

One of my coworkers always wants to know what projects I am working on. He will be talking to me, but I can tell he is trying to read what is on my desk or my computer screen. I find this annoying but don't know what to do.

Simply turn over, or lay a file folder casually across any notes or papers lying on your desk, while this person is chatting with you. You can hit the "page down" button on your computer, which will move any wording out of the range of the screen. If the person comes up behind you, finish what you are doing (hit the page down key or save the document and clear the screen), then turn around and say, "Just had to finish that up; what can I do for you?" There are also screen covers for computers that can be purchased for people who work with confidential information. These screens make it difficult for people to read what is on your screen while you are working.

There is a nosy coworker who bugs me all the time about where I am and what I am doing. How can I get him off my back?

Simply agree with him. If you are returning from lunch an hour late because you were running an errand for your boss and your coworker approaches you and says, "Returning from lunch a bit late, aren't you?" merely smile sweetly and reply, "Yes, I certainly am." He can't argue with that, can he? By agreeing with him, you will throw him off; by not stammering out an excuse for your tardiness, you will frustrate him a little, too. He will tire of his game when he realizes that you won't play—then he'll be off to bait someone else.

EFFECTIVE WAYS TO DEAL WITH CONFRONTATIONS

Confrontations may be cunningly subtle or outright angry, abusive attacks. If the attack is expected, you can, and should, be prepared for it. For instance, if you and this person have had minor run-ins before, you should know that your actions could trigger a confrontation. You must also be prepared to handle unexpected confrontations.

I was accused of holding up an expense report because I didn't like the person who submitted the report. This is untrue. Two receipts were missing and I had sent a memo requesting either the receipts or a written explanation—company policy before it could be processed. I was so shocked by the verbal assault on me, in front of my boss and coworkers, that I just sat dumbfounded, unable to defend myself. He ended his verbal assault by saying he "wanted his expense reports processed on time in the future" and walked off. Everyone acted as if they hadn't heard or began shuffling papers. I got up and went to the bathroom and burst into tears. What should I have done?

Be prepared when you think something you have done may trigger an angry response. Know what you are going to say and present your side in a clear but level tone (don't raise your voice). If the attack is totally unexpected and you are afraid to say anything because you may burst into tears, simply say, "Excuse me, please" and walk (shoulders straight) to the ladies room to recoup—this gives you time to assess what's happened and plan your counterattack. It also stops the angry diatribe directed at you.

Another way to handle this type of situation is to offer sympathy to the attacker, "If that's the case, I can understand why you are so angry. Let me look into the matter and get back to you." Or, perhaps, "I can see you're angry right now. What if I get back to you with some answers so we can discuss this problem later."

Whatever you do, don't get caught in a screaming match. Avoid personal insults.

In any confrontation, try to calmly assess the situation:

♦ Did you know the attack was coming? Is it something that has been brewing for weeks?

◆ Who is doing the attacking? Your boss? Another secretary? A person from another department? Where it's coming from will also have a bearing on how you will react. Departmental rivalries often cannot be avoided. If the marketing and accounting departments have been feuding for years, you'll become the enemy just by being in the department.

<hr>

6-10

WHAT TO DO WHEN YOU ARE ANGRY AT YOUR BOSS

My boss can be very difficult to work with. I knew this when I took the job. I find that instead of talking back, I suppress my anger, which causes my skin to break out and itch like crazy; my doctor finally figured out what was causing this condition. My doctor says I have to let the anger out, but I don't know how. Is it appropriate for me to let my boss know that I'm angry with him?

There is no reason to hold your anger inside. Anger is a natural human emotion. If you let go with little pieces of anger when something happens that upsets you, you will feel much better. The best thing to do is to go with your gut instincts. For instance:

◆ If your first reaction is: "Why are you bringing that up now?" then go with it.

◆ If your first reaction is: "How am I supposed to do that, when I am supposed to finish this first?" then go with it.

◆ If your first reaction is: "I'm going to punch out your lights and break your face," hold up, head for the restroom, and cool off.

My boss is much too nitpicky. For example, she wants all her file folder labels to line up perfectly. I am not exaggerating. It seems to me that she focuses on minor details too much. To me, it is more important to be able to find the file than to spend hours just to make sure all the labels are perfectly in line. Her secretaries usually quit after about three months. I can't afford to quit, but she is driving me crazy. The Human Resources department knows she is hard on secretaries, but they just keep hiring new ones. Is there anything I can do to solve the problem?

Complaining won't help much. Why don't you try to do things the way the boss wants? Even if it is nitpicky and takes you hours, your boss is paying you to do that very thing. So, do it—with a smile. Lots of bosses have quirks that will set them off; learn to deal with it. It is a growth opportunity for you. Besides, it is always good to be known throughout the company as the only secretary who could work with so-and-so; it will enhance your reputation.

I had (what I thought) was a good idea for processing work orders that come through my department. When I explained it to my coworkers, they said my boss would never go for it. I told him my idea and he rejected it. He made me feel silly and stupid. Now, I am not comfortable working for him. I feel he has a low opinion of me. Should I ask to transfer or just start looking for another job?

What you are feeling is misplaced anger. You are mad at your boss because he made you feel silly and stupid. If you quit your job, you will be proving he was right. What was a crushing blow for you could have been a routine moment for him. Did he explain why your idea wouldn't work? Maybe he really thought it was smart of you to try to figure out a way to improve the order processing—you may have really impressed him. You don't know how he felt. You know only how you felt. Anger can distort your perceptions.

Everywhere in our company they are pushing teamwork, but our boss will call us in and give us identical assignments and then wait to see which one of us can do it the fastest. Instead of working together, we are constantly working against one another and I end up angry at my boss as well as my coworkers. I would like to tell Human Resources what he's doing because morale in our department is so low everybody quits at the first opportunity. What should I do?

If you are having difficulty working with your boss, talk to someone in Human Resources. But don't do it in a judgmental or whining manner. Be specific. State specific projects and name the others who were involved. Human Resources cannot act without specific information. They will probably agree that this person needs to attend a few seminars on the proper way to manage and motivate people. The turnover rate in your department is another indication that something is wrong.

I can't stand my present boss. I am transferring departments next month. What should I say to him, if anything? He really needs lessons in management. I want to tell him, "You're a lousy manager." Do you think I should?

It's not a good idea to burn any bridges. However, when you leave you might want to have a chat with him and tell him that you realize the two of you did not always see eye to eye but that he challenged you and you learned a lot working for him (you don't need to mention you learned what not to do). If you have the opportunity to discuss the situation in your former department with a representative from Human Resources, please do so, but once again, be specific, state details. Human Resources people know that sometimes personality clashes do occur, and it is not necessarily a reflection on either one of you.

6-11

COPING WITH YOUR BOSS'S TEMPER

My boss has a terrible temper. I was warned when I was hired, but I didn't think it would bother me. However, it does. He will have a screaming fit and yell. Once he even threw a three-ring binder against the wall, and it broke open and all the papers spilled out. Because he brings in a lot of accounts (money) to the company, the top brass overlooks his problem. I can't afford to quit this job but never knowing when he will throw a tantrum (or what might trigger it) is making me a nervous wreck. Is there anything I can do?

First of all you must realize that the anger is not directed at you. This type of behavior, while juvenile and even infantile, is often tolerated when the person is making a lot of money for the company or when the person is in a position of power. Is there anything you can do? No, there is nothing you can do to suddenly make this person nice and pleasant to work with. Try to stay out of his way when he is in a "mood" or "temper" or when you know something is about to set him off.

You can control your response to the temper outbreaks. Don't run off to the bathroom crying. That only adds to the furor he is creating. Simply try not to react much at all. Other than that, there is not a lot you can do to control the situation. You can ask for combat pay—if you are well paid it may help you tolerate his temper tantrums a little better.

<hr>

6-12
HANDLING NOISY COWORKERS

I sit near a group of people who work for another department. They are always very noisy, laughing and joking all day. My job is very demanding. I find the noise distracting. Also, I don't see how they can get any work done. If I sat around laughing and talking all day, I would get in trouble. Because it is a large group of people, nobody in my department wants to say anything. Is there power in numbers?

Probably the reason they have not been reprimanded is because, despite all the laughing and joking, they must be getting their work done well. Humor is a great stress reliever. It's a smart way to relax the atmosphere and cut the pressure. The entire department seems to share a camaraderie, which indicates they work as a team. On the other hand, your work and your work style seems to require quiet and freedom from distractions. Perhaps you can ask for a change in work space, explaining your need to your boss, rather than complaining about them. If a move is not possible, you or your boss may want to discuss the problem with that department's supervisor.

<hr>

6-13
WHEN YOU'RE ASKED TO DO WORK FOR ANOTHER MANAGER

I work in a fairly large office and each secretary has to relieve the receptionist for lunch and breaks about one day a month. When I was relieving for lunch, one of the other executives came out and gave me an assignment because her secretary was at lunch. It was a five-page report she had dictated. Just because I was the only one around, I got stuck with it. I wasn't happy and I guess it showed. Why couldn't it wait until her secretary got back?

When you are relieving at the reception desk, you are considered public property. If there is a tape player and word processor at the reception desk, there is no reason you should refuse to do the project. You should have accepted the project gracefully. You would have been viewed as a competent assistant and a team player. Now this particular person will remember your negative attitude (and at the right opportunity may mention it to your boss); when a boss starts receiving negative reports on your behavior, it usually affects your chances for promotions, raises, or both.

Because I get my work finished on time, I am constantly asked to help out in other departments. How do I refuse to take on a project for another department when they ask?

Most companies like to think their employees are part of a team, and as a member of the team, are willing to help out when a department needs you. However, if you are frequently asked to help out because your work is finished, it could mean (1) that you don't have enough to do and they should consider someone part time for your position or (2) the other department actually needs full or part-time help because they are unable to do their work without constantly "stealing" someone from another department. You are being paid to work for the company whether it is for your department or someone else's. Accept the responsibility to help out. This is a great networking opportunity.

One of the vice presidents asked me to work on a special project. I tried to tell her that another secretary was just as capable as I and could easily do the job, but she wouldn't listen. Why me?

Why not you? You need to listen to the response your suggestion received. The vice president really wanted you to perform the task, even if someone else was just as capable of performing it in your eyes. In the vice president's eyes, you were the only one she wanted working on the project.

Handle the project as instructed. Farming it out after you were explicitly requested to complete it could be viewed as insubordination. If anything happens to the project, you will have compounded the error by not following instructions.

Again, this is one of those situations where you can take either the negative or the positive approach. The negative approach is the "why me?" syndrome. You can feel taken for granted and unimportant. The positive approach is the "why not me?" attitude. You can feel pleased that the vice president knew you would handle the project just as she wanted it, no exceptions.

6-14

SCHEDULING CONFERENCE ROOM TIME

Every large office has conference rooms. There is always one conference room that is a little bigger or a little nicer and everyone wants to use it for their meetings. How do you decide who gets which conference room?

Part of my job is to schedule conference room time. I ask how many people will be in attendance, how long will they need the room, if "outsiders" will be present (if there are outside guests, we sometimes order refreshments), if they will need audio/visual equipment, etc. Based on that information, I tell them which conference room is available. Some people schedule their meetings in advance. Suddenly a vice president will call and say he needs a conference room fast and I have to kick out someone who had scheduled the room weeks earlier and give them a smaller room. I don't think this is fair to the people who schedule in advance. Is there anything I can do?

As a matter of fact, there is. You are in control; you are in a power position. It is true that frequently management needs to call a meeting on the spur of the moment, and you should certainly cooperate. You should remember, too, that rank does have its privileges. If you come head to head with a vice president, you will probably be the loser. However, if you suspect that these meetings were scheduled in advance and someone simply forgot to call and reserve a meeting room, it is up to you to make a decision. Making decisions always carries a risk so make sure it is an informed decision. If the meeting has been scheduled for a long time and outsiders will be attending, put the vice president in one of the smaller rooms. If questioned, explain that so-and-so had reserved the larger conference room weeks ago and clients will be attending. If the vice president is having a staff meeting, explain your reasoning (and the need to reserve the conference room early). However, if the vice president insists on kicking out the other meeting, simply notify the other person that their meeting has been rescheduled to Conference Room B due to an unexpected meeting scheduled by the vice president.

People often eat lunch in our conference rooms and leave the table messy. Crumbs, papers, dirty cups are left behind. When I schedule a meeting, I can't tell if the room is clean or not; some are even located on other floors. But, boy, do I hear about it when they walk into the messy conference

room for their meeting. It's not my job to clean the conference rooms. What can I do?

You realize a problem exists but you are doing nothing to help solve it. In effect, you are saying, "It's not my job. My job is just to schedule the conference rooms." Why don't you try to solve the problem? Could someone from Facilities check the rooms each morning and each afternoon to be sure they are clean? Maybe people should not be allowed to eat in the conference rooms. Do you have a lunchroom? Think of a solution that you can present to your boss. Instead of saying, "It's not my job," tell your boss about the problem and how aggravating it must be to walk into a messy conference room; then suggest a solution. Your boss may be too busy with other matters to tackle the problem of the messy conference rooms and will appreciate your suggestions.

My problem is not with employees who eat lunch in the conference rooms and leave them messy, but with the top executives. It looked as if they had had a food fight with those little mayonnaise and mustard packets. Another meeting was scheduled in that room later in the afternoon and when the attendees for the meeting walked in, they were appalled. What can you do when it's the top executives who have no table manners? I had to call building maintenance workers to come up with soap and water and clean the room.

Everybody has a boss, and the top executives are no exception. Since you had to call building maintenance to clean up, it means your company will be charged for the cleaning. Find out how much it cost (probably through the Facilities department). Approach your boss with what happened at the meeting and how much it cost to clean it up. Then state that a certain department should be charged the cleaning fee and that he should be told that he will no longer be allowed to use that conference room until his (and his friends') table manners have improved. Let's face it, not a lot of business is getting done in this type of meeting.

I had reserved the conference room at 10:30 A.M. for my boss's meeting, but Joe, another manager, said he wanted a quick staff meeting and would be out by 10:00 A.M. However, at 10:00 he was still in there. When I checked at 10:15, he was still in there. You guessed it, they didn't leave until after 11:00. I had to scramble around and get another conference room for my boss. I was mad, but he just laughed it off. What should I have done to get Joe out of the room?

At 10:20 you should have opened the door and said that Mr. Zulewski's meeting was going to begin at 10:30 and the attendees would be showing up any minute. Could he please end his meeting (or move it to Conference Room B, which was now available) so you could begin setting up. If he refused to vacate the conference room, you should certainly have arranged for a backup meeting room (Conference Room B), but you should also let your boss know what happened and how you handled the situation.

6-15

HANDLING CONFLICTS THROUGH NEGOTIATION

To negotiate means to bargain to reach an agreement. A good negotiator is someone who can create a "win-win" situation. The person who can bring two differing sides to an agreement, with neither side feeling as if it had given in, is rare indeed.

Our company is going through some hard times and my boss said not to expect an increase in salary this year. My raise was low last year, and I was really counting on an increase this year. Asking for a raise seems futile, but quitting seems just as futile because all companies seem to be cutting back. Is there anything I can do?

The goal of negotiation is to solve whatever problem or conflict is facing you. Don't ask (or worse yet, demand) an increase in pay. Sit down with your boss and explain your financial situation and ask what you can do to increase your salary. Tell her you want to earn what is fair for your position and that you know she doesn't want to pay you anything that would be less than fair. This approach might make your boss more agreeable to exploring other options, such as increasing your duties or upgrading your position in the department. Maybe she will suggest you return to school and that the company will reimburse you for the classes; better education translates into better pay.

My boss told me my work had been slipping and I had better start paying attention to my job if I wanted to keep it. I know I have been making a lot of mistakes lately, but I am getting divorced (no one at work knows). I have two small children and we are going to move to an apartment as soon as I sell the house. I am an emotional wreck. I don't want to tell him because I

don't want it to sound as if I am looking for sympathy and making excuses for my poor performance. Instead I end up arguing with my boss and defending my mistakes.

You need to sit down and talk to your boss. Tell him about the divorce and the reason for your errors. Explain that you understand he's concerned about your poor performance and that you are, too. Negotiate some solutions. Perhaps some of your work could be farmed out to another department or taken over by another secretary for a few months. Maybe your boss will be able to allow you to work flexible hours for a while. Your company may have a crisis-counseling program that can also help see you through the divorce. You don't know what options can be arranged until you explore them.

I want to extend my child-care maternity leave because the person I hired to take care of my child won't be able to start work for another month. Our company has been firm in not extending maternity leave so I dread even asking my boss. Should I just call in and quit?

You need to stop for a moment and focus on the real issue. The real issue is not to get your maternity leave extended, but to make sure your child is taken care of properly. Sit down and explain what has happened and ask your boss for his input. You may be able to work out a part-time schedule, or someone in the office may know someone who could provide temporary child care. Your boss may ask management to rethink their policy on the extension of maternity leave. Don't eliminate any options that may be available.

6-16

COPING WITH COMPANY LAYOFFS AND TAKEOVERS

Rumor has it that large layoffs will hit the office staff soon. I can hardly concentrate on my work. What will I do if I lose my job? What if I can't pay my rent?

Layoffs, downsizing, rightsizing—no matter what trendy word is used it still means that people are going to lose their jobs. Many companies find it necessary to lay off portions of their work force. If you are afraid you will lose your job in the next layoff, don't sit around and worry; take some positive steps to prepare yourself for the future.

- Get your finances in order. Pay the minimum balance on your charge accounts and put every penny you can into a savings account. You may need that money to live on until you can find another job.

- Update your resume. Make sure you list any educational seminars you have attended or software programs you are familiar with.

- If you need to finish school, this is the time to go back. Begin a class that will help you find another job or enhance your present knowledge.

- Make sure you are computer literate. Becoming familiar with the popular software programs used in your company might be your key to survival.

- Begin networking. If you are not a member of a professional organization, now would be a good time to join one. Let your friends know there is a possibility of a layoff and you may be in need of any assistance they can give.

- Check the resources available at your local library. You can check newspaper ads and job guides. Several libraries are now on-line with a computer service that lists jobs available in your area (or all over the country).

I didn't get laid off, but several of my friends did. Now I feel guilty because I have a job and they don't. How do I deal with the guilt?

What you are feeling is survivor's guilt. It's the reason people always slow down to gape at an accident scene. They are not really morbid; they are thinking, "It could have been me; but it wasn't. I'm safe for now." Offer as much help and support to your friends as you are able to give.

I didn't get laid off, but my best friend did. Now she won't even speak to me. She acts as if I'm the one who laid her off. What can I do?

Sometimes friends who are laid off resent those who are employed. Try to be understanding. They have been wounded and are in a state of shock. On one level she knows you had nothing to do with her being laid off, but on another level, she resents you for having survived. Help your friend get through this by offering your assistance in helping her find a job, perhaps helping her with her resume or just being there when she needs to blow off some steam.

Rumors have been circulating about layoffs in our company. I work in Human Resources and have typed up some reports that confirm there will be some layoffs. One of my best friends is on the list to be laid off. She is thinking of buying a new car and I want to tell her not to do it. Should I tell her so she can start looking for something now?

It's tough to be in the position you're in, but your allegiance belongs to the company. They have trusted you with this information because they respect your integrity. If you tell your friend, she may resent you for telling her. Her boss is the one who should tell her. He hired her, he has been responsible for her work, and he must be the one to tell her about the layoff. Don't jeopardize your position or your integrity.

I work in Human Resources and suddenly everyone is my buddy and wants to go to lunch with me because we are going to have some layoffs and they want to pick my brain. Do they really think I'm that naive?

No, they don't think you are that naive. They are that desperate. They are hoping you will leak some information on the layoffs, such as which department will be eliminated or when the cuts will begin. Protect the confidentiality of your position and don't have lunch with anyone you don't consider a true friend.

With all the rumors going around about layoffs in my company, I can't concentrate on my job. I just sit and worry and make mistakes I never made before. What can I do to improve my performance and stop worrying?

Worrying about whether you will be laid off or not will not change the outcome. In effect, you are using all your energy to worry instead of performing your job. You have no control over the viability of your company, but you do have control over your job performance. Concentrate on your job and what needs to be done today. Exercise to relieve some of your stress. Avoid caffeine, tobacco, and alcohol. When you find your concentration slipping and you begin to worry, say, "What will be, will be, and worrying won't change it, so I may as well get on with what I have to do."

Rather than worrying, try to think about what is right with your life right now. Notice the good things going on in the world instead of the negative things. Begin to network. Take up a hobby that interests you.

I survived one job cutback at our company last year, but it looks as if we might be having another one. I feel that if I can survive this one, the worst will be over. I've got that awful feeling in the pit of my stomach and a lot of nervous energy. I almost had a nervous breakdown last time. How can I survive emotionally?

First, keep yourself physically healthy by eating nutritious foods and avoiding caffeine, tobacco, and alcohol. Exercise daily to work off some of that nervous energy. Keep your mind (as well as your body) occupied. Channel some of your frustration in a positive direction:

- ◆ Volunteer to help out at a hospital or the library or anyplace you're needed. Helping others will keep you from focusing on your own problems.

- ◆ Take time to get involved with your children's activities or school projects.

- ◆ Keep a journal and write down your innermost feelings about what you're going through (you may be able to turn it into a bestseller one day).

- ◆ If you feel like crying, then cry. Get it all out. Crying is a great tension reliever. A good cry can make you feel renewed.

My company is in the middle of a takeover. Rumors are flying like crazy. My last three bosses quit and number four is an interim boss until the new people take over. The first day I worked for him, he asked me to type up his resume. The more people I talk to, the more confused I get. Some people say I should start looking for another job right away, others say the new people will get rid only of management types, that the secretaries are probably safe. Then someone else said when her cousin's company got bought out they closed the regional office and moved everything to Chicago. Should I look or take a chance and stay?

What have you got to lose if you stay? Things are always a little crazy when a company is being bought out or taken over, but things should settle down once the deal is completed. Nobody knows what the future will bring. Sure, the new owners may close the office, but they may also enlarge the office. And, if so, they will probably need experienced secretaries familiar with the company's operating procedures to help them through the transition period. Make a list of probabilities and possible outcomes to help you make your decision.

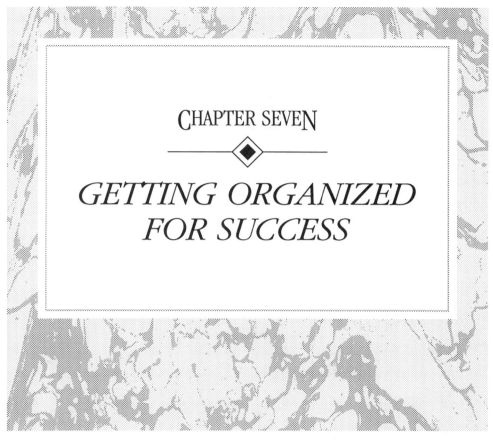

CHAPTER SEVEN

◆

GETTING ORGANIZED FOR SUCCESS

Organization is one of the keys to success at any job. An organized secretary stays on top of deadlines. At any given time, she can give a capsulized view of what's going on in the department, such as, who's meeting with whom, where the meeting is at, what the topic is, and where the files are. Being organized is not only an art form, it's a necessity.

7-1

SORTING THE MAIL

When mail is unorganized or sorted improperly, it can spell disaster for both you and your boss.

My boss gets a lot of mail, not only from within the company, but from outside as well. What is the best way to sort it?

107

Colored folders are a big plus in prioritizing the mail, although manila folders may be substituted. Colored folders are easily recognizable and are hard to lose on your boss's desk. Follow this technique:

Five-Folder System		
RED	-	Urgent, contains faxes, express-mail items, telexes, plus any memos requiring action
GREEN	-	Items requiring signature
BLUE	-	Reports (financial, sales)
ORANGE	-	Important reading, background information
YELLOW	-	Magazines, office newsletters

If five folders are not necessary, use this three-folder system:

Three-Folder System		
RED	-	Action/important
BLUE	-	Information
GREEN	-	Signature

Within each colored folder, arrange the items by priority. This comes with experience, of course, but obviously a request from the CEO of the company would be considered RED material.

Mail is delivered twice a day in our office. The first delivery is U.S. mail. The second is interoffice. My boss likes to take her afternoon mail home to review. Any tips to handle this?

Two sets of files are required, labeled A.M./P.M. or 1, 2. A rubber band keeps the evening stack together for easy briefcase loading.

My boss is a customer-service manager. Each piece of mail is equally weighted, with few receiving preferential treatment. However, time is an issue. We really need to respond to Monday's mail before tackling Tuesday's mail.

The color-coded approach will work here too. However, when each piece of correspondence is equally important and time is the issue, your folders need to represent days of the week. Monday may be green, Tuesday yellow, etc. You and your boss will know at a glance if all of Monday's correspondence has been handled.

My boss is a paper factory. One piece goes in and three come out. I've been waiting until the end of the day to clean his "out" box, but that doesn't seem to be working. Sometimes there are notes for things he wanted done today. The end of the day is too late. How can I keep up?

Try retrieving the mail from your boss's office three times each day (first and last thing, plus noon-ish). Thumb through it for important items, sorting as you go. Items to be copied and distributed go in one folder, filing is placed in an A-Z expanding file. Any piece of correspondence that requires action on your part (getting a copy of an invoice, for example), should go in your "in" box as well as any letters to be word processed. Be sure to set up a system with your boss on rush items, such as using a red pen or flagging items with a sticky "rush" note.

Most of the letters my boss receives have files, some of which are bulky. I'm never sure whether I should pull them or not.

Try to anticipate your boss's needs. If a letter arrives that you know has a small file, pull it out and attach it. If the file is too bulky to pull and attach, or perhaps your boss wants the file only upon request, pencil the file title in the margin followed by the question, "Shall I pull?" The boss's memory is then jogged as to the existence of the file and she has the option of reviewing it. Another option is to locate the latest piece of correspondence or newest report and attach it rather than the entire file.

Should I highlight or underline my manager's mail? And if so, what should I highlight?

Highlighting is quicker than underlining. Highlighters are available in a variety of colors that do not show up on photocopies. Some items to highlight are:

- a date for a meeting (make a pencil notation in the margin "calendar noted" followed by your initials)—then remember to note the calendar.

- a deadline—"We need this report by the end of the month." (Put a copy in your follow-up file for two days before the report is due.)

- information requests—"Send us a list of all your regional offices." If it is a request you can handle, prepare the reply, then next to the highlighted sentence write "letter attached for your signature."

Highlighted Items

DATE: Month/Date/Year
TO: Lynda Abegg
FROM: Peggy Grillot

Just a reminder that I need your **figures** for the **monthly sales report** no later than **Monday, March 28.**

7-2

FILING FOR QUICK AND EASY ACCESS

It's not enough for the mail to be organized; the files need to be organized as well. An efficient secretary is able to quickly retrieve needed items, whether they're stored in folders, binders, or even on the computer system.

I store all my boss's reports in file folders, but the reports keep slipping out and then they are out of date order. Any ideas?

Three-ring binders are perfect for holding frequently reviewed reports or files. The information is at your boss's fingertips without searching through folders or file drawers. Place new reports in front of old ones or pitch old ones (with your boss's permission, of course) so she always has only the latest documents. You can bind obsolete reports with brads and file them until they can be safely tossed. Don't store clumsy binders in file drawers.

I have file folders full of claim forms. I have to search through stacks of claims to find the ones I need. They are filed by date, with the most current form on top. If someone is looking for the "Smith" claim, it could be in the middle or on the bottom, depending on when it was received. Is there a better system for retrieval?

Quick retrieval is possible, even when you have several files in one folder. Since most correspondence is filed horizontally, it is almost impossible to read the name of the person or company without pulling the entire file out. Write the name in pencil horizontally lengthwise across the correspondence, as well as other key information—such as date, type of sales, agent, etc. — anything that is unique and would help to identify this letter once filed. Now you can thumb through the letters and/or claims quickly without removing the folder.

Quick Retrieval Method

Smith file
Month/Date/Year

I type so many letters each day, I have trouble keeping track of them. My boss frequently will ask me to locate a letter he wrote last month to "that firm in Colorado," but we file by company name. Is there something that can help me?

Make a copy of each letter you type for your reading or chronological file. File this letter by date in a three-ring binder or file folder. There is no need to keep any backup material or enclosures. Keep that information with the original file. Your file is just a chronological one. You will easily be able to find the letter to "that firm in Colorado," even though the name of the company or contact person is not initially available. You can also use it as a reference to check information sent to other departments or companies. The number-one rule is to *never* permanently remove letters from the chronological file. If someone needs a copy, photo it and put the letter back in its proper date sequence.

Our files are jammed. Ordering more cabinets is not the answer. I need to clean house, but where do I begin?

By law, some files have to be kept for a certain length of time. Companies also have their own rules as to how long certain files should be retained. Before you purge, do your homework. Find out what the rules are. Once you have identified files that could be pitched, find out if your office provides storage for older files. If so, you're saved. Box up the older files and send them down to storage, with an explicit note that your boss is to be contacted prior to discarding. Any time you are asked to retrieve a file from storage, keep it with the current ones. Eventually, the only files boxed will be ones with no activity. Then your boss can be approached with, "These files have been in storage for one year with no activity. Can they be discarded?"

My boss starts a file for everything. I seem to be making file folders for one or two sheets of paper. It's hard to find correspondence when there are so many folders. I need something more simple.

Keep a file folder for miscellaneous letters or reports received, a catch-all file. There is no reason to start a separate file for every single piece of paper that comes across her desk. Put these miscellaneous reports and letters into this folder and every ten days or so, skim through it. As more pieces of paper are accumulated for a particular topic, then a new file can be started. For others, eventually you will be able to toss about 90 percent of the material, reserving only 10 percent for permanent filing.

I hire temporaries to fill in whenever secretaries are on vacation. When the secretaries return, they come to me because they can't find a document

stored by the temporary. Because there are many work stations involved, I need something that is easy to monitor.

Create a new directory on the hard drive and instruct the temporaries to store all their documents there. Or give the temps a floppy diskette for all their work. Whenever the permanent employee returns, she should be able to find all the documents and then store them wherever they would be normally.

I work in an office with shared work stations where no one is allowed to store documents on the computer hard drive. Everything is on floppy disks. I'm not used to this and keep losing information.

Have several diskettes. Label them by managers or by type of correspondence such as letters, reports, or executive summaries. The small 3 1/2" diskettes high density (H.D.) are more durable and hold more information than the 5 1/4" diskettes. Invest in a storage box and use it. Always return the diskettes to their storage container. Less handling means less wear, which translates to less chance of lost data. On a regular basis, delete old documents. Remember to keep diskettes away from magnets, which can erase information. Do not remove a diskette while the computer drive light is on. Removal too early can scratch the surface of a diskette, making certain tracks unreadable.

Remember that diskettes wear out. One that you've been using for a year can suddenly become unusable. Transfer documents to newly formatted diskettes on a regular basis—annually at least, more often if the diskette is heavily used, that is, if documents are added and deleted daily.

I have my own computer but no printer. Although I store my documents on the hard drive, I have to load my documents onto diskettes to print. Then it seems I lose my floppies. This is frustrating since sometimes I make formatting changes as I am printing my document and the latest version is not on my computer.

Label your diskette with your name. Your diskette will easily find its way back to your desk once people know to whom it belongs. Use 3 1/2" H.D. diskettes whenever possible. They hold more information and are more durable. If you make additional changes to the document on the floppy diskette before final printing, move or copy this revised document back onto your computer's hard drive. Make this a never-fail routine. This way, if a diskette is misplaced or becomes unusable, you still have the latest version available on your hard drive.

As more and more people exchange information via diskettes, always keep backup files of important documents in case there's a hard-drive failure or a computer glitch involving unreadable sectors or lost data.

7-3

KEEPING ROUTED MATERIAL MOVING

Subscriptions and multiple copies of large documents are costly. Routing material is often an inexpensive way to pass along outside publications and company documents to a large number of people.

My boss is on every routing list imaginable, from daily papers to weekly bulletins to monthly magazines. She never has time, and our office librarian is constantly hounding me for routed material that has disappeared into her office.

Make a table listing every publication your boss has requested to see. List frequency and whether anyone else in the department reads the publication.

Sit down with your boss and show her the table. Chances are she has lost track of all the publications she has requested to review. Gently remind her that since her schedule is so heavy and free time is limited that perhaps

Publications List		
NAME OF PUBLICATION	FREQUENCY	INDIVIDUAL
The Wall Street Journal	Daily, except Saturday, Sunday, and legal holidays	Bodeaux
Business Week	Weekly	No one
Fortune	Biweekly	Chameko

some selective purging is in order. Ask her to reevaluate which ones she wants to see and which publications her name can be removed from.

My boss collects routed items. Journals, magazines, special reports, you name it, are stacked behind his desk for future reading. Some are months old and have lost their timeliness. Any suggestions?

Keep items for no more than one cycle—two at the most. Check the dates.

Suggested Routing Cycle	
Daily	1 day 2 days at the most
Weekly	1 week
Biweekly	2 weeks

Move the rest out. If the publication really was important, your boss would have read it by now.

Certain routed publications are horded by my manager. I've tried moving them, but every once in a while he comes back to me looking for that "missing" magazine that I continued routing. Then I get chewed out. Now, I am afraid to touch his office. How do you keep the material moving yet hold onto some items at the same time? It just doesn't seem possible.

See what magazines your boss holds onto. Do any publications frequently appear? If so, get your manager his own subscriptions to those publications.

For publications that appear randomly, photocopy the table of contents and continue to route them. If your manager wants to read an article at a later date, you will have all the information you need to purchase that particular issue if it's still on the newsstand or order a back copy from the publisher or even borrow it from your library.

If anyone else in your department is on that list, eliminate your boss from that publication. Ask coworkers to flag any articles that may be of interest to your boss and to give those magazines to you.

I would like to help my boss stay current with her reading. Is there anything I can do? She has stacks of subscriptions in her office, but she really doesn't have the time to look at all those publications.

Ask her what she is looking for. Familiarize yourself with topics of interest to her either personally or professionally. Many individuals are conducting research on a particular topic. Scan the table of contents of these publications. Anything of interest, flag it.

A modem and communications software coupled with an online service allows you to access newsclipping services. Just log in key words, such as your company's name, for example, or specific topics, and let the computer do the work. The system can search old publications as well as new ones. Once you've printed out all the older information, the system can be set up to print out any new clippings on a daily basis. Your boss stays on top of the current situation and so do you.

7-4

PLANNING A CONFERENCE CALL

In order to save money, our company is making more conference calls. I can spend hours trying to get everybody together. Some are in different time zones. Others are on vacation or not in the office. There always seems to be a lot of confusion. People get upset because they are on hold too long while I am trying to get everyone on the line at the same time. My boss thinks I am disorganized and it's my problem. Meanwhile, I'm at the end of my rope. Is there anything I can do?

You can prepare a conference call planner similar to the one used for meetings.

◆ List each individual who should be included in the conference call.

◆ Note the city and time zone.

◆ List a backup person for anyone who cannot be part of the call due to vacation, business travel, etc. Call and ask the individual who his or her backup is.

◆ Enter the phone and fax numbers. Once a date and time has been selected, fax everyone a reminder that the conference call will be at 10:00 A.M. CST (central standard time) on Wednesday, March 9.

◆ Make sure the list contains the secretary's name and don't be afraid to ask for her assistance as well. The secretary will be the person responding to your requests and reminders. The secretary will make sure her boss is in place for the call.

By using this type of formatted information sheet, you can then give your boss a list of the people who will be involved in the conference call, as well as whether the department head or a designated backup will be participating. You will be more efficient and there will be less confusion.

7-5

ORGANIZING YOUR BOSS'S OFFICE FOR MAXIMUM EFFICIENCY

How your boss's office is organized affects the flow of paperwork. Take the time to analyze his work habits, those of his colleagues, and of his subordinates. Then adjust accordingly.

My boss's desk is always messy. I try to put his phone messages in the middle so he will see them, but sometimes they are overlooked. Then he gets mad when he finds out the call he has been waiting for came through an hour ago. Even though I show him the message, which somehow got stuck under a pile of papers, he feels it's my fault. Yet he also gets mad if I try to straighten up his desk. What am I supposed to do? It's a no-win situation.

You are supposed to see that your boss gets his telephone messages and that they do not get lost in the mess of papers on his desk. Order a small message holder that you can put either next to his telephone or in a designated spot on his desk. All phone messages go into it. Because it holds the messages in a clamp, they are up and out of the pile of papers on his desk. You may find that keeping the message holder on the corner of your desk works well. He can check them on the way into his office and let you know that he is aware of all his calls.

Keep all important or urgent messages on the top of the stack. Write important or urgent phone calls that must be returned right away on a different color paper or perhaps on an index card so that they are noticeably different from the regular messages.

People put memos and reports directly on my manager's desk, bypassing me. I need to know what's going on. When I don't review her mail, I lose touch. How can I get her staff to route all information through me?

Have your manager issue a memo to her staff saying that all her mail is to be given to you. Then enforce it. Position your office as close to her office as possible. Do not allow your manager to have anything vaguely resembling an "in" box on her desk. And be sure your "in" box is clearly labeled and highly visible.

My boss doesn't want his desk top cluttered with an in/out box. I put his mail folder along with accompanying files on the corner of his desk. At the end of the day, he returns the mail folder to me. Sometimes, though, he hangs onto some items. Any thoughts as to where pending files can be stacked without cluttering up his desk?

Invest in a desktop organizer, which has slots to store files vertically. Place this organizer either on his credenza or perhaps near his phone, wherever easy access is possible. The files are visible and won't get lost. Check this organizer weekly to find out if a response is overdue, then remind your boss. If he objects to having the organizer anywhere in his office, try using his desk drawers. Use a right-hand drawer for his "in" box and a left-hand drawer for an "out" box. His desk and office are uncluttered, yet his mail is kept flowing.

While my director travels, I try to clean up her desk, but there are reams of half sheets with handwritten notes. I'm afraid to pitch anything for fear of losing an important phone number or note. Your thoughts?

A "desk notes" file could be utilized to hold any stray pieces of paper. These notes should be dated if possible. After a reasonable period of time, you should be able to purge items in this folder without fear of losing important information.

7-6

ORGANIZING YOUR WORK SPACE FOR MAXIMUM EFFICIENCY

I am overwhelmed by paper. My desk is always a cluttered mess. Worse yet, I have lost important papers and files. What can I do?

Start with your desk. Use a two-tiered mailbox to plan your work load. Leftover projects can be placed in the top bin, while incoming projects are placed in the bottom one. At the day's end, all projects are moved to the top bin and placed in order of importance. Read on for other tips.

My desk top is too small. I don't seem to have enough room to spread out.

Since your desk is also your work space, you need to be organized. Memos and reports should be placed in an A-Z expanding wallet folder until they can be filed. Set aside specific filing time, such as each day following lunch or every Thursday morning. Items awaiting responses should also be kept in folders. And remember to work on one project at a time. When completed, file that project away and start another.

My work area is cluttered and it makes me look inefficient. What can I do?

Analyze how you're using your work space. Items used daily should be within arm's reach, either on your desk or perhaps next to your computer terminal. Items used weekly should be nearby, but not necessarily on your desk. Items used monthly can be kept farther away. The top of a more distant file cabinet would be appropriate.

Remember, too, that an overabundance of plants, photos, candy dishes minimizes effective use of your desk area, creating a cluttered, disorganized image. Be selective. One or two personal items, for example, a photo and a small plant, are acceptable,

Your work space is just that—your work space—so don't clutter it up.

7-7

TIPS FOR TACKLING ANY PROJECT

I'm spinning my wheels at work, running to the copier every five minutes because I needed six sets, not five, of a particular document. I start typing, get interrupted by a phone call or other emergency, then have a hard time remembering where I've left off. Sometimes I begin a new project, even before the old one is finished. Help! I know I need to get organized, but how?

A few tips will put you on the right track:

- Have a folder for all copies that need to be made and have no real urgency. Run copies all at once whenever possible.

- Items to be mailed should be placed in a folder and brought to the mailroom in a group, not individually.

- Place documents to be filed in an "A–Z expanding-wallet" organizing folder. Set the filing aside for a particularly quiet time of the day, not when the phones are ringing off the hook.

- Unless you have to fax a document immediately, put it aside to fax at off-peak periods, such as right before lunch, when there is less chance of having to wait.

- Make sure you understand the directions for a complicated project *before* you begin working on it.

- Whenever possible, avoid typing a complex document or heavily edited charts when your day is extremely hectic, such as when you're filling in for a coworker who is out of the office.

- For projects that are time consuming, try breaking them up into parts so you can stop to do other work without losing your place or your momentum.

- Don't waste time by making unnecessary trips. A walk to the copier room may be coupled with delivering outgoing mail to the mail room. Plan ahead.

- Use the phone to check general information instead of walking over to another's office.

Once you start thinking in an organized fashion, it will seem second nature to streamline. Always be open to change. A system designed now may need to be revised with the addition of another manager or coworker or may perhaps have to be modified when a copier is added that is closer to your office. Always be on the lookout to improve procedures.

7-8

HOW TO STAY ON SCHEDULE

Sometimes others perceive an organized and efficient secretary as one who has time on her hands for another project. Don't be caught by the "little project" nightmare.

There's one individual in our office whose secretary leaves before me. He knows I work later and does not hesitate to ask me to type one more memo before leaving the office. However, its my job to see that all the overnight mail pouches for our field offices get out on time, and I start gathering everything around 4:30.

I really don't mind helping out once in awhile. But it has become routine now to type one more memo. Then I end up racing to get the overnights out. How can I say, "can't the typing wait until tomorrow?"

Respond with, "I have to get the overnights ready for pickup first. Could I type your memo first thing in the morning?" Let the individual know that an extra typing job will be handled after the overnights are completed. Otherwise, you will be unable to meet your deadlines, causing you to look inefficient and disorganized.

7-9

CREATING DAILY PLANNERS, WEEKLY SCHEDULES, AND YEARLY VACATION LOGS

Even the most organized secretary loses touch without a "to-do" list. Create one not only for your boss, but for yourself as well. The format can easily be adapted to accommodate weekly schedules and yearly vacation logs.

The executive I work for is disorganized. She comes in each day without a good idea of what's on the day's agenda. I know what reports are due, but need some direction from her to get the project done. Somehow it seems we should be able to work better as a team, but how?

A "to-do" list should be prepared each day. This "to do" list should serve as a daily planner showing which tasks to tackle first. It will provide the organization your manager needs.

Try typing the Daily Planners on colored index cards. These cards are small enough for your boss to prop up on her desk, by her phone, or tuck under the edge of her desk blotter, but large enough to contain brief notes regarding the day's appointments.

Daily Planner

9:00 A.M.	Meeting with Marketing to discuss new products. (Take yellow folder.)
10:30	Staff meeting in General Conference Room to discuss salary review. (Manila folder)
11:00	Respond to general correspondence: Grant letter, McGilray memo, Newton quote
11:30	Luncheon meeting with new service engineer at Water Street Inn
1:00 P.M.	Open
4:00	Leave office; dentist appointment at 4:45 P.M.

Index Card Daily Planner

Monday, January 18

10:30 A.M.	Human Resources update, Conference Room 102 Eva, Wade, Logan, and Linda
11:00 A.M.	Review financing budget for new product line, Conference Room 301 with accounting staff
12:00 P.M.	Lunch with Ms. Marlowe and Mr. Williams, Marquette Restaurant

Reminder: Call California office regarding Committee Meeting agenda.

My boss makes appointments and forgets to tell me about them. Sometimes she comes in late because she had an early appointment with someone that I knew nothing about. Meanwhile, her boss has been calling and I'm forced to cover. Of course, this not only makes me uncomfortable, but I appear inefficient. Suggestions?

Keep an appointment calendar for your boss and a duplicate calendar in your office. Refer to your duplicate calendar when scheduling meetings or appointments, but check your boss's calendar frequently so you can update your own calendar and log any meetings or appointments she has scheduled to prevent conflicts. Always use pencil when entering information to facilitate erasing and rescheduling with ease, and place a check mark next to those items in her calendar that you have already noted. Another option is to use a computer calendar program. When your boss returns from a meeting, ask her if they scheduled the time and date for the next meeting.

Any quick way to keep track of the numerous projects my boss is working on? He likes to be able to see where he is now, what's due tomorrow, and what can wait.

Keep a computer log and print it each week. He can take the listing with him so he can check the status of all projects at a glance.

I need to track the location of at least five managers who report to my boss. They travel and are in and out so much sometimes that I feel as if I'm trying to track a swarm of bees, buzzing off in all different directions. Is there a way to restore a semblance of order to this chaos?

A weekly location status report is an excellent way to track a medium- to large-size group. This report has the days of the week running across the top with the names of the managers running down the left-hand margin. Each Friday, ask all the managers to log in their travel plans for the next week and to indicate a contact person and phone number. Distribute this report to the department or post it in a visible spot. If anything urgent materializes, the traveling party can easily be reached.

If schedules do not change on a weekly basis, then perhaps a monthly location status report would be more suitable. Use the same principle, except compile information on a monthly basis. Drop in specific travel dates followed by the information.

Location Status Report
Week of 3/12–3/18

NAME	MON. 3/13	TUES. 3/14	WED. 3/15	THURS. 3/16	FRI. 3/17
DiVito		Seattle Mr. Gibbons (A/C)xxx-xxxx		Milwaukee Ms. Haydorn (A/C)xxx-xxxx	
Drews	<----------------	Management Seminar O'Hare Hyatt Regency (A/C)xxx-xxxx	---------------->		
Koban		Phoenix Ms. Clay (A/C)xxx-xxxx		Los Angeles Mr. Shea (A/C)xxx-xxxx	
McKine	<----------------	--------------------	Vacation	--------------------	---------------->
Roarke	Ft. Wayne Ms. Clemons (A/C)xxx-xxxx	---------------->	<----------------	Indianapolis Transmission Training Class	---------------->

Vacations are always a problem. With seven people in the department, it seems everybody always wants the same weeks off or selects the same vacation day to make long holiday weekends even longer. My boss feels that I should be able to handle this, but how do I make it fair?

For the first year, start off by seniority. Those with longer service within the department get first choice. However, next year, those who did not get first

Monthly Location Status Report–June

NAME	WEEK OF 6/3	WEEK OF 6/10	WEEK OF 6/17	WEEK OF 6/24
B. Adams		6/9 S. Newton Chicago Hyatt (A/C)xxx-xxx		6/25 vacation day
S. Jones			6/16-6/19 Las Vegas Hilton (A/C)xxx-xxx Marketing Convention 6/20 vacation day	
K. Kelley	6/5 L. Johnson Dallas (A/C)xxx-xxx			

choice will. Everybody gets what they want at some time—every other year or however long it takes to work through the rotation.

The annual vacation schedule is an expanded version of the weekly (or monthly) location status report. Vacation forms can show either the whole year or an excerpt with weeks listed across the top with room to jot down individual names along the left. Single vacation days are listed as dates. Weeks are shown by V's. Legal holidays are shown as a date followed by an H. If your company has personal days, these dates can be followed by P's.

Vacation forms provide an at-a-glance synopsis of who's scheduled to be off when and is a valuable aid for tracking a large department. A copy should be posted for employee review. This eliminates interruptions such as "When did I schedule my vacation, was it the week of the 23rd or the 30th?" And be sure to file the form at year end, in order to gently remind individuals when scheduling vacations who is in line to receive first or second choice the following year.

Marketing Department Vacation Schedule
November–January

Staff by Seniority	11/04	11/11	11/18	11/25 11/28H 11/29H	12/02	12/09	12/16	12/23 12/24H 12/25H	12/30 01/01H	01/06	01/13	01/20	01/27
Gregory			11/22V					V	12/30V 12/31V				
Roxanne		11/15V						12/23V 12/27V	V				
Shannon								V					
Carl								V	12/30V 12/31V				
Bill						12/13V		12/26V					
Vanna			11/22V			12/13V	12/20V		01/02V 01/03V				
Emily		11/14V		11/27V				12/26V 12/27V	V				
Tim		11/15V							01/02V 01/03V				

7-10
PLANNING AND COORDINATING MEETINGS

My boss often holds in-house meetings. He normally schedules these for midday. We give everyone plenty of notice, yet it seems that attendance is often poor. People arrive late and the meeting never starts on time, or worse yet, they forget. How can I change this trend?

Try having breakfast meetings, where you provide muffins, rolls, and coffee. Or try scheduling the meeting for odd times, such as 10:10 A.M.—a number that sticks in the attendee's mind because it's different. Let people know how long the meeting will last—say until 10:30 A.M. Do start and finish on time, even if everyone is not there at the onset. As soon as word gets out that your boss's meetings are prompt, your stragglers will clean up their act. For those on networked computers, you could also send a message to all attendees reminding them of the meeting.

In-house meetings are an important part of my position. My job is to make sure the logistics are handled properly. So far, I've been winging it and I've been incredibly lucky. How can I make this task run more smoothly?

The ability to plan and coordinate meetings is an essential part of your position. Whether it is a meeting for five or fifty, be sure you know exactly what will be needed to ensure the success of the meeting. The following checklist should help you with your planning.

- Know the meeting dates/times (alternate dates, if applicable). Ask for an agenda.

- Know the exact number of people attending or which departments will be represented.

- Discuss beverage and food considerations. Will the meeting break up prior to lunch? Will muffins and coffee be all that is needed? Does anyone have a restricted diet?

- Will audiovisual equipment, flip chart, chalkboard, VCR, or TV be needed?

- Make sure that extra chairs are available, in case there are unexpected attendees.

  ◆ Water pitchers and glasses are a must for lengthy meetings.

We have numerous meetings off site. My previous company had in-house conference rooms. Now that I have to go outside, I don't feel comfortable handling the arrangements. What should I be looking for when scheduling these meetings?

If an outside location is selected for the meeting, do the following:

  1. Contact several sites to check availability, rates, amenities, and the size of their meeting rooms.

  2. Once a site is selected, confirm all arrangements in writing. Set forth all the details arranged, what is expected, and the prices quoted. Give your boss a copy of this correspondence so she will know exactly what to expect.

      Details of the arrangement should include:

      ◆ hotel reservations for out-of-town attendees

      ◆ special equipment such as overhead or slide projector with extra bulbs and screen, podium, microphone, flip chart, audio-cassette player, VCR, and TV set

      ◆ paper and pencils, water pitcher and glasses

      ◆ whether smoking is permitted or where a smoker may smoke

      ◆ food arrangements—whether there will be muffins/sweet rolls available with coffee prior to the start of the meeting, luncheon service brought in, refreshing the ice/water

  3. Send a memo to attendees that includes not only the date(s), topic(s) to be discussed, time and location of the function, but directions to the hotel as well. Use north, south, east, and west as opposed to right or left as the attendees may be approaching from different directions. List landmarks, including one if they've gone too far. An explanation of how to handle expenses may be included. State mileage or travel time. If the site is 45 minutes from downtown, let the attendees know so they can plan appropriate travel time. Always give a time frame for the length of the meeting. Whether it is a two-

hour meeting or an all-day seminar, the people involved will be better able to schedule their time.

My boss is attending a conference in another city, and I was asked to assemble material to ship to a booth in which we are exhibiting some of our promotional material. I don't have a clue as to how to handle this.

Remember to ask the five W's—who, what when, where, and why. Ask *who* is hosting the show. *What* should be sent? Find out *when* and *where* the exhibit show is taking place. *Why* is this show important?

The answers to these questions will dictate what type of time frame is involved. Call the convention center or the organization handling the exhibit. Know where to send advance shipments and whom to call if you have a question. Remember to ship early to allow for unforeseen delays. Material is often stored in a warehouse until time to set up the exhibit. Do you have any special setup requests, such as electrical outlets, unusual carpeting, or special signs? What time has been allotted for exhibit-booth setup? Have enough people been assigned to assist in the setup? The same is true for dismantling the booth. Have arrangements been made for the return of unused material?

Make a list of all the brochures you think should be displayed, followed by a potential quantity. Display racks or stands make for a nice exhibit, so check with your marketing department to find out if any are available. Most exhibit shows hire firms to handle all the arrangements, from skirted tables to electrical outlets and phones.

Once you have made a list of what you think you should ship, touch base with your boss to find out if your list is complete or if there are any additions. Next, you will need to see the person in charge of these promotional items to make sure the quantities are available. Start boxing them up as they become available. Clearly label boxes that contain display items or those that contain giveaways or promotional items. Be sure to label the boxes *Box 1 of 6, Box 2 of 6,* etc.

Plan to ship an additional box containing office supplies such as paper, pens, stapler, staples, shipping tape, and return labels. Prepaid overnight mail labels and envelopes are also useful.

Once the shipment is assembled, make a list of each box and its contents. Although this may seem time consuming, it really is worth it, particularly if someone else will be setting up the booth. She will know immediately how many boxes to anticipate, what the overall shipment should weigh, and exactly what is in each box.

Shipping List

Shipped [date] 6 boxes via [name of carrier] weighing 213 lbs. to [destination]:

1 box	44 lbs.	10 display racks 2 boxes of pens 1 stapler and staples 1 roll of packing tape 1 sheet of return labels 3 pads of paper
1 box	30 lbs.	power tool brochures (1,000)
1 box	25 lbs.	lawnmower brochures (500)
1 box	50 lbs.	snowblower brochures (750)
2 boxes	32 lbs./ea.	coffee mugs (250 box)

Ask that all overages be returned to your attention. Once the return shipment is on site, make a list of all the items that were returned. This can be used as a benchmark for the next exhibit show. Maybe you'll find out that you ran out of the power-tools brochure, but that you had plenty of lawnmower brochures left. Next time you ship to an exhibit booth, you'll know to add more power-tool brochures and cut back on the lawnmower ones.

7-11

HOW AND WHEN TO FAX A DOCUMENT

Are fax sheets really necessary? They seem like a waste of money.

The answer is—it all depends! You are correct. On the surface, they do appear to waste paper, which translates to money. However, there is some information that is vital to the receiver, particularly when a fax is received incomplete.

Some companies use a rubber stamp on the face of the document to indicate the following items:

Fax Stamp

DATE: _____   PAGES: _____   FAX: ___
TO: _____
COMPANY: _____
PHONE: _____   FAX: _____
FROM: _____
COMPANY: _____
PHONE: _____   FAX: _____

Generic self-inking fax stamps can be purchased from office supply stores. Customized ones can also be ordered. Sticky notes with this information are also available. No need to permanently mark your original copy with a rubber stamp. If the information is on a sticky note, your original remains intact and can be photocopied without having to block out the fax stamp.

Other companies use a fax cover sheet, particularly when short notes to the receiver, either handwritten or typed, are needed. Items usually contained in a fax cover sheet are shown on the sample on page 132.

Still other companies use only half sheets for fax cover sheets. They prefer not to waste a full sheet of paper if the information can be condensed to a half sheet.

Is it cheaper to fax or to call?

Faxing is faster and may be cheaper when taking into account leaving voice mail messages or being put on hold. However, the choice depends on the message. Some phone messages may be misunderstood, whereas a written note or letter more clearly explains the situation. Then there are times when a voice mail message says it all.

Fax Cover Sheet

To: Name _____
            Company _____
            Fax _____ Phone _____

Date: _____

    We are sending _____ pages, including this cover sheet. Please call the number shown below if all the pages are not received.

Message: _____
_____
_____
_____

From: Name _____
           Company _____
           Fax _____ Phone _____

I tried for two days to get a fax through. I finally gave up and sent it express mail. I still don't know what went wrong.

Dial the fax number and listen. You may be surprised to learn "that number has been changed to . . ." or that you have been dialing the wrong number.

If the phone just keeps on ringing, it may be the fax machine is out of service or out of paper. And remember, it doesn't hurt to call the recipient's secretary to verify the number and ask if there's anything wrong with the fax machine.

If you still can't get through by the end of the day, express mail any items that you have been unable to fax. Express mail has different classes of service, so be sure to select the one right for you. The package can be delivered first thing. However, if you know the recipient will be traveling, afternoon delivery may be acceptable, which saves a few dollars.

7-12

WHEN YOUR MANAGER TRAVELS

My boss travels frequently and I end up spending most of my time making travel arrangements instead of focusing on important letters, reports, and projects that must be completed quickly. What should I do?

Tell your boss the situation, and ask her if you can use a travel agency. A travel agent will save you a lot of time by taking care of the following:

- Maintaining a profile sheet listing the traveler's preferences, such as aisle seats or whether or not any special meals are required; frequent-flyer numbers can also be logged into the computer so they are immediately accessed when travel plans are made

- Making hotel/motel reservations

- Handling car rentals or land transportation

- Delivering tickets billed on the company account as well as handling flight changes or cancellations

- Providing information regarding foreign travel requirements such as visas, immunizations, shots, etc., as well as preparing forms for passports

- Arranging limo service to/from home to the airport or to the hotel

My boss has just taken on a new assignment and he'll be traveling to foreign countries monthly. Just how should I organize his paperwork?

Color-coded plastic folders are great. Use one for each country he will be visiting. Include an itinerary inside along with any files or information he plans to discuss or present. For example, blue could be used for France, green for England. Encourage your boss to use these same folders for any reports or information he receives while traveling.

My boss needs to take an itinerary with him when he travels. Just what goes on an itinerary?

Itineraries should include:

- Type of transportation to airport, whether he'll be driving and parking his car, or the time his limo will be picking him up

- Dates and times of his flights and the name of the airline he will be traveling on; whether seating has been preassigned or if check-in is required; list whether meal service is provided

- Local transportation to final destination, whether it's a rental car, taxi, hotel courtesy bus, or private car

- Hotel accommodations, including addresses and phone numbers; include the price of the hotel room, any confirmation numbers, if the room was guaranteed for late arrival, anything to make sure he will receive what was ordered

- List of local contacts, phone numbers, meeting sites, and agenda

Sample Itineraries

FEBRUARY 2		FEBRUARY 3	
		9:30 A.M.	Sam Waters will meet you in the lobby and transport you to Smythe & Smythe, Inc; meeting with CEO Rita Johnson et al re French Operations
10:00 A.M.	J&J Limo will pick you up at home; confirmation #J23234		
11:00 A.M.	United Airlines Flight 555 to Washington National; meal service; low-fat, low-cholesterol; check-in required	10:30 A.M.	Tour of proposed site
12:30 P.M.	Land at Washington National, in Washington D.C. Take taxi to Sheraton, 4345 E Street N.W., (202)xxx-xxxx; single room, $109 plus tax	12:30 P.M.	Lunch to be arranged by Sam Waters
		2:00 P.M.	Resume discussion of marketing plans; file attached
6:00 P.M.	Dinner; Sam Waters will pick you up at the Sheraton; his number is (202)xxx-xxxx	5:30 P.M.	Sam Waters to drive you back to airport for 6:45 P.M. flight
		6:45 P.M.	United Airlines Flight 545 to Chicago O'Hare
		7:45 P.M.	Flight arrives; pick up baggage; call J&J Limo to confirm pickup; confirmation #J12345

I've just begun working for a frequent flyer who often has to change her original flights while traveling. Any tips to make her life easier?

Lots of frequent flyers carry the *Official Airline Guide (OAG) Pocket Flight Guide* or the *Sky Guide*. That way, if one flight is cancelled, she knows immediately what other flights are available. If your frequent flyer doesn't want to carry one of these guides, list alternate flights on the back of her itinerary.

My boss travels frequently. Weekday trips are usually not a problem. I try to arrange same day fly in/fly out, but weekends are a mystery. I never seem to know which way to go. Should I book a Saturday-night stay because the airfare is cheaper or just have him fly in on Sunday?

Find out if your company has a set policy regarding Saturday-night stays. Your company may have a policy to book the cheapest travel arrangements possible, which may include flying in on a Saturday and staying overnight.

If there is no set policy, then the easiest way to resolve this is just to ask your boss what he prefers.

We have a corporate travel department at our company that makes all hotel and airplane reservations. Recently, my boss returned from a trip and informed me that the hotel reservations weren't made. He was mad. I can't afford to have this happen again. How should I handle this?

The only way to be absolutely sure that the hotel reservations are made is either to make them yourself or call the hotel to verify.

My boss had connecting tickets from the wrong city, and unfortunately I didn't catch the error until he had already left. How can I prevent this from happening again?

Travel agencies make mistakes too. Always check the tickets to be sure your boss's itinerary and tickets match. Check the departure/arrival dates and times. An incorrect date on a ticket or the wrong connection can ruin a business trip.

My boss is attending a meeting in another city. The packet of material for this meeting is so large he needs a separate suitcase to carry it. I know he won't want to bring it on the plane. Any suggestions?

If the material is ready a day or two before the meeting, send it on ahead. You could express mail it either to his hotel, to the meeting site, or to the individual's attention who is hosting the meeting. Make sure the package clearly identifies to whom the package is being sent.

Shipping Label

Mr. James J. Jamieson
c/o The Hamilton Hotel
3333 Park Avenue
Chicago, IL 60606
(Scheduled to check in as guest on 10/25/XX)

My new boss travels frequently, and he receives a large quantity of mail. What's the best way to organize his mail?

First, take care of all the mail you can handle yourself and keep a record in case you or your boss needs to refer to it. Then, make folders to hold reports and data received during his absence. For example:

- action—requires a response
- signature
- financial reports
- general correspondence
- future meetings and appointments

You should also find out who has signature authority in his absence and who can handle routine matters while he's traveling.

Keep a list of all correspondence received in his absence.

- 1/15　　　　　Received contract from Johnson company; forwarded to legal for review and processing

- 1/15　　　　　Sales meeting rescheduled for the 23rd. Date noted on your calendar

- 1/16　　　　　Received order from Mercury; forwarded to Order Department for handling

Phone calls can be listed in the same way:

- 1/15   Tom Black—re lunch on the 28th? Your calendar was open, so I said okay tentatively.

- 1/16   Dr. Mary Watson—needs to discuss your upcoming presentation; her phone is xxx-xxx-xxxx.

7-13

PREPARING YOURSELF FOR A BUSINESS TRIP

Our company takes part in a huge convention in Las Vegas each year. I've been asked to work in our convention booth, but I don't know exactly what to expect. This is my first year attending the convention. It's four days and three nights in a city I've never seen. How should I prepare myself for the trip?

Expect to work long hours. If the convention runs from 8:00 A.M. to 5:00 P.M., you'll probably be working 7:00 A.M. to 6:00 P.M. Some tips from the convention-wise are:

- Find out from accounting what expenses need receipts (usually over a certain dollar figure). Take a blank expense report form to log your expenses. Make sure your airline tickets and hotel accommodations are within the company's guidelines. Remember that cash advances not spent on business-related expenses will have to be paid back upon your return.

- Wear comfortable, low-heeled shoes. Plan to bring at least two pairs that match all outfits. Rotating footwear will provide some relief for sore feet. Some companies permit their staff to wear athletic footwear instead of heels to eliminate the stress involved with standing and walking on cement floors all day.

- Provided your company does not have any restrictions, charge meals to your room. This eliminates the need for carrying large amounts of cash or running up your charge card.

- Be pleasant to everybody.   This may sound trite, but you never know whom you will meet.   And don't judge people by the clothes they wear.   Many executives may elect to wear sports clothes at a convention, avoiding traditional business suits.

- Try to be helpful when fielding questions.   However, if you can't answer a question on site, ask for the individual's business card.   Write the question on the back.   Tell her you will get the answer when you return to the office.   Be sure to follow through.

- Set up file folders for each department. You can use the folders to drop business cards or literature to be sorted and distributed when you return.

CHAPTER EIGHT

◆

WORKING SMARTER

By working smarter, you'll be able to accomplish more in less time. Then you'll have that extra time for tricky projects or for rearranging an existing system into something that's much more streamlined and efficient. By working smarter, you'll be able to keep track of your boss's projects and assist whenever necessary—all because you have the time! Working smarter means devoting enough time to a project to do it and do it right, but not more time than is necessary. By combining time-saving techniques, delegating tasks, sharing responsibility on projects, you have effectively taken control of your position as secretary and key time manager. Don't let time manage you.

8-1

STREAMLINING YOUR JOB

My boss agreed I'm overworked and stretched to the limit, but our budget says no new hire for any reason. What now?

Make a list of all your functions. Then streamline your job. Find out if any reports can be eliminated because the information is not used or is already provided in another form. Are there overlapping duties? Do you and another secretary track sales? Perhaps you could use her figures, thereby eliminating one function. Keep a log to find out what duties take up most of your time. Then decide how to streamline those duties. Become super organized.

What type of office supplies and equipment can help me streamline my job and save time?

It depends on what you use on a regular basis. A few items to keep handy are:

- A three-hole punch. Rather than using the central one located by the copier, get your own.

- A personalized fax stamp or cover sheet with the company's fax number and your boss's name and phone number on it. Having those items already filled in will save you lots of writing time. Another option is a fax modem package on your computer, which allows you to send a fax directly from your terminal.

- A pencil sharpener. No more running to accounting to borrow one. And both you and your boss's pencils will always be sharp and ready for use.

- A Rolodex® with phone numbers added, deleted, and updated daily. No more fumbling around for Ms. Wilson's new direct-line number.

- Reference books, a dictionary, quick hyphenation book, maybe a general style guide, whatever you need to make your job go smoothly. Have a grammar hotline number available for those hard-to-answer questions. Remember, too, that your local library is a great resource and will find answers to difficult questions. Use it.

- Order extra binders to have on hand for those last-minute projects that need to be bound. No rummaging around in the office supply cabinet only to find out no binders are available.

- A box of blank formatted diskettes to transfer information from your computer to someone else's.

Time-saving items you may want the office to have are:

- Copier machines that can handle two-sided copy, collate, and staple. They can also reduce or enlarge copy as needed.

- Fax machines that can be left unattended. Some fax machines need to be babysat because often the machine misfeeds, which is a real time waster. In the long run, if the company knew how much time was wasted by employees standing around watching their copy go through, they would buy a more reliable machine.

- A folding machine, for those projects small enough to be photocopied on site, yet still needing to be folded.

- Access to a full service copier shop for large copying needs.

- Preprinted express-mail forms. To type in a return address on ten forms is a real time waster. Now multiply that by ten or fifteen others who are sending out their own express-mail items. If your company sends lots of express-mail items, you may want to investigate directly linking via a dedicated computer to an express-mail service. The express-mail computer can be located centrally, and users type the mailing address, select the type of service, and weigh the package. With a flick of a button, the package is automatically entered into the mainframe allowing instant tracking capabilities, and a bar-coded label is generated to affix to the package. Cost savings are available to volume users.

- A centrally located paper slicer that works. Slicers with a dulled cutting edges should either have the blades sharpened or replaced.

- Three-hole punch paper available for those in-house copy jobs that will eventually be held in a binder.

- A heavy-duty three-hole punch and stapler.

8-2

DELEGATING TO SAVE TIME

Squeezing ten hours of work into an eight-hour day is an art form. Learn to manage your time by delegating tasks that don't require your personal attention or expertise.

I can't seem to delegate, and I have a real need for "hands on" involvement for every job or project. Because I won't delegate, I get bogged down. How can I make myself let go of a project?

Even the most efficient secretary will have problems maintaining an even work flow if she insists on doing everything herself. The secretary who hangs onto everything not only hampers her own production but stifles the growth of junior secretaries as well. Practice giving away "pieces" of a job. Learn whom you can trust to take the same care as you do.

I know I should be delegating more, but who has the time to show someone the ropes?

Delegating involves training. Delegate the first time when you have a little breathing room and can explain the project thoroughly and show what's to be expected. If you start with small manageable pieces, such as asking the receptionist to contact individuals regarding an upcoming conference call, you will soon find that the pieces all fit one entire task, such as actually setting up the conference call with the phone company and sending out memos to all participants.

I really could use some help on this complex document I've been working on for the past month. However, I'm reluctant to turn over any piece of it for fear of introducing an error into the package.

It's much easier to work on a complex document if you've created it, using your own word-processing style. Finish word processing the document yourself, but delegate proofreading, photocopying, and verification of figures to others.

Next time you have this project to work on, delegate portions of the package to others so that they will learn how to format the document.

8-3

TIPS FOR TIME MANAGEMENT

My normal quitting time is 4:30 P.M. I'm staying later and later just to get my daily tasks done. Everybody else seems able to leave on time. Why can't I?

Analyze how you spend your day. Do you find yourself chatting for ten minutes at a stretch? If you do that four times a day, you've suddenly lost forty minutes. Multiply that by a few five-minute phone chats or three-minute walks to the copier room, and now you've lost an hour. Track your typical day. You may be amazed at how you fritter away the time. Then at the end of the day, you're caught with incomplete tasks and a mound of paperwork that needs to be filed.

Do you spend too much time shuffling through papers? Handle each piece of paper *once*.

If, after analyzing your daily habits and streamlining procedures, you still find yourself staying late, maybe your work load has increased. Delegating to coworkers or perhaps the hiring of additional help (either temporary or part time) may help. You will need to present concrete facts and figures to justify an addition to staff. All the background work you did to analyze your work habits can now be used to support your request for additional help.

It seems my coworker is able to handle twice the workload as I am able to. She works for four managers, whereas I work for only two. How does she do it?

Efficiency is an art. Wasted motions should be identified and eliminated. When photocopying, do you bring your folder to do it all at once? Be sure to close the cover on the copier. This uses less toner, which saves money. Time is saved since the machine will not have to be out of service often to replace the toner cartridge or to have costly repair bills.

Do you have to fax a few documents? Were you able to use the fax stamp instead of a cover sheet? By doing so, you will eliminate the need to send a cover sheet, which saves you time and your company money.

Don't print until it's right. When typing a memo, do you use spell check and view it prior to printing? Short memos can be adjusted so they're properly centered before printing. How about double-checking any dates contained in the memos? This may save you from reprinting the memo.

I work in the marketing department, and we write newsletters. Lots of time and energy is used to edit on paper. The corrections then must be inputted into the system and proofed. I keep thinking there must be an easier way, but what is it?

On-line editing is now common. Instead of editing on paper, have your boss enter her corrections right into the computer. The redline method on your word-processing system or strikeout feature can be used to compare texts.

I work in a marketing office. We do lots of personalized mailings with time-sensitive material. How can we improve our delivery?

Bar coding the zip should help. The mail gets to its destination quicker and there is less chance of misdirected mail. Bar coding may be available in your word-processing program. Or a software package may be purchased.

I still have the report on my desk that I was to complete yesterday. My boss is angry with me because it's not done, and finance has moved the meeting up a day. I don't feel it's my fault. I've been very busy. Now what?

You should have definite objectives that you plan to accomplish every day. Then do them. Stay focused. Don't tackle any other projects until you've either reached the end or hit a midway point. You'll spend less time trying to figure out where you left off when you pick up the project again. If the report had been your primary objective yesterday, it wouldn't matter whether the meeting was moved up. It would be done and you'd be working on your next project.

8-4
SETTING PRIORITIES

How do I determine who's important, what's important, and what I can put off until another day?

For who's important, watch your boss. See how she treats certain individuals. Watch how quickly she responds to requests for information or returns phone calls. Ask to see an organization sheet. Familiarize yourself with administrative assistants' names associated with certain managers as well as your boss's superiors and subordinates. There's a pecking order in every organization. Learn it.

To determine which tasks or projects need your immediate attention, assess daily what needs to go out and what can wait. Does your boss need to respond to a memo by today? Is a report due for an upcoming meeting? Has your boss returned that urgent phone call for information? Is there a resulting fax from that conversation? Figure out how much time is needed to complete each project and you'll know what you need to start working on immediately. If possible, delegate tasks that you don't have to handle personally so you'll have the time to complete special projects or last-minute assignments that require your expertise.

Get a feel for what your boss shrugs off and what shifts your boss into high gear. You might want to make a list of regular tasks and projects and ask your boss to number them in order of importance.

8-5

HOW TO STAY ON TOP OF YOUR WORKLOAD

When I first come in, people start asking me questions, such as where are the files for the 10:00 A.M. meeting or who has the handouts? My day is off to a hectic start and I feel so disorganized.

Prepare a "to-do" list for each day. Ideally this list should be prepared prior to leaving the office the night before. It doesn't necessarily need to be written and can be prepared mentally.

Prepared the night before, it gives you the opportunity to gather all the files and handouts needed for the 10:00 A.M. meeting.

On the way to the office, practice recalling what's on your "to-do" list. The better your recall powers are, the more comfortable you'll be fielding questions when you walk into the office.

I still don't have a feel for what has to go out today and what can wait. I have been here six months and still seem to be doing things at the last minute.

Visualize what you think should get out today. Then ask your boss what he expects to get out today. Compare and mentally note the areas in which your responses were different. Remember that for future reference.

Check the progress of the projects. Learn which ones require immediate attention, which ones have to be mailed today, and which ones you can safely put aside. After a while, you will develop a better feel for what's important and what can wait.

I lose track of the things I wanted to do first. I know there must be a trick to stay focused, but what is it?

Steno pads are great resource tools. Keep your daily "to do" list here, as well as log any phone calls or notes. Cross off items as they are completed. At the end of the day, any items outstanding can be copied to the next clean page and numbered in order of importance. Rubber band the pages as they are completed. The steno book can be used to review a week's activities, a month's, even a year's, depending on how long you keep it.

Any tricks to end the day? I am usually pretty well worn out, but I need to stay on top of things.

Don't leave your work area a mess. Take a deep breath and plan for tomorrow.

- ♦ Check your calendar to see what is scheduled for the next day. Make a note of what needs to be prepared.

- ♦ Check the schedule for the balance of the week to help you plan better.

- ♦ Organize your desk. Take a few minutes to sort through the papers. Those items not completed can be placed in the center of your desk under a paperweight—near your steno book with notes for the next day's activities.

8-6

PLANNING AHEAD FOR MAXIMUM EFFICIENCY

There's only one of me and I'm being pulled in a hundred different directions. Right now, for example, I'm in the process of assembling 50 binders for the marketing meeting next week. I'm supposed to type, photocopy, three-hole punch, make tabs, and insert into labeled binders. I honestly don't know if I can do it all by next week.

Once the typing is complete, analyze the tasks involved to complete the project, such as:

1. Photocopy all materials

2. Three-hole punch

3. Create tabs

4. Assemble

5. Insert into labeled binders

If you have trouble segmenting the tasks, plan the project backwards. "I know Mr. Tushkowski wanted the report in binders, which means I need to make tabs. The copies will need to be punched or copied on three-hole punch paper. He said he needed 50 photocopied sets." Decide if anything can be farmed out.

For example, photocopying could be done by your facilities or mail-room staff or even an outside print shop. Run the project on three-hole punch paper to eliminate a step. Now items #1 and #2 have already been completed.

Item #3 is easily handled on an electric typewriter with a repeat function key. Use sticky note paper to keep the tab inserts from slipping in the typewriter. After the tabs have been typed once and programmed, keep inserting a new blank tab sheet and hit the repeat key. One word of caution. Check your master set of tabs before printing the other 49. A typographical error or an omission caught after you've done all 50 is costly and time consuming.

Binder labels needed for item #4 can easily be done as 24-up labels on a laser-jet printer. The labels can then be pasted on the front of the binders. If the side of the binder is to be used, these sticky labels can also be placed on top of the regular inserts.

By breaking the job up into small pieces, the once overwhelming task becomes manageable and simplified.

I can't believe it! I just ran 100 copies on punched paper only to find out that there was a mark on the copier glass. It looks like correction fluid. And of course, the mark was located in a crucial spot, obliterating some financial plan figures. Now I need to rerun the sets and we're running low on punched paper. I'm so mad I could scream.

Go ahead and scream if it'll release some of the tension. However, you will still need to run the replacement sets.

After the fact, it's easy to tell someone what they should have done. *Always* check the copier glass. Run one copy and take the time to look it over. One page could be upside down, crooked, or needing to be reduced. One quick check can save a lot of work.

Sometimes the problem is not so obvious as correction fluid on the glass. At one office the copier cut off all the page numbers, which were properly positioned. The copier was out of alignment. The secretary didn't have to rerun the sets, but she did have to pencil in page numbers on 20 sets. It pays to check your master copy before running the balance.

I work in a marketing office. We do lots of personalized mailings with time-sensitive material. How can we improve our delivery?

Bar coding the zip should help. The mail gets to its destination quicker and there is less chance of misdirected mail. Bar coding may be available in your word-processing program as a macro. Just be sure to update as needed.

8-7
───────────
HOW TO ASK FOR TEMPORARY HELP

I really have too much to do. There's not enough of me to go around. Is there any help for me?

If you're already stretching your work day by coming in early, staying late, and cutting your lunch hour (short tricks all secretaries use on an occasional basis to get things done), then perhaps you need to consider getting help. Analyze how many additional hours you are working over and above your normal work schedule. If you are putting in an additional 45 minutes a day, this equates to a half day for a temporary worker on a weekly basis. Maybe it's even more. Whatever the figure is, be sure you are able to document it. For example, if you have been working late for the last three months, add it all up. You'll probably be surprised at how much it is.

        With memo in hand, talk to your boss about additional support. It could be a temporary, once a week. It could be a part-time college student hired to come in on Mondays. Whatever the end result, be sure to come in armed with detail, followed by positive suggestions and a definite plan for which work a temporary could handle for you.

        "I called Personnel, who has a temporary, Suellyn, wishing to work four days a week. Currently she is working in Marketing three days a week. We could have Suellyn on Thursdays. I feel very comfortable that I could provide her a full day's work. That media project would be perfect for her. I haven't had time to start it and she could use it as filler. No commitment is necessary as to length of time. If the situation changes, we just need to let Personnel know a week ahead of time that her services are no longer desired, and she's released."

MINIMIZING INTERRUPTIONS FROM COWORKERS

One of my coworkers likes to corner me in the morning and tell me *all* her escapades. I'm not a morning person for starters, plus I resent the fact that she catches me for ten minutes at a crack. Is there any polite way to break off this conversation?

Change your habits. She obviously knows where you'll be and when you'll be there. If she's been catching you at your desk first thing, take that time to clean out your boss's in box or do some filing.

If that doesn't work, look at your watch and say, "Gee, Ms. Reynolds is expecting a report from marketing. I'd better check on it," and quickly make your get away.

Help! A few fellow workers have decided that I have a friendly ear, and they stand by my desk for excessive periods of time. At first I was flattered. Being new, I was eager to be accepted. Now my work is beginning to suffer. How do I get rid of these people without hurting anyone's feelings?

If you want to cultivate the friendship, make arrangements to meet for lunch. "I'd love to chat, but I really need to finish this report. Let's get together for lunch and you can tell me all about your weekend."

It's not politically astute for me to tell my gabby coworkers that I don't have time to listen. I don't want to appear unfeeling or arrogant either. Any suggestions for gently removing them from my work area?

Try one of the following techniques:

- Start or resume typing.

- Shuffle papers on your desk.

- Get up from your desk and pretend to search for a file in the cabinet, which forces the interloper to either follow or hopefully get the hint and disappear.

- Say you must make a phone call and start dialing.

- Say your boss is waiting for this, grab a piece of paper and walk into his office.

- Grab your "copies to be made" folder and head for the copier.

8-9

WHAT TO DO ABOUT FREQUENT INTERRUPTIONS FROM YOUR BOSS

I just can't seem to stay focused. Just when I think I've got all the enclosures straight for one project, my boss interrupts me with yet another memo to type or letter to fax. What can I do?

It's not what you can do—it's what you need to say, "Do you need that right away?" Said at the right time, you may save yourself a trip or two to the fax machine or a search through the files or even shifting gears to type something else. Maybe you only need 15 more minutes to finish up the mailing. Those six little words will not only find you those 15 minutes, but will allow you to concentrate on one project from beginning to end, without interruptions, with fewer errors. Interruptions cause errors, and errors cost time!

8-10

MANAGING YOUR TIME WHEN YOUR BOSS IS AWAY

My boss is traveling and I need a project or two to keep busy while he's gone. Any suggestions?

Here are a few suggestions:

- Try to answer all routine correspondence.

- Bring your filing up to date.

- Clean out his office if you know what can be tossed.

- ◆ Schedule yourself for a seminar.

- ◆ Teach yourself some additional features available in your current word-processing software package or learn a new package.

My boss will be out of the country for the next three months. I've been assigned to work in another department during his absence. I'm a little put out. Doesn't management recognize that there is still work to be done, even if my boss is gone?

Management knows the mail doesn't stop and the phones still ring. However, management also feels that some free time is bound to occur. A negative attitude can be disastrous to your career. What happens if your boss decides to transfer? You may need to find a new place for yourself.

Treat this as a great networking opportunity. Learn how another department works and decide whether or not you would like to work there. You'll be able to meet new people. And more important, new people will be able to see what type of an employee you are—diligent, conscientious, accurate, team player.

My boss travels a lot. When he is in town, I often end up staying late to wrap up last-minute projects. When he is out of town, my boss has given me permission to leave early. My coworkers view my leaving early in a different light. It seems to be causing some resentment as I appear to be the recipient of preferential treatment.

Although your boss's suggestion to leave early is nice, it appears to coworkers that you are receiving preferential treatment which can cause problems, the most serious of which is lowered morale.

If you merely say you have permission to leave early, it sounds more like an excuse. Your boss needs to make it very clear to his subordinates that it is acceptable and appropriate for you to leave early.

8-11

USING YOUR DOWN TIME PRODUCTIVELY

Sometimes my workload doesn't fill out the whole day. I hate to say it, but sometimes I stroll over and talk to my coworkers. I know that this doesn't look good, but what can I do?

Don't chitchat with your coworkers. Instead of having one person unoccupied, now there's two. Check your project folder. This is where you
would have jotted down tasks that you wanted to tackle at some future
time. Some other activities you might wish to tackle are to clean out the
filing cabinet, make new file folder labels, or even set up binders for
those oversized files. Familiarize yourself with some new features on
your computer.

Whatever you do, *don't* disappear into the rest room to kill some time
or take extended coffee or lunch breaks. An overloaded secretary is sure
to notice your lack of activity and mention it to her boss.

If you have exhausted all your projects, check with your boss.
Perhaps he has something he's been wanting to get off his desk. If he
continually doesn't keep you busy, tell him. Maybe he has a problem delegating work. Your volunteering may make it easier for him to release
some tasks.

Where do I go if my boss has run out of projects?

Find out if you may volunteer to assist in another department. Be sure to
get clearance first. She may not want anyone knowing she doesn't keep
you busy all day. If you do take work from another department, exercise
the same care as you would with your own boss's work. This is a good
way to gain additional exposure and a possible promotion. Let your work
and your reputation speak for you.

**My boss won't let me do work for other departments. However, his work
load is not enough to keep me busy at times. I'm open to suggestions.**

If your boss forbids you to do another department's work and yet he doesn't
keep you busy all day, then learn to pace yourself. Keep a pile of papers
scattered on your desk so you look busy. In some offices, a clean desk is a
sign you have nothing to do. Don't talk on the phone with friends, another
sign you are not busy.

Know how much work actually goes on in your boss's office by watching the inflow and outflow of mail and the number of business calls made
and returned. Take your cue from him. If he doesn't have enough to do,
your constant requests for projects will only aggravate the situation. If he
puts forth a *busy* image, then so should you. Learn to look busy. Write an
advertising campaign for your company. Volunteer to work on the company newsletter or secretarial task force.

HOW TO STAY CHALLENGED

I've noticed in our company that secretaries are not leaving, raises are limited to cost-of-living increases, and promotions are few. How can I keep myself challenged? I really love my work environment, the benefits are great, but boredom is just around the corner.

Job switching or cross training may be the answer to your boredom dilemma. Sometimes the only moves left are lateral ones. Lateral moves will keep you challenged and interested. When growth and advancement opportunities begin to appear within your company, you will be well armed with a diversified knowledge of all the operations of the company.

Our department recently posted a newly created administrative position. I was amazed at the number of internal candidates who applied, even though for some it was a lateral move. Why are so many people interested if they won't make any more money?

Money isn't everything. People watch the growth areas. You mentioned this is a newly created position. Obviously this department is growing, while other departments may be shrinking. Smart people want to get into the growth areas.

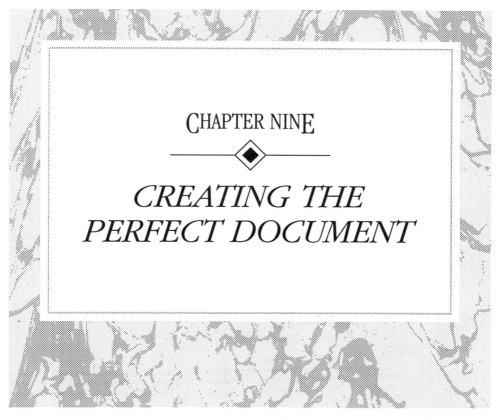

CHAPTER NINE

◆

CREATING THE PERFECT DOCUMENT

When you're creating a document of any kind, your job is to produce quality copy quickly and efficiently. What does your finished product look like? Are your letters properly centered? Do you know how to stretch short letters and condense long ones? Can you properly format a complicated report? Do you proofread all your documents?

Errors, whether typographical, grammatical, or format-related, not only reflect upon you, but on your boss as well. You must be sure that you can handle any project with the expertise necessary to produce top-notch work every time.

9-1

DETERMINING PROPER MARGINS

I have seen varying margins on letters lately. Some seem too wide, some seem lopsided. What are the margin requirements?

155

Every letter should look like a picture on a page. A letter typed too high or too low gives the recipient the wrong message. Short letters, only a few sentences, can be stretched by making the margins wider and the lines of text shorter. Double spacing the text is also an appropriate way to stretch short letters. Long letters can be condensed by changing to a smaller font or point size, or simply by making the margins narrower. Line spacing also can be reduced to less than 1, such as 0.9. However, be careful the letter doesn't look scrunched, making it difficult to read.

Should I right-justify the text of correspondence? What about hyphenation? Is there an industry standard?

Reviews are mixed regarding justification and hyphenation in letters. Some executives feel that the letters look too perfect and lack that personal touch as a result. This may be especially important to an individual in marketing who would not want his mail to look like just another form letter.

Some bosses prefer justified margins, with hyphenation turned off. Hyphenation is usually viewed as a space-saving mechanism and not necessary in short documents. In long reports, however, the opposite might be true—with hyphenation on—to save space, but with justification off. Justified documents are harder to read because words and spaces are stretched.

Look at some old correspondence. See what your predecessor did. If there is no company standard, perhaps that might be a suggestion for the secretarial task force to study.

9-2

TYPING ENVELOPES

In the office, the secretaries have been discussing the placement of addresses on envelopes. Some of the younger secretaries don't believe me when I say there are rules for envelopes too.

Addresses on a No. 10 envelope should be 4 inches from the left and 2 inches down from the top. The word "Personal" or "Confidential," if used, should be placed two lines above and just left of the address.

Confidential Envelope

Confidential

MR. ALLAN WADE
EXCESS COMPANY
1313 DEXTER LANE
CHICAGO IL 60606-0720

Post office regulations prefer the address typed all in capitals, with no punctuation between city and state, to facilitate optical letter sorting. No more than two spaces should appear between the two-letter state code and the zip code.

How should a foreign address be typed? I've heard conflicting reports as to where to put the country.

Current postal regulations state that the country should appear on the last line of the address.

Foreign Envelope

MS. L.J. ALLEN
WADE GRAPHICS
5555 LOGANS RUN
MELBOURNE 3000
AUSTRALIA

9-3

TIPS FOR ERROR-FREE PROOFREADING

I realize that my job is to produce error-free copy, but too many errors have been slipping through and ending up in the finished product. Do you have any tips for sharpening my proofreading skills?

If you follow these simple guidelines and tips, your proofreading skills will greatly improve:

- ◆ Don't be fooled by the length of a document. Short documents, including letters, need to be proofread as carefully as long ones.

- ◆ If time permits, once the document is keystroked and printed, shift gears. Open the mail or file correspondence. Then go back and proofread. You won't be tempted to read from memory, which often happens when proofreading a document or letter right after keystroking.

- ◆ The simplest way to catch keyboarding or transposition errors is to run spell check. Most if not all word-processing packages now have a program that catches spelling errors. Even short documents can hide errors. So be sure to run every document through spell check. Remember spell check can tell only whether the word is spelled correctly. It doesn't catch word substitution errors, such as "to" for "too" or "if" instead of "is." Also, it won't catch grammatical errors. They are your responsibility.

- ◆ Try reading the document backwards from the end to the beginning to catch errors. They will be easier to spot because you won't be reading for content.

- ◆ Another method for catching typographical errors is to start proofing in the middle of the first line. Read to the right. When you reach the end of the line, again start in the middle and read to the right. This way, you are reading only one half of a line at a time. Once you're finished reading the middle to the right side of each paragraph, go back and read from the left side to the middle of each paragraph.

Proofreading from the Middle

This is a sample of proofing **starting in the middle of the first line**. Read to the right. When you **reach the end of the line, start in the middle** and read to the right.

Once you're done, **you're ready to go back and read from the left** side to the middle of each **paragraph**.

- Look for the obvious. In January, usually the year is wrong. Address and phone numbers warrant double checking. Math errors are common. And yes, watch your letterhead. One company has several subsidiaries, each with its own letterhead. It's very easy to turn out a perfect letter—on the wrong letterhead.

- Whenever possible, have someone else proofread the document. Sometimes no matter how many times you look at it, as the originator, you are oblivious to the errors.

- If errors still slip through after you proofread your documents once, try reading them twice. This is time consuming, but in the long run, the finished error-free product is worth the time and effort. Use your first read-through to catch typographical errors. Don't assume that the spelling program will catch everything. It doesn't. Remember, spell check catches only misstrokes. Omissions and number errors can and will occur. Read the document the second time for content, punctuation, and overall format. This is the time to put on your grammatical hat. Is each sentence complete? Do the verb and the subject agree? Is the punctuation correct? Look at the format of the letter. If indentions are used, are they consistent? If it's a two-page memo, does the first page break at a good point? A third read-through may be needed for those documents that contain statistical data, numerical tables, or unfamiliar terminology.

- Identify the types of errors that are slipping through and you will know what to watch for.

- Plan your proofreading during quiet times—first thing in the morning before the office is fully staffed or during the lunch hour when most of your coworkers are gone—to avoid interruptions and distractions.

- To help you concentrate on the task at hand, try printing the letter or document on different colored paper. You'd be surprised how the grammatical errors jump out at you.

- Try reading the document quietly out loud to yourself to help focus your concentration.

- Take a one-day proofreading seminar. These seminars keep you abreast of what's going on in the field, as well as teach techniques to sharpen proofreading skills.

My job involves proofreading the company newsletter. I share a cubicle with another coworker. Interruptions are constant, and many times I end up reading the same paragraph two or three times. If I had a door, I would close it. Any suggestions to eliminate interruptions?

Hang up a sign or tent card on your desk that reads "Please no interruptions. Working on deadline." You could even include a time when you will be available—or leave a piece of paper for them to sign and you'll return the call.

If you do get interrupted by a phone call, mark where you left off either by placing a small dot on the copy (if someone else has the original or you know that another original will be run) or place a sticky note on the copy.

Is there a tool available within my word-processing package to help me proofread?

Sometimes referred to as strikeout or redline, your word-processing program may have such an option to compare documents. If your system doesn't have one readily available, there are software packages that act as another set of eyes, comparing documents by highlighting the changes.

We publish executive reports on an annual basis. These documents are 100+ pages in length with lots of tables. Any proofreading tips for a document of this size and complexity?

Proofreading large documents usually requires special care. Most proofreaders go through large documents several times. For example, one read-through might be for grammatical errors, another for formatting problems, and yet another for checking page numbering and headers.

Be sure to double-check the table of contents for accuracy. It's amazing how often errors are found there. Also be sure to check sentences between pages. Read the last line of each page and the first line of the following page. Does the transition make sense? Is the thought complete? If not, a line may have been dropped.

If pages contain minor changes, such as correcting a word, the pagination should not change. A mental red flag should go up if the top and bottom lines of the original page and the corrected page are different.

The proofreading checklist provided is helpful when proofing large reports or documents.

Proofreading Checklist

CHECKLIST	FIRST PROOF	SECOND PROOF
Is the title page correct? Look for misspellings, capitalization errors, incorrect dates, or improperly centered text.		
Is the table of contents correct? Double-check the headings and page numbers to ensure accuracy.		
Are page numbers consecutive throughout? Hint: right-hand pages should be odd.		
If odd/even headers or footers are used, are they on odd or even pages?		
If hyphenation is used, verify that the words are correctly hyphenated at the end of the line.		
If justification is used, are line endings consistent? Gaps at the end of what should be wrapped copy indicate hard returns, which should be removed.		
Are tables/charts placed near their first reference and numbered consecutively?		
If numerical tables appear within the document, are the numbers aligned, the text proofed for misspellings, and calculations performed so that the totals are correct?		
If an index is needed, have the entries been verified?		
If an appendix is to appear, is it properly placed?		
Is some type of reference code or date needed to distinguish this version from an earlier one?		

I've been asked to proofread for another department a 20-page document that was hyphenated and paginated automatically by the computer system. What should I watch for?

Word-division errors are fairly common. Remember the 2-3 strategy. Never leave fewer than 2 letters at the end of a line or fewer than 3 at the beginning of a line. Words of five characters or less should not be divided. See the following example of incorrect word division:

> This new product will generate 1,000 new sales on an a-
> nnual basis. How can we accomplish this? Frankly, our new i-
> tem will sell itself.

If annual is to be split at all, it should be *an-nual*, and *item* should never be hyphenated. Remember computer-generated word hyphenation is never as accurate as operator-assisted hyphenation.

Two tools a secretary should never be without are a word-division guide and an up-to-date dictionary.

- ◆ A word-division guide should be used to verify hyphenation. A dictionary normally should not be used for word-division questions; because it's so large and cumbersome, it takes too long to look up a word.

- ◆ A dictionary should always be used, however, for those words not listed in the word-division guide. Don't guess. The dictionary should also be used to verify the definition of unfamiliar words. When in doubt, find it out.

- ◆ Remember: you can add acronyms, technical words, and proper names to your spell checker. Just be sure the word is correctly spelled when you add it.

- ◆ Become familiar with standard proofreading symbols. Be sure your boss and coworkers are familiar with them also. It will facilitate making corrections if uniform symbols are used. Some common proofreading symbols are:

Common Proofreading Symbols

⟋	Insert	⌐	Move left
⌒	Close up	⌐	Move right
℘	Delete	⊙	Period
⟋	Change as indicated	‖	Align
↰	Change order	≡	Capitalize
∿	Transposition	⊕	Comma
#	Space	¶	New Paragraph
↜⊃	Move copy	∨	Superscript
—	Change as indicated	∧	Subscript
_	Underline or italicize	m̄	M dash
⬭	Spell out	n̄	N dash

9-4

FINDING GRAMMATICAL ERRORS

No matter what I do, my documents still contain grammatical errors. I give up. Of course, my boss's cohorts are quick to point out these errors in meetings or briefings, wherever there's a crowd.

Are the errors contained in your documents ones that you just failed to catch in proofreading or are they mistakes that you failed to recognize as errors?

If you did not recognize a grammatical error, a refresher course might be in order. Contact your local educational facility to see if classes are offered.   Your company might even agree to pay for the class.   Ask your boss or Human Resources about tuition reimbursement benefits.

Several grammar software packages are available.   They are used in conjunction with your regular word-processing package.   Pick one that is compatible with your software.   Once a document is typed and spell checked, just run it through the grammar package.   Most grammar packages are menu driven, offer many features, and are easy to use.   These packages work with different writing styles, from business to technical, but remember they are just aids to better writing.   They can point out awkward sentence structure or grammatical errors, but, as the editor, you make the final decision.

Are there any grammatical or editorial publications worth subscribing to? I work in the Public Relations department and need to stay up to date with styles and terminology.

Subscribe to an editorial newsletter or purchase an up-to-date style and/or usage book.   Antiquated editorial styles date not only you but also your boss and your company.   For example, many words once hyphenated are now written without the hyphen.   Coworker is one such word.   Even the rules regarding commas have changed.   March 1995 is the standard, not March, 1995.

Just how current is your company image?   When your boss can be heard only through her written word, make sure all correspondence carries a contemporary tone.   Don't be caught in a time warp.

9-5

DECIPHERING UNCLEAR OR MESSY HANDWRITING

My boss's memos are usually three or four handwritten pages, with lots of squiggles, red marks, and arrows. He travels a lot, so I can't always ask him what his squiggles mean. His handwriting is indecipherable most of the time. What can I do to produce an error-free document quickly?

The best solution would be for your boss to get a computer or a tape machine so you won't have to read his handwriting.   If that is not feasible, try the following techniques:

- Focus on one paragraph or sentence at a time. As each paragraph or sentence is completed, lightly pencil through it with an *X* or draw a line through it. That way you will be able to see if you missed any copy.

- Become familiar with your boss's handwriting styles. Does he make wide loops on his *i*'s so they look like *l*'s? Does his *w*'s look like *m*'s? Recognizing his writing quirks will help you to decipher his hieroglyphics.

- Suggest that your boss write on every other line so that editing can be done with minimal disruption to the general thought process. Encourage your boss to use another color ink when editing so you can pick up the changes quickly.

- Ask your boss to read the memo to you. Make notes as needed. Make your own arrows where the original ones seem unclear.

- Type the document and leave a blank where you are unable to read a word or follow an arrow. Once the entire document has been keystroked, go back and reread that sentence. Sometimes the missing word or phrase will jump out at you. Otherwise, try to decipher the leading characters. Just knowing the word begins with a *thr* may give you enough of a clue to fill in the missing word. Most word-processing packages have an option to look up words beginning with certain letters.

- As a last resort, if the document is not confidential, ask a coworker. Sometimes what looks illegible to you may be legible to someone else.

With my boss's long letters, I find that I sometimes type sentences that are incomplete or confusing. These aren't caught by spell check, because the words are spelled correctly. It's just that the sentences don't make any sense.

A grammar software package would catch the fact that the sentence structure is wrong. However, if your company is not interested in investing in additional software at this time, try the ruler approach. When keystroking from a handwritten document, the ruler should be just below the line of copy you are typing. Allow extra time for keystroking, though, as you will need to lift your hands from the keyboard frequently to move the ruler down. Magnifying rulers that enlarge the typing line are also available. These actually sit on the current typing line, magnifying the text.

And after a document is typed, *always* read it. Don't assume you've typed it correctly. When proofing a tricky document, use two rulers, one on the handwritten document and one on the typed document. Compare each line carefully.

9-6

KEEPING YOUR COMPUTER SKILLS UP TO DATE

Sometimes I feel computer illiterate. I learn all the applications only to find some newcomer knows additional features that I never knew existed, such as blocking a portion of a document and spell checking only that portion. How can I keep up with technology changing so quickly?

Subscribe to a word-processing magazine for your software package. If this is not possible, that is, if your word-processing software does not publish a magazine, subscribe to one of the other large word-processing magazines. Many applications may be transferrable to your program. If not, you may be able to persuade your office to switch over to another word-processing package or to purchase additional software packages for which there is a demonstrated need.

Remember word processing is an ever-changing art form. You wouldn't expect your doctor to cease learning about the latest cures and treatments in medicine. An executive secretary needs to keep up with the technological changes in the industry.

We just switched word-processing systems. I hate to admit it, but I haven't been using the spell-check option because I don't know how. I know this would save me time, but can't seem to find the time to learn it. Now what?

"I don't know how to use it," is not a positive statement. You will be seen as someone who is unable to keep up with technology. Don't be computer illiterate. Learn the ins and outs of your system now. One- or two-day seminars are available as well as evening classes offered by local community colleges. In the meantime, if you don't know the system, read the manual or ask a colleague to help you.

What are some other software packages that might be helpful to me?

Communications software allows you to send and receive faxes or files directly from the computer. It facilitates transmitting information from one office to another in a timely fashion without rekeying information.

Grammar or editing packages, identify grammatical errors. The software makes suggestions as to how the report or memo could be improved. The final editorial decision, however, is made by you, the user. The package can be customized by selecting certain features.

Data bases are available to manipulate large amounts of information. The packages allow the user to perform specialized sorts. One possible use would be to provide labels in a certain zip-code range to mail a marketing brochure.

Scanning software allows the user to scan typed documents and/or graphics, capturing the information onto diskette. This software is particularly useful for scanning those long documents that were not accompanied by a diskette. However, the captured text or graphic usually requires some clean up.

Calendar programs, as discussed in Chapter 1, Building a Relationship with Your Boss, can be set up to record daily tasks, weekly projects, or monthly logs. An alarm feature can be activated to alert the user to check the daily calendar to avoid missing an appointment or forgetting a deadline.

Graphics packages allow the user to add visual features to text. This can be in the form of bar or pie charts, clip art, scanned images, as well as free-hand artwork. Graphics are particularly useful in the publishing industry, technical works, marketing presentations, etc.

Design or border packages contain page borders, drop caps, as well as some predefined column layout for newsletter design and blank resumes. Design packages can be used for adding impact to the printed word.

Spreadsheet software allows the user to keep track of figures. The spread-sheets can be programmed to total columns and project percentages. For newsletters, it's easy to keep track of layout and design, printing, and mailing costs. Even though many word-processing programs have math capabilities, spreadsheet packages are much easier to use for large numerical projects.

Is your PC sluggish? *Disk optimizers* are available to make files segmented by use into contiguous ones. Frequently changed oversized documents are stored wherever disk space is available. The document may be splintered into five, eight, or even ten smaller segments, with pointers leading from piece A to B to C. Optimizing your hard drive on a regular basis keeps your PC performing at top processing speed.

Interchange diskettes frequently among locations? You may want to invest in *virus scanning* software. This software scans all incoming diskettes to verify they are virus free. If a virus is detected, these packages remove it. Undetected viruses have a wide destructive range, from replicating until all available disk space is used up to actually changing numbers in spreadsheets.

Need to do organizational charts? There's a package available. Have a diskette you need to convert? There's software for that too. Contact your local computer software dealer for a detailed explanation of what's available to help you.

My friend works for a company that just purchased PCs for all their secretaries. She said word processors are obsolete. What's the difference between a PC and a word processor?

Single task stand-alone word processors have now evolved to personal computers, and PCs do so much more than just word process. Letters can be faxed to various locations, spreadsheets can be created, and databases can be designed. Some offices have linked or networked all their computers to send messages to other work stations or to share documents.

9-7

SOLVING COMMON COMPUTER PROBLEMS

My spell checker stops at my boss's name, the company's name, etc., which wastes time. Any time-saving suggestions?

Customize the speller by adding your own words. Before entering the word, however, double-check that what you want to add is indeed spelled correctly. Of course, incorrectly spelled words can and should be deleted promptly, but that takes time. Do it right the first time.

I work in a legal office that uses a lot of trade names. Any help for me? My spell checker stops at the first occurrence of each name, slowing down productivity.

Remember to add words to your speller. However, if you feel you waste too much time adding words, maybe you need to examine additional software packages designed to include trade names or specific terminology such as legal terms or foreign phrases. Carefully assess any supplemental program for compatibility with your current package, user's ease, and whether or not it suits your needs. Ask the systems expert in your company for input; he or she might be able to recommend a package. Otherwise use our handy software checklist when comparing packages.

Software Checklist

	SOFTWARE PACKAGE #1	SOFTWARE PACKAGE #2	SOFTWARE PACKAGE #3
Compatible with current word-processing program?			
Easy to use?			
Can perform application(s) desired, such as containing trade names, etc.?			
Can perform additional applications desired but not necessary, such as Latin?			
Was the product demonstrated?			
Is the software returnable?			
What is the price?			

Don't settle for less than what you want. Ask for product demonstrations.
Compare various systems.

**I work in a medical office. The terminology is highly specialized and diffi-
cult to spell. My speller doesn't contain even one fourth of the words I
need. Of course, I realize I can add words to my spell checker, but there
must be an easier way.**

Believe it or not, there is a medical dictionary supplement available just for
you. This supplement is used in addition to your regular speller. However,
as with any supplemental software program, be sure it is compatible with
your current word-processing package. Use the software checklist on page
169 for evaluating it.

**I was on vacation and a temporary filled in for me. Now my spell checker
doesn't pick up all the errors. A coworker told me that the temporary
added words to my dictionary. Now what can I do? I'm near tears as yet
another document has been returned with an individual's name misspelled.
I just can't seem to catch all the errors myself, and I relied on my spell
checker to flag proper names for me.**

Don't throw in the dictionary just yet. Most spell checkers not only allow
users to add words but to delete them as well. Follow the instructions
shown in your manual for your package or ask your systems specialist for
help.

For example, the entries may be listed alphabetically in a supplemental speller. Deleting may be as easy as retrieving the file and
removing the incorrectly spelled word. If your supplemental file is too
large and contains numerous errors, it may be simpler to delete the file
and start over.

Periodically check your supplemental speller and purge on a regular
basis. You, too, may be guilty of hitting the wrong key—adding words when
you only intended to skip or edit.

**A coworker password protects her sensitive documents. She's seriously ill
and I've been asked to work on some of her documents. However, I don't
know her password and neither does her boss. Is there any way to unlock
a password-protected file without knowing the password?**

Call your word-processing hotline number for suggestions. They may be
able to walk you through an unlock program.

If they are unable to help you, utility packages are available that can decrypt some password-protected files. Of course, these utility package are not recommended by your word-processing manufacturer.

In the future, suggest that all secretaries let their bosses know their password.

I worked hard on a report to the board of directors, but a line was dropped from the final printing. Now I look incompetent and, unfortunately, so does my boss. Where did I go wrong?

The problem probably occurred when you were correcting individual pages. When printing from the screen, sometimes pagination is not set and the page rolls with additions or deletions. The best way to avoid this is always to check the beginning and ending lines on a page. Do they match the previous copy? If that had been done, chances are the dropped or rolled line would have been caught. Remember: the closer you are to a project, the less likely you are able to catch errors. Ask a coworker to proof your changes.

I was making some changes on a document for the CEO. His secretary was on vacation and he asked me to work on this project for him. He was so anxious for the final copy that he was removing it from the printer before I had a chance to look at it. I was afraid there might be errors. Actually, I never did get to see the entire finished project. How should I have handled this?

There's nothing wrong in saying, "Here, if you wait a minute I'll proof those changes," and then begin immediately. Another thought is to reprint the entire document after the CEO has left and reread it then. If you find a mistake, you can quickly reprint the entire document and just hand him the whole package. Just ask the CEO to pitch the entire old version.

Help. I've deleted a file that I shouldn't have. Can I get it back?

Yes. The more recent versions of DOS actually have an undelete feature built in. If your DOS is an earlier version, utility programs are available that have this feature. Become familiar with either how this program works or with someone who can walk you through the software.

The sooner you attempt to undelete a file, the better the recovery rate. If you wait even ten minutes and use the computer, some of the clusters may become overwritten, making the undelete unsuccessful.

If you must purchase a utility package, find one that is compatible with your word-processing package. Be sure this package is bought and installed before you need to use it.

Help! In our office, secretaries are asked to help out in different departments. I gave one secretary a document on a diskette to update with corrections. I've done this before and *never* had a problem.

When she returned the document on diskette, I just copied it onto the hard drive. A few days later when I called up the document, imagine my surprise to find out that the document was blank. Now what? This document represented weeks of work. I'm afraid this might mean my job. Did I lose it?

You could have lost it. A few general rules are needed.

Rule #1: For documents worked on in other departments, *always* have the individual save the document on her hard drive. When she has finished working on it, transfer it back to the original floppy diskette. If the diskette bombs, the document is still accessible on her hard drive. The document can be recopied onto another diskette.

Rule #2: Always retrieve the document before you save it on the hard drive. You would have found out up front that something was wrong with the document, without losing the version you had on the hard drive.

Rule #3: Remember the later versions of DOS have recover or undelete commands. Utility packages are also available that help to retrieve or recover documents. However, success is dependent on how soon recover procedures are done. The success rate is better if done immediately.

Recently another division sent me a diskette in the mail along with a word-processed document for inclusion in our presentation package. I just threw it in my "to-do" box, thinking I'd get to it later. When I finally got to it, I couldn't read the diskette. Luckily it was a short document, which I ended up keystroking. I know I handled this poorly. What should I have done?

Whenever you will be working from another's diskette, immediately check:

1. that the document is on the diskette. You may find out the diskette is blank, which means the secretary either did not properly copy the file or sent the wrong diskette.

2. that the document can be retrieved on your system. Just because a file exists on a diskette doesn't mean you will be able to access it.

Occasionally the message "incompatible file" may appear or "file inaccessible" or "bad sectors." All these messages spell trouble; you will not be able to retrieve the document.

With some word-processing packages, you may also need to know under what software system the diskette was created. The document may need to be converted prior to using. And, as with any conversion, sometimes it doesn't work.

One secretary received a 15-page speech along with a diskette, which she threw in her "to-do" pile. A few days later when she finally attempted to retrieve the document, she found she needed to convert it first. However, she didn't know which software package the document was created under. After four attempts, the document finally converted. But what if she had been unable to convert the document? She would have been forced to type and proofread a 15-page document—under pressure.

We often send documents on diskette to other facilities. Our office-supply manager keeps ordering unformatted diskettes. I absolutely hate taking the time out to format them. How can I get the office manager to see my point and order formatted ones?

Details are what sells your idea. Do a price comparison. Find out how much a box of formatted and a box of unformatted diskettes cost. For example, if you allow one minute per diskette to format, a box of ten translates to ten minutes of your time to format without interruptions. Tell the office manager your findings. Time is money.

I didn't realize that all the diskettes ordered had to be formatted until I used one. It couldn't have happened at a worse time. Three people were standing around my desk waiting for information to be copied onto them. How should I have handled this?

Check your supplies carefully. For diskettes, the box usually states whether or not they're formatted. Load one of the new diskettes into your computer and try to copy a file onto it.

If you happen to get a box of unformatted diskettes, format the entire box right away. You won't have to worry about which ones are formatted and which ones are not. In the long run, it's a time saver.

Check with your systems specialist for the proper way to format diskettes. The size, 3 1/2" versus 5 1/4", as well as low versus high density

dictates the type of formatting command to use. Because an incorrectly formatted diskette can result in lost data in the future, be sure you know how
to format blank diskettes properly.

**I can't find a document that I moved from another person's hard drive. I
remember copying it, yet it's just not there. Worse yet, I deleted the original once I knew I copied it. What do I do now?**

How did you move it from one machine to another? Did you copy it onto
a diskette? See if it still exists on the diskette.

Where did it go? You probably copied it into a nonexistent directory.
The computer does move it, but since there is no directory by that name,
it's gone. Check to see if it defaulted to the hard-drive directory.

As a future safeguard, always check the directory to which you moved
the document to be sure it exists. Once confirmed, it is then safe to delete
the original. By making this step a habit, you'll lessen the chances of losing a document.

**I can't believe I did it! It was a particularly hectic day. I had two diskettes
in my hand. One had information on it. The other needed to be formatted.
Well, I switched diskettes and formatted the one I needed. Is there any way
to get back my information? Will undelete do the trick?**

Unfortunately, no. Undelete only works on erased or deleted items.
Formatting reconfigures the diskette, making it brand new.

Use a "write-protect tab" on diskettes that you want to keep intact.
This tab prevents copying or changing documents on your master diskette.
If you had had the write-protect tab on your diskette, you would have not
been able to format the diskette.

On 3.5" diskettes, using the write-protect feature is easy. In the
upper left corner, there's a rectangle with a square tab that slides back and
forth. To write-protect your diskette, slide the tab up, which exposes a
square opening. To unprotect a diskette, slide the tab down, covering the
square opening.

The 5.25" diskettes do not have a square tab. Instead, these diskettes
have a notch on the right side. By placing a tab over the notch, you have
write-protected the diskette. These self-stick tabs are normally included
with each new box of diskettes. Be sure to place the label flat so as not to
catch on anything in the disk drive, which could result in a costly repair bill.

Again, to unprotect a 5.25″ diskette, simply remove the self-stick tab, exposing the notch.

Always view the directory of a diskette before formatting. Again, by taking a few seconds out to view the directory, you would have been alerted that you switched diskettes. At that point, you could have easily removed your master diskette and replaced it with the blank one you wanted to format.

Unless you kept a backup diskette for your master document, you'll need to re-create everything. Your office may have a scanner that will allow you to scan a previously typed document and save it in ASCII.

When our satellite marketing offices send in their reports, my boss insists that a diskette accompany them. In reality, the diskette rarely accompanies the project. Several phone calls later, I finally track down the individual responsible for sending the diskette and I request one. On short reports, I could rekey it without too much trouble. I don't understand my boss's obsession with diskettes.

Every time you need to rekey information, you run the risk of introducing errors. Perhaps he's using the diskette as a safety mechanism. If there are errors in the reports, they were caused by the author of the work, not the assembler of the package.

Think of it this way. Let's say your time is worth $20 an hour. Maybe the document will take you an hour to type and an hour to proof. That's $40. Now remember, the diskette has already been created and is just waiting for you. The only cost involved is express-mail charges.

Develop a form to accompany the monthly reports. Send it to all satellite locations. List on the form the due date, to whom the report should be sent, and of course, in bold letters, the fact that the diskette is to accompany the report.

Transmittal Reminder

Reminder: Your monthly sales reports must be received no later than the **15th of every month.** Questions regarding these reports should be directed to LuAnn Phillips at (708) 555-1212. Please use this form to accompany your report.

Mail the report to: LuAnn Phillips
                             The Excellent Company
                             303 Main Street
                             Headquarters, IL 60000-6497

_____ **Diskette enclosed. (Diskettes are required in order to facilitate assembling the final document.)**

This report is from:

_____

_____

_____

Phone No.: _____

_____

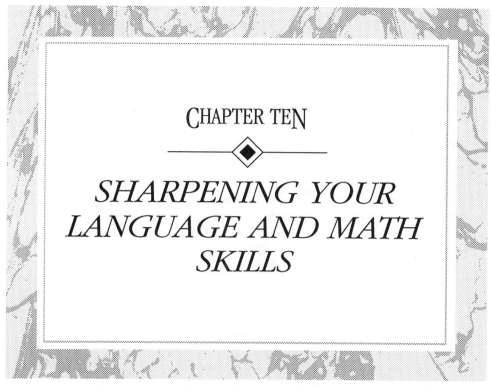

CHAPTER TEN

◆

SHARPENING YOUR LANGUAGE AND MATH SKILLS

Our language is constantly changing. New words are added, other words deleted. The gender issue has made us aware of how language can change our perceptions. The primary purpose of any language is to communicate. Knowledge of the mechanics of punctuation and grammar is of principal importance in order to create correspondence that will communicate thought and ideas clearly and concisely. Put your best image forward. Don't allow poor grammar or misspellings to damage your reputation. This chapter reviews punctuation and grammar basics and addresses some of the new trends for business communication in the twenty-first century.

10-1

GRAMMAR AND STYLE FOR THE TWENTY-FIRST CENTURY

I know what I learned in school regarding grammar and punctuation but that was over 20 years ago. What type of writing style is acceptable in the business world today?

Short sentences containing fewer than 20 words written in simple, concise language in active voices, are the best.

I thought grammar rules pertained to all types of writing, but our communication area frequently uses a different style from the one used for business purposes. Are different grammar rules used for business writing than those used by a publisher?

Business writing is on the cutting edge of style and format change. New words are constantly entered into our vocabulary from the business community. Remember when there were no such words as *downsizing, rightsizing, palimony, legalese*; when *okay* was considered slang; when *ain't* wasn't in the dictionary? Remember when judgment and acknowledgment had an "e" in them? New acronyms are also turning up; *PC, CD, PMS,* and *AIDS* are just a few.

Business writing can be a little more flexible and creative, but people who work in the communications area, in particular, must follow the more rigid demands of formal written presentation demanded by their profession.

I notice that often the periods have been dropped between the letters of acronyms or certain abbreviations. Is this a new trend?

There is a trend in business writing toward simplicity and it is acceptable to drop the periods from acronyms and abbreviations—write CPA, AM, PM, PO Box.

10-2
REVIEWING THE PARTS OF SPEECH

I recently landed a new job working in an editorial department. I've been out of school for some time and when my boss talks about using a different adjective or adding an adverb, I am lost. What are the definitions?

There are eight basic parts of speech. Use this poem to help you remember the definition of each one.

1. **Nouns** name people, places, things,
    as *Smith, New York, potatoes, wings.*

2. **Pronouns** are used in place of nouns:
    I think; *she* sings; *they* work; *he* frowns.

3.   **Adjectives** add something to the nouns,
        As *old* New York and *little* towns
        And don't forget that *many, few,*
        and numbers and articles are adjectives too.

4.   **Verbs** come next—the words that tell
        of action, being, and state as well;
        To *work, become, exist* and *curb*—
        each one of these is called a verb.

5.   **Adverbs** add something to the meaning
        of adjectives, as *brightly* gleaming.
        To verbs they also add a thought,
        As when we say "was *nearly* caught."
        And last, an adverb has the chore
        Of making other adverbs tell us more
        Than one alone could hope to tell,
        As in, "She sang that *very* well."
        To find an adverb, this test try:
        Ask *How?* or *When?* or *Where?* or *Why?*

6.   **Prepositions** show relation,
        as *with* affection, in *our* nation.

7.   **Conjunctions**, as their name implies,
        Are joining words; they are the ties
        That bind together day *and* night,
        Calm *but* cold, dull *or* bright.

8.   **Interjections** are words that show
        Sudden emotion, as Alas! Ah! Oh!

        Thus briefly does this jingle state
        The parts of speech, which total eight.[*]

Permission granted by The English Language Institute of America, Inc.

PUNCTUATION POINTERS

When is it appropriate to use a semicolon instead of a comma?

A semicolon indicates a short pause. Ideas that are not independent enough to be separated by periods and are not closely enough related to be separated by commas are separated by semicolons. In other words, the semicolon is a cross between a period and a comma. When typing, one space follows a semicolon.

Basically, semicolons separate the clauses of a compound sentence. But there are definite rules for using semicolons to join clauses:

1. The sentences joined must be related in thought.

2. Each clause joined by a semicolon must make a complete statement.

Jane is a wonderful teacher; she wants to learn to type one day.

This sentence is a compound sentence, but are the two thoughts related? Jane being a wonderful teacher has nothing to do with her wanting to learn to type. These two separate ideas should *not* be joined by a semicolon. The sentence should probably read, "Jane is a wonderful teacher and she would like to learn to type one day."

Jane is a wonderful teacher; she received the PTA Teacher of the Year award last year.

Here, the two sentences joined make a complete statement. They are also related in thought so it meets the "semicolon two-rule test."

A *conjunctive adverb* joins two long independent clauses together and should also be preceded by a semicolon. Don't let the phrase *conjunctive adverb* throw you; it simply means another thought will follow. Some common conjunctive adverbs are:

accordingly	indeed	on the contrary
besides	likewise	otherwise
consequently	moreover	similarly
furthermore	nevertheless	therefore
however	notwithstanding	

We received the order late; therefore, we were unable to ship it before the end of the month.

We have the complete sentence, *We received the order late,* but the conjunctive adverb *therefore* tells us there is more to follow and will take the form of a conclusion or result.

Semicolons are also used when commas cannot separate groups clearly or with enough emphasis. For example:

Please read the following chapters over the holidays: Chapter 12, pages 85 to 102 inclusive; Chapter 13, pages 106 to 115; and Chapter 14, pages 122 to 130.

When should I use a colon?

A colon indicates a longer pause than a semicolon. A colon at the end of a sentence indicates that something will follow to explain or to complete the idea. A formal introduction of a list of items should be followed by a colon. For example:

Please note the following requirements necessary for a good meeting: private conference area, agenda, overhead projector, and refreshments.

A long or formal direct quotation or question should be preceded by a colon. For example:

His exact words were: "An agenda should be provided to each member of the team."

When typing, two spaces follow a colon.

When should I use a dash instead of a colon?

A dash is used to express a sudden and unexpected change of thought:

Susan has always been interested in travel—and very wealthy men.

Our research shows—and we find this most unusual—that our new product is finding acceptance with a great number of working women.

The dash may also be used before or after a series or a summary:

A racy sense of humor, street smarts, and unique directing—these are the characteristics that have made his films so great.

Note: Never use a dash at the beginning of a line. If you are typing a sentence and the dash falls to the beginning of the next line, either move the dash to the end of the preceding line or move the whole word to the next line.

Once and for all, where does the punctuation go, inside the quotation marks or outside?

Basically, periods and commas are placed inside quotation marks while semicolons and colons are placed outside quotation marks unless they are part of the quotation.

Note that the question mark is placed inside the quotation marks when the sentence quoted is a question. In the sentence, *"Who's there?" she called,* the question is part of the quotation and belongs inside the quotation marks. In the sentence, *Is it true they named the new mall "Prairie Plaza"?,* the question mark is placed outside the quotation marks.

A person I work with is always sending memos with those three little dots in the middle of a sentence. Exactly what are they supposed to mean or do?

Those three little dots (spaced periods) are called ellipsis marks and are used to indicate that one or more words have been omitted from a quotation. For instance,

Poe wrote "'T'was on a midnight dark and dreary . . ." and it still sends shudders down my spine.

When the ellipsis marks are at the end of a sentence, add one for a period. Remember three in the middle, four at the end.

Ellipsis marks can also indicate a kind of fading away:

He desperately wanted to call her, but morning faded to evening, days turned into weeks, months into years . . . .

Advertisers use ellipsis marks to separate short groups of words for emphasis:

Do it now . . . Do it Right . . . Call the dealer in your area.

A question mark or exclamation point may follow ellipsis marks:

Did she write the truth in her diary . . . ?

If a sentence ends in a word like *etc.* do you add another period to show the end of the sentence?

No. One period at the end of the sentence is enough. However, if an interrogative or exclamatory sentence ends with an abbreviation, the question mark or exclamation point follows the abbreviation period:

Should I write to all the members, guests, employees, etc.?

Inside the sentence, an abbreviation period is followed by any mark that would normally be used:

Should I write to all the members, guests, employees, etc.; or were they notified earlier?

Does the period go inside or outside parenthesis marks when the parenthesis ends the sentence?

If it is part of a sentence, the period follows the parenthesis:

Everyone planned to attend the meeting (but the marketing people were delayed).

However, if it is a complete sentence enclosed in parentheses, then the period goes inside.

Everyone planned to attend the meeting. (Last year the marketing group did not attend, however.)

10-4

REVIEWING PLURALS AND POSSESSIVES

Lawless Language

We'll begin with a *fox*, and the plural is *foxes*,
But the plural of *ox* should never be *oxes*.

One fowl is a *goose*, and the plural is *geese*,
But the plural of *moose* won't therefore be *meese*.

So also for *mouse*, the plural is *mice*,
But for house it's *houses*—we never say *hice*.

And since the plural of *man* is always called *men*,
for the plural of *pan*, why can't we say *pen*?

Then *one* may be *that* and *three* may be *those*,
Yet *rat* in the plural is never called *rose*.

And the masculine pronouns are *he, his,* and *him*,
but imagine the feminine, *she, shis,* and *shim*!

So English, I fancy, you all will agree,
Is the most lawless language you ever did see.

—Anonymous[*]

[*]*Permission granted by the English Language Institute of America, Inc.*

If a word ends in "s" does that mean it is plural and requires a plural verb?

As you can see from the poem, plurals can be very confusing. Just because a word ends in the letter "s," does not mean it is plural. The verb "is" (which ends in "s") is always singular. Remember the "s" in "is" stands for "singular." Many words ending in the letter "s" require a singular verb:

Politics is interesting. Economics is boring.

I have trouble with apostrophes. I am always getting confused, especially with plurals and possessives. How can I keep my apostrophes straight?

The apostrophe mark (') is used to show omission of a letter, possession, and some plurals. Use these guidelines:

♦ If it is a singular word that shows possession, simply add *'s*.

   The dog's toy, Mr. Martin's house.

♦ If the word shows possession but already ends in s, you have two choices. You may add only the apostrophe or you can add *'s*.

   It was my boss's idea or *It was the typists' responsibility* (the responsibility of more than one typist).

♦ If it is a plural word that ends in *s* (but does not necessarily show possession), add only the apostrophe.

   It has taken five days' work.

♦ Use an apostrophe to distinguish between joint and separate possession.

   Bill and Toni's presentation (joint) or *Bill's and Toni's presentations* (separate).

♦ The apostrophe is also used to indicate a letter or a number that has been omitted.

   He'll be there on time; the '90s promise to be interesting.

10-5
CAPITALIZATION

I don't capitalize people's titles, but my boss always insists on it. Who is right?

Capitalize professional and business titles that precede a proper name: Mayor Larson, President Clinton, Vice President Gore. However, if the title follows the name, it should not be capitalized: George Larson, mayor; Bill Clinton, president of the United States; Bradley Edwards, vice president.

Am I supposed to capitalize the name of the seasons? When I write, "We plan to complete the budget before fall," it looks funny.

The names of the seasons are not capitalized—spring, summer, fall, and winter—unless they are personified. For example, *Winter's cold wind chilled our souls.*

———— 10-6 ————

HYPHENATION

If a proper word is hyphenated, am I supposed to capitalize both words?

Do not capitalize any part of a hyphenated word that would not ordinarily be capitalized. For instance, mid-August, pre-Gothic, French-speaking. Note that hyphens have been dropped from most words beginning with prefixes, such as coauthor, nonstop, cosponsor. Hyphens are still used with the prefixes *self, ex,* and *all*: self-control, self-image; ex-spouse, ex-representative; all-important, all-inclusive.

I am totally confused about hyphenating words. Why is *year to date* hyphenated sometimes and at other times it is not?

Hyphens are used to join two or more words to form a single, compound adjective. For instance in the phrase, *year-to-date* sales, one can quickly see that *year-to-date* describes (an adjective) the sales. However, in the sentence, *In the year to date, the sales of the Division have been flat,* the phrase "year to date" is not describing, anything, but is stating a fact. Hyphens make several words into one adjective. Other examples are:

- She is a high-powered executive. (what kind? high-powered)

- It is a once-in-a-lifetime deal. (what kind? once-in-a-lifetime)

- There are 75 full-time sales people. (what kind? full-time)

Hyphens are used in joining certain prefixes to nouns. Janet has a poor self-image.

Hyphens can also indicate a range; *delivery will take 5-7 weeks, we should have an answer in 4-5 hours.* However, if the words "from" and "to" are part of the sentence, do not use a hyphen. Delivery will take from 5 to 7 weeks.

Note, when keystroking a document for a printer or when using a graphics software program, the "en" dash is used to indicate range.

A compound noun in which both nouns refer to a person or thing is hyphenated to give the words equal value; *city-state, secretary-treasurer, lawyer-banker.*

10-7
GUIDELINES FOR CORRECT WORD USAGE

I get confused about when to use the word *principal* and when to use the word *principle*. Is there a simple way to remember the difference so I don't have to keep looking them up in the dictionary?

Principal (noun) means "chief participant or head." The princi*pal* of the school is your *pal*. *Principal* also means "money" (What is the amount of *principal* outstanding on the loan?) and money is your *pal*. As an adjective, *principal* means "most important" as in *the principal reason for the change.* Anything important is your *pal*.

Principle (noun) means a "rule, law, or doctrine." She is a woman of high *principle*. What is the *principle* of gravity? Remember that rules and laws are not your *pal*. Anything that is not your pal is a *ple*.

What is the difference between *a*ffect and *e*ffect?

Affect (verb) means "to influence." Will this new law *affect* our policy?

Effect (verb) means "to bring about." This new law will *effect* a change in our policy.

Effect (noun) means "as a result of." What *effect* did this change have on our policy?

When do you use *who* and when do you use *whom*? I still get those two confused.

Use *who* when it is the subject of the sentence:

Who sent this letter? The girl with the brown hair is the one who speaks no English.

In this sentence use *who* because it is the subject of *speaks* in the clause *who speaks no English.*

Use *whom* when it is the object of a verb or preposition: *You are the one to whom I am speaking.*

Whom shall we send to the meeting? Object of the verb *shall send.*

Where is the person from whom you received the roses? Object of the preposition *from.*

A frequent cause of confusion occurs in questions when *who* or *whom* precedes the verb. In order to tell which form of the pronoun is required, change the question to a statement:

Whom shall we send to the meeting? We shall send whom to the meeting.

It makes it easier to see that *whom* is the object of the verb *shall send.*

Use *whom* as the subject of an infinitive. The infinitive must always be in the objective case:

Bill is the man whom we thought to be your new supervisor. (Subject of the infinitive "to be.")

When should I use *among* and when should I use *between*?

Between refers to the relationship of *two people* or things.

The exchange of information between *John and Susan was interesting* or *The exchange of information* between *John's department and Susan's department was interesting.*

Among refers to the relationship of a group or more than two people or things.

The exchange of information among *the participants at the seminar was interesting.*

What is correct, *all right* or *alright*?

All right means "acceptable, safe, yes." The list of attendees looks *all right* to me. *Alright* is not *all right*; it is a misspelling of *all right.*

Can you tell me when to use *compliment* and *complement*, *complimentary* and *complementary*?

Compliment means to flatter; *complimentary* means to express praise.

Complement means to complete or make perfect; complementary means to complete or supply something that is missing.

I would like to compliment *(flatter) your* complementary *(complete) color scheme.*

We have a full complement *(complete) of wine on board and are awaiting any* complimentary *(praise) comments on our choices.*

I got into an argument with another secretary because my boss always uses the word "irregardless." She said there is no such word. I don't want to embarrass my boss. Who is right?

Irregardless of what anyone thinks, *regardless* is a better word. Why say "irregardless" when simply "regardless" will do? However, note that even though "irregardless" is considered poor form, it is now in the dictionary—it means "regardless."

Can the words "infer" and "imply" be used interchangeably?

These two words are frequently confused, yet their meanings are very different. To "infer" something is to arrive at a conclusion after listening or observing something. It also means to surmise or guess.

To "imply" means to hint or guess at something without stating it outright.

The manager implied [hinted] *the employee would be getting a raise.*

After reviewing the success of Sue's marketing program and the profits it generated, the manager inferred [deducted] *she would get a bonus.*

Please go over when it is correct to use "sit" and when it is correct to use "set." I always get them confused.

Sit is an intransitive verb that means to "assume or be in a certain position." This verb never takes an object. If you say "I will let the letter *sit* where it is" can you substitute the word *place* for *sit?* You wouldn't say "I will let the letter *place* where it is." Therefore, *sit* must be right.

Set is a transitive verb that means to "place or put." It needs an object. In the sentence *Colleen set her bowling ball on the floor* can we substitute "place" for "set." *Colleen placed her bowling ball on the floor.* Yes. Therefore, "set" is correct. Note that the object of the verb "set" is "ball."

I just got a letter that stated "enclosed is a small *momento* from the meeting." Isn't it supposed to be *memento*?

You are correct. A *memento* is a souvenir or something that reminds us of the past. There is no such thing as a *momento*.

What is the proper usage of the words "accept" and "except"?

Accept is a verb that means to receive something.

   I accept your apology; I accept your invitation; I accept the terms of the contract.

   Except means to exclude.

   The contract is fine except (excluding) Item 12. The change in policy will except (exclude) anyone hired after June 1993.

   The word "except" is also a preposition.

   Everyone arrived on time except Ellen.

When do you use the spelling "capital" and when do you use "capitol"?

Capital means just about everything. If you say *That's a capital idea,* you mean it is excellent or outstanding. *Capital* stocks are shares issued by a corporation. *He invested his capital (money) in bonds.* The *capital* of Illinois is Springfield. The thing to remember here is that *capitol* refers only to a building. Use a capital "C" when *capitol* refers to the building in Washington, DC, where the Congress of the United States convenes. Use a small "c" when it refers to the state legislature building.

What's the difference between *stationary* and *stationery?*

Stationary is an adjective that describes something that is in a fixed position; it will not move. An office building, a stove, or a garage would be *stationary* objects.

   Stationery is a noun that refers to office supplies or paper, pens, pencils, letterhead, and envelopes. Remember station*ery* and pap*er*.

When my boss dictates he will often say something like, *Susan, John, and myself will attend the conference*. I changed the word *myself* to *I*. However, I also get memos from people who say *The conference attendees will be John, Susan, and myself.* I know it should be *John, Susan, and I*. It seems to be pretty widespread, at least in my company. Has a rule been changed or something that I don't know about?

When incorrect grammar is used over and over, people begin to accept it as correct. Even those who know better begin questioning the proper usage. This must be what is happening in your company. Pronouns ending in self or selves should never be used as subjects. You would not say "Both myself and my sister received awards." *Myself* cannot be a subject. The sentence should read "Both my sister and I received awards."

Perhaps the confusion came about because "myself" is used to intensify the pronoun "I". *I, myself, saw her get on the train.* However, *myself* should never be *substituted* for the pronoun "I." Myself is also used as a form of "me" as direct or indirect object of a verb or preposition.

I bought myself a gift or *I thought only of myself.*

10-8

SPELLING RULES-OF-THUMB

I am a poor speller. Do you have any tips that will improve my spelling?

Train yourself to become a super speller by using these guidelines:

1. Sharpen your visual memory. Some people say a word may "look" wrong even if they don't know how to spell it. Make a list of words used in correspondence that you have trouble spelling. Keep it close to your word processor and study the list daily. By forming a strong visual impression of these words, you will be able to reproduce them accurately. Update the list by adding new words.

2. Practice writing (or typing) the word or list of words over and over until it becomes automatic. For instance, when you write a letter to your mother, you automatically write the words "Dear Mom." You don't stop to think how the words are spelled; it is an automatic process. By writing or typing the words that give you trouble, you will be able to develop an automatic response.

3. Learn the basic spelling rules by reading this chapter and apply the rules to the words that give you trouble. By understanding the structure of the word and learning what spelling rules apply, you will learn to spell correctly any word that gives you trouble.

What is that old spelling rule about "i before e." I know there is more to it but I can't remember it.

The rule is:

> *i* before *e* except after *c*
>
> or when sounded like *a*
>
> as in *neighbor* and *weigh*

While this little rhyme covers most words, there are some exceptions: *neither, leisure, foreign, seize.*

If a word has a long "i" sound it is usually *ei: height, stein, feisty.* However, when followed by an "r" use *ie: fiery, hierarchy.*

If the word has a short sound, use *ie: mischief, friend, patient.* The exceptions include *heifer* and words that end in *eign* or *feit: foreign, counterfeit, sovereign.*

If you're unsure (or confused) check your dictionary for the proper spelling.

What is the correct way to spell *supersede*. I have seen it spelled *supercede* so many times, I am starting to spell it that way. What is the spelling rule for words that end in "ceed"?

There are only three verbs that end in *ceed.* They are *succeed, proceed,* and *exceed.* Think "To *succeed,* don't *exceed* the speed limit as you *proceed.*" All others end in *cede; precede, intercede, recede. Supersede* is the *only* word with an ending of *sede.*

The spelling in business correspondence seems to be getting worse. Today, I received a letter with the word *superintendant* instead of *superintendent*. If people don't know the correct way to spell a word, why don't they take the time to look it up?

A person working under pressure to prepare a document quickly is more likely to make errors; that same person is also less likely to take the time to check the spelling in the document. Sadly, many people believe they spelled the word correctly. Spelling errors could be corrected easily if people would only utilize the "spell check" feature on their word processors, or take the time to look the word up in the dictionary.

Whether a word should be spelled with an "ant" or an "ent" on the end can be confusing. Words that seem to cause the most trouble are superintendent, dependent, persistent, and insistent. By using the sentence, "the persist*ent* superintend*ent* is depend*ent* and insist*ent* on collecting the *rent*," may help you remember they all end in *ent.*

I have trouble remembering when to drop the "e" and add "ing" and when to leave the "e." Is there some simple rule I can follow?

The rule is quite simple. When a word ends in "e," drop the "e" before adding a suffix that begins with a vowel. In other words, you don't want to put two vowels together. The vowels are a, e, i, o, u, and sometimes y (the letter "y" is almost always a vowel unless it is the first letter of a word).

Drop the "e"	**Add "ing"**
write	writing
prove	proving
encourage	encouraging
state	stating

However, you keep the "e" if you add a suffix beginning with a consonant. A consonant is any letter that is not a vowel.

state	stating	statement
encourage	encouraging	encouragement
replace	replacing	replacement

Other suffixes that begin with a consonant (retain the "e") are *sorely, profusely. widely*. Exceptions include *only, truly, awful,* and the *dge* words: *acknowledgment, judgment, abridgment*.

I have had some bad experiences using spell check. If you make a typo, say you type *is* instead of *if,* spell check won't catch it. After all, *is* is spelled correctly. Will it ever get to the point that a computer feature will be able to differentiate between a word that is spelled correctly but that does not belong in that sentence?

Grammar check is now available for most word processing software. It can do some of the things spell check can't, like differentiate between words and their meaning within a sentence. While spell check can correct any misspellings and will catch most of your typos, it does have its drawbacks. This poem, *Spellbound,* by Penny Harper has appeared in various newspapers and emphasizes why you should not rely entirely on your spellchecker.

Spellbound

I have a spelling checker.
It came with my PC.
It plainly marks four my revue,
Mistake I cannot see.
I've run this poem threw it,

I'm sure your please too no.
It's letter perfect in it's weigh,
My checker tolled me sew.

I get confused typing prefixes. In the word misspell, I add an "s" but in the word disappoint, I don't. How can I tell when to add that extra "s" and when not to?

Think of the basic root of the word. The word *spell* begins with an "s." When you add the prefix "mis," it ends in an "s." Therefore the word is correctly spelled "misspell". The root word of disappoint is *appoint*. The prefix *dis* when added to the word *appoint* becomes *dis*appoint. Notice that if the root word begins with an "s" and you add either *mis* or *dis*, it has two s's. This also holds true with the prefix *dis*. If the root word begins with an "s" and you add *dis*, the word will have a double s.

misspell	dissatisfy
misstep	disservice
misstate	dissolve

However, if the root word begins with a letter other than "s," there is no double s.

mistake	disappoint
mishap (from happening)	disapprove
misconstrue	disappear

10-9

FOREIGN WORDS AND PHRASES

My boss uses "i.e." in correspondence as well as "e.g." I am not sure exactly what they mean and if I am using them properly. Can you explain what they mean and how they should be used in correspondence?

An abbreviation, *i.e.* is Latin for *id est*, which means *that is*. The abbreviation *e.g.* is also Latin for *exempli gratia* or *for example*. In the past both *i.e.* and *e.g.* were used only in footnotes and technical reports. In correspondence, instead of using the abbreviation *i.e.*, it was preferred to simply use *that is*. However, due to persistent use in correspondence, both abbreviations are now accepted wording in most documents.

Is it okay to use "per" in letters? It sounds old fashioned but I don't know what to substitute.

When *per* is used in *per* hour or *per* day, it serves a useful purpose. Try to avoid phrases such as "As *per* your recommendation," or "As *per* your letter." It sounds old-fashioned. Instead, say *"Regarding* your recommendation," or *"In accordance with* your letter." Avoid using *per* to mean *by*.

What does *per se* mean?

In Latin *per se* means "through itself." It translates to a sense of being of or by itself. For instance, "This bracelet is worth little *per se*, but much to me, for it belonged to my sister."

My boss uses the phrase *quid pro quo* in his reports. I have an idea what it means from the way it is used, but is it appropriate to use it in letters?

Quid pro quo is Latin and means for a fair return or consideration. It is appropriate to use well-known foreign phrases in general correspondence.

10-10
PROPER PRONUNCIATION

Sometimes I don't pronounce words properly and this makes me very self-conscious. Is there anything I can do to overcome this problem?

Regional variations in speech are very distinctive. Practice accurately sounding out the words you often mispronounce so you won't fall victim to "the lazy slur." Check your dictionary for help in pronunciation and repeat sounding out the word. For example, try pronouncing entrepreneur. Practice saying it phonetically. The first part of the word "entre" is pronounced "ontra." The second part "pre" is pronounced "pra." The final part "neur" is pronounced "nure." Entrepreneur is pronounced "ontra-pra-nure."

So many people run their words together so that whole sentences sound like a one-syllable word. Can you remind people to pronounce each word and/or syllable so their sentences don't become one big blur?

What words are commonly mispronounced in your area? Do you pronounce words clearly? Don't use prONUNICATION shortcuts.

Don't say *waitruss* for *waitress.*
Don't say *jever* for *did you ever.*
Don't say *jeet?* for *did you eat?*
Don't say *toljuh* for *told you.*
Don't say *notchet* for *not yet.*
Don't say *wanta* for *want to.*
Don't say *wunnerful* for *wonderful.*
Don't say *ax* for *ask.*
Don't say *reperzentative* for *representative.*
Don't say *childern* for *children.*
Don't say *athalete* for *athlete.*
Don't say *realator* for *realtor.*
Don't say *careflee* for *carefully.*
Don't say *wuz* for *was.*
Don't say *warsh* for *wash.*
Don't say *terlet* for *toilet.*

If you're having problems with grammar and punctuation, local educational facilities offer refresher courses. There are also a number of correpondence courses that are excellent.

As secretarial status has expanded and changed, so have the requirements for these positions. More and more secretaries are responsible for preparing spreadsheets and are expected to utilize their analytical capabilities. Don't let math anxiety keep you from achieving an executive-level position. This mathematics section should be helpful, but if you are still having trouble, sign up for a refresher course. A mathematics course can also improve your problem-solving and decision-making abilities because math teaches you to think analytically. It may be that mathematical concepts you were unable to grasp earlier in your career may now seem interesting and even fun.

10-11

TIPS FOR TYPING NUMBERS

When typing figures in columns, be sure the digits line up. Dollar and percent signs appear only on the top line and on the total line of a column.

Sample Numerical Columns

TYPE OF EXPENSE	JANUARY	FEBRUARY	MARCH
RENT	$2,500.00	$2,500.00	$2,500.00
ELECTRICITY	727.31	635.90	822.30
TELEPHONE	375.25	260.40	343.90

If cents are not used, drop the decimal and the two zeros.

Normally spell out numbers one through ten, except when larger numbers are used. Then consistency applies.

> *We have had ten applicants for the job.*
> *Marketing has received orders for 1 crawler and 15 loaders.*

Another exception is page and table numbers, which are expressed as figures.

Always spell out numbers that start sentences.

> *Forty children went on the field trip.*

Or reword.

> *Nineteen ninety-one was a profitable year* can be rewritten as *The year 1991 was a profitable one.*

Estimates or approximates are usually written as words.

> *Our meeting will have approximately twelve hundred attendees.*

Numbers are used with percentages.

> *We cut the budget by 5 percent.*

Use A.M. or P.M. after times.

> *The meeting will be held at 10:00 A.M. in Conference Room 1739.*

Fractions should be written as figures when used with whole numbers.

> *The office averages 27 1/2 calls an hour.*

Without a whole number, use words to express fractions.

> *The pie was three fourths gone.*

10-12

BRUSHING UP ON THE BASICS

I never was very good at math in school. My boss has asked me to figure out the markup on some new equipment that cost $4,895. Last year he was able to buy the same equipment for $4,695. I know that the price has gone up $200 just by subtracting $4,695 from $4,895. But the percentage of increase baffles me.

You're halfway there. Divide the difference by the *original* amount, $200 divided by 4,695 = 4.3 %. The answer on your calculator will actually read 0.042598509. However, remember the rule. To find the percentage you *drop the first digit and move the decimal point two places to the right,* which will place it between the 4 and the 2. And since the number after the 2 is a 5, round up to the next highest number, so your answer reads 4.3%.

$4,895
 4,695
——————

$200 $200 ÷ $4,695 = 0.042598509 = 4.3 percent

An even simpler method, saving the subtraction steps, is to divide the larger number by the smaller one. Remember to drop the first digit and move your decimal two places to the right.

$4,895 ÷ $4,695 = 1.0425 = 4.3 percent

By dropping the first digit, moving the decimal point two places to the right, your answer is 4.25, rounded to 4.3 percent.

Salaries are either figured on a monthly or yearly basis. How can I figure out what I make a week if my annual salary is $24,000?

Since there are 52 weeks in a year, divide your salary by 52. The answer is $461.54 per week.

If you wanted to take it a step further and figure out what you make on an hourly basis, next divide your weekly rate by the number of hours you are scheduled to work (overtime doesn't count in this example). If you normally work 40 hours, you would divide $461.54 by 40 to get $11.54, your hourly rate. To double-check your math, multiply your hourly rate by 40 and that answer by 52, and you should be close to your original annual salary of $24,000. Sometimes the pennies get in the way and the answer doesn't exactly tie out.

Once you know your hourly rate, you can even figure out what you make in a day. Multiply your hourly rate ($11.54) by the number of hours you work (8 in this example), which equals $92.32.

I worked five hours overtime last week. I'd like to figure out how much extra I made.

You need to know your hourly rate. If you haven't already figured that out, see the previous example.

Since you worked 5 hours overtime and the standard rate is 1.5 (time and a half), you actually are getting paid for 7.5 hours = 5 hours × 1.5 overtime rate. Now you need to multiply your hourly rate, let's use $11.54, by the number of hours you worked, 7.5. You earned $86.55 extra, less taxes.

I work for a small company and am responsible for the office-supply budget. I have been instructed to cut the budget by 5 percent. How can I figure that out?

You would multiply the amount you spent last year, which is the budget, by the percentage amount, 5 percent, to find out how many dollars to cut.

Let's say your budget was $4,000. Multiply $4,000 by 5% = $200. Your budget would be only $3,800 this year, which is $4,000 − $200.

To figure out what you should spend on a monthly basis for office supplies, divide the new budget amount, $3,800, by 12 months, to get $316.67 a month.

Now how to figure out what to cut. Secretaries are in a great position to pinpoint areas to save money. At one company, the secretary found out that she could save the company $300 per year by simply ordering green plants for the office instead of flowering ones. The company liked having the flora, but did not realize the cost involved.

Another secretary suggested the company could save money by signing a maintenance agreement on the computers rather than paying each time one needed repair.

10-13

PREPARING EXPENSE REPORTS

The accounting department is a lot like the IRS, rule oriented and sticklers on accuracy. Accounting expects that all rules governing expense reports will be complied with. Original receipts for all expenses over a certain dollar amount are also needed. Expense reports should add, horizontally and vertically. If your boss has lost a receipt or his report doesn't add, talk to someone in accounting. Make sure your boss's expense report is correct *before* it's submitted. That doesn't mean accounting can't or won't still bounce it for another infraction of the rules, but you're reducing the odds.

Domestic

As part of my job, I prepare my boss's expense report. This is a first for me. In the past, my bosses prepared their own reports. Just what can I expect?

Expect to receive lots of receipts, in all shapes and sizes. On the back of the receipt, jot down important items, such as the date and what the receipt was for. Business meals can be a problem if your boss forgets to note who was there and the purpose of the luncheon meeting.

Drop the receipts into an envelope or expanding folder until you're ready to post the entries. However, don't wait until the last minute to begin compiling the information. Expense reports should be prepared on a timely basis, once a week for people with heavy travel schedules. Arrange for Friday mornings, for instance, to be expense-report day. If you don't submit expense reports weekly, stay current. Log in the receipts you have received. This will make the process easier and more accurate.

Prepare a reference list that shows mileage to regular locations or facilities, such as branch offices, monthly business meetings, etc. Note whether tolls are involved.

Before you begin entering data onto the expense report, organize the information by date to keep items in the proper column. Hotel bills usually are broken down into several categories: telephone calls, meals, room charges, tips.

My boss travels a lot. At the end of her trip, she returns with a wad of receipts and no notations. Often, accounting hounds us for that missing receipt. Sometimes the receipts turn up in some pocket or notebook. How can I get my boss to be more organized?

Expense Report

Employee: <u>William J. Luczak</u>   Date: <u>June 14, Year</u>

Date of Trip: <u>From June 1, Year</u>   To: <u>June 11, Year</u>

Reason for Trip: <u>Tour potential sites for new venture</u>

Original receipts must be attached for transportation, hotel, and each separate expense of $25 or more.

Date	6/2	6/3	6/4	6/7	6/10	6/11
Auto Mileage @ $0.28/mile			11.20			
Transportation						
Air	645.00			808.00	377.22	
Taxi/Limo/Bus				42.00		
Tolls/Parking						
Hotel/Motel	157.07			270.31	166.63	
Meals including tips						
Breakfast		15.44				
Lunch	32.26			32.81		23.25
Dinner	56.57					
Other Tips	2.00			4.00		
Telephone/Fax	45.25					
Entertainment			100.95	323.88	123.48	
Miscellaneous				150.00		
Total	938.15	15.44	112.15	1,631.00	667.33	23.25

Date	Explanation of Entertainment and Miscellaneous Expenses	Amount		
6/4	Richard Longly	100.95	Total Expenses	$3,387.32
6/7	Tiffany Ward, Wade Foyt, Enrico Delviano, Linda Logan	323.88	Subtract: Travel advance	1,000.00
6/7	Cress Creek Club dues	150.00	Subtract: Direct charges to company	1,830.22
6/10	Mary Trumbell	123.48	Balance due company	--
			Balance due employee	$557.10

Employee Signature:_____ Date:_____

Authorized By:_____ Date: _____

If your boss is disorganized, she's not likely to change. However, you can help make things easier for her. She needs a central location to put all her receipts while traveling. She also needs a central place to write down expenses. The location can be an envelope, a clear plastic folder, the inside pocket of her daily planner, any place that is convenient for your boss. The place to write down expenses should be kept with the receipts themselves. That way, when another receipt is added to the pile, it is easy to jot down the facts in the notebook. Some bosses prefer a blank expense report or a little spiral notebook for making notes. Ask her what her preference is and then get her one.

Preparing Foreign Travel Expense Reports

I just started working for a person who travels overseas. I'm nervous about foreign currencies. What is an exchange rate and how do I convert foreign currency to dollars?

When the U.S. dollar is stronger, it buys *more* of the foreign currency. However, in some countries, the foreign currency is stronger and it will take more U.S. dollars to purchase it.

All foreign currency must be converted to U.S. dollars. The exchange rate is simply the domestic price of foreign currency or the price we in the United Sates pay for foreign monies based upon the supply and demand for the currency. Because of all the importing and exporting among nations as well as foreign investments, a rate of exchange had to be developed. Since 1973 a flexible foreign-exchange rate has been used based on the supply and demand of the currencies. If you don't know the conversion rate for a particular currency, it is available though your local bank or an online service available via modem through your computer. It is also printed in the business section of major newspapers and looks something like this:

FOREIGN CURRENCY CHART

	U.S. $ VALUE		UNITS PER U.S. DOLLAR	
	MONDAY	TUESDAY	MONDAY	TUESDAY
ARGENTINA (PESO)	1.01000	1.01000	.9900	.9900
AUSTRALIA (DOLLAR)	.70300	.71290	1.4225	1.4027
AUSTRIA (SCHILLING)	.09304	.09254	10.7500	10.8100
BELGIUM (FRANC)	.03180	.03162	31.4500	31.6300

By multiplying the "U.S. $ Value" column by the "Units Per U.S. $," your answer should be 1.00 or extremely close to it.

$$1.01 \times .99 = 99.99, \text{ which rounds to } 1.00 \text{ for Argentina}$$

So now that I know the conversion rate for the Argentina peso is 1.01, how do I write that figure? I'm confused. What do I do with the "Units per U.S. $" figure—anything?

There are two ways to express conversion rates. It can either be expressed as a percentage—the "U.S. $ Value" column, or it can be expressed as a figure of how many to the dollar.

For example, using the Argentina peso, how many pesos would you get if you converted $50?

$$\$50 \times .99 = \$a49.50 \text{ or}$$

$$\$50 \div 1.01 = \$a49.50$$

Note the use of the "$a" sign. Just as in the United States we use the dollar sign to refer to our money, in Argentina it's the "$a." Some other foreign-currency symbols are shown in the chart on the following page.

My boss just came back from a trip to the United Federation of Germany. He said the exchange rate on the day he converted his money was DM1.52. He knows he spent DM3,161 for the hotel. What is that in U.S. dollars?

DM1.52 = $1.00 or $\dfrac{\$1.00}{DM1.52}$, which is equivalent to $1.00 ÷ DM1.52 = 0.66.

The next step would be to multiply 0.66 times the amount spent, which would be DM3,161 x 0.66 = $2,086.26.

Check your math by multiplying 0.66 x DM1.52 to see if it does equal $1.00 or very close to it. In this case, it will equal $1.0032.

My boss recently spent three days in London and two days in Brussels. How do I enter all this on his expense report?

Foreign Currency Symbols

Country	Symbol	Currency
Argentina	$a	peso
Australia	$A	dollar
Austria	S or Sch	schilling
Belgium	BF	franc
Brazil	C or Cr$	cruzeiro
Canada	Can$	dollar
China (Mainland)	$	yuan
China (Taiwan)	NT$	dollar or yuan
Denmark	Kr or DKr	krone
United Federated Germany	DM	deutsche mark
Egypt	£	pound
France	F or FF	franc
Greece	Dr	drachma
Hong Kong	HK$	dollar
India	Re (plural Rs)	rupee
Ireland	F	pound
Italy	L or Lit	lira
Japan	Y or ¥	yen
Mexico	$	peso
New Zealand	NZ$	dollar
North Korea	W	won
Norway	Kr or Nkr	krone
Poland	Zl	zloty
Saudi Arabia	R or SR	riyal
Singapore	S$	dollar
South Africa	R	rand
South Korea	W	won
Spain	Pta or P (plural Pts)	peseta
Sweden	Skr or Kr	krona
Switzerland	SFr	franc
United Kingdom	UK£	pound
United Federation of States	R or Rub	ruble

The simplest method is to use the foreign currency as it is, add all the pounds, francs, or whatever and convert the total amount of currency to U.S. dollars. This saves time because you don't have to convert each line item. Remember, though, to add all like currencies. It won't work if you try to add pounds to francs.

Foreign Expense Report

Name:_____ Department:_____

Business Purposes of Travel:_____

	SUN	MON	TUES	WED	THU	FRI	SAT
Date	3/25	3/26	3/27	3/28	3/29	3/30	3/31
Travel from		Chicago	London	London	London	Brussels	Brussels
Travel to		London			Brussels		Chicago
Airfare		$500.00			$200.00		$500.00
Ground Transportation		$20.00					30.00
		31.60£					
Car rental							
Hotel-room		355.50	355.50£	355.50£	6200BF	6200BF	
Hotel-tips		31.60	31.60	31.60	620	620	
Breakfast			23.70	28.44		465	
Lunch			47.40	63.20	930	1240	
Dinner		94.80	316.00	126.40	3100	6200	
Entertainment							
Expenses-Auto					9300		
Telephone				31.60			
Miscellaneous							
Subtotal							
Total		$520.00	744.20	636.74	$200.00	14725BF	$530.00
		513.50£			20150BF		

Foreign Exchange Rate £ = $1.58; BF 31 = $1.00

Amount Due Employee	1924.44£	=	$3039.92
	34875BF	=	$1125.00

Deduct Cash Advance   ($1000.00)

Direct Charges to Company $1250.00

Amount Due Company/Due Employee $1914.92

Purpose of Trip: Visit London & Brussels to discuss new sales plans

Employee's Signature _____ Supervisor's Signature _____

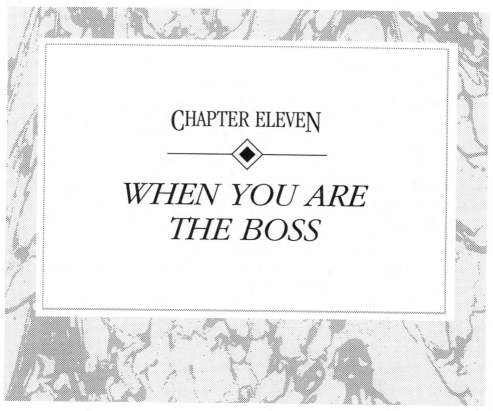

CHAPTER ELEVEN

◆

WHEN YOU ARE THE BOSS

When you become a manager, you will be faced with new challenges and opportunities as you begin to grow into your position. This move up probably will make it necessary for you to adjust your work style as well as your on-the-job relationships as you become more skilled in your new role. Within a short period of time, you will see your own management style developing, based on tried-and-true guidelines, common sense, and your own unique way of dealing with people, making decisions, and solving problems.

MAKING THE TRANSITION TO SUPERVISOR

I've been offered a promotion. Tied to the promotion is the responsibility of managing the secretarial pool, which now consists of three full-time and two part-time people. The supervisory duties have me in a quandary. I've never been a supervisor before and the thought of managing people and giving instructions frightens me. Are there general guidelines I can follow in the beginning so I can start off on the right foot? I really hate to turn down this job.

Keep in mind that if management didn't have confidence in your abilities, they wouldn't have offered you the promotion.

Make a list of all the attributes you admire in other bosses or supervisors. What really makes them exceptional? It might be that they are understanding, sympathetic, noncondescending, able to accept responsibility without shifting the blame, etc.

Now make a list of your qualifications and skills. You may be surprised how many overlap. Make a mental note of those traits you feel you are lacking but would like to acquire. Be sure to work on developing those traits as you begin your new supervisory role.

Taking on additional responsibilities is never easy. But it is a way to keep growing and challenging yourself. The first step, making the decision, is the hardest.

Ask your boss if you may attend a seminar for people in supervisory positions. These seminars are always available to increase your skills. Don't be afraid to admit the need for additional schooling in areas where you feel your skills are deficient and could be improved.

I've just made the transition from secretary to manager of the word-processing pool. I now supervise some of my friends and am unsure how to approach my new position. What can I do to increase my chances of success?

Act like a supervisor. If a situation warrants a decision, be prepared to make one. Don't shirk your responsibilities. Your staff will be looking to you for guidance. If an error is made, don't blame others. Own up to your mistakes. Learn from them, but don't dwell on mistakes.

Look like a supervisor by dressing professionally. While it may be fine for the word-processing pool to wear coordinated slack outfits or skorts, your wardrobe should consist of classic suits and dresses and a few interchangeable blazers and skirt sets.

11-2

HOW TO BE AN EFFECTIVE MANAGER

I was recently promoted into an administrative-assistant position from executive secretary. The problem is my predecessor, who was promoted out of

the position. She is always doing and saying things to make me look incompetent. Why can't she be happy with her new job and leave me alone?

Some people have trouble letting go of the familiar. She, too, is learning a new job. She may be feeling incompetent and is bolstering her ego at your expense. Ask her to lunch or coffee and tell her you appreciate her extensive knowledge but her comments hurt. Assure her that you need her input during this tough learning phase and will call when you can use some advice.

Basically, you need to lay out a game plan:

1. Tell her how much you appreciate her knowledge and expertise.

2. Explain in detail how her comments and/or actions are undermining you at this critical learning point.

3. Ask for her cooperation and help.

If this doesn't work, ignore her inappropriate behavior. One of the first things you learn working in an office is that some people just won't cooperate. You wouldn't have been chosen for the position if the boss didn't have confidence in your abilities. Make checklists to be sure you won't forget important items and/or project report dates, etc., until you feel you are in control of the position. Work slowly and accurately. Ask your boss for feedback on how you are doing. Remember, he is the one you have to please—you should be soliciting his comments and critiques.

I supervise some friends. Sometimes they take advantage of the situation. They ask to leave early and take unscheduled days off. I know they are using my friendship and I should do something, but what?

Your inaction has given them permission to continue their present work behavior. Have a departmental meeting to outline the rules. Go over the problem areas such as abusing sick time, unscheduled days off, excessive personal phone calls. Remind them that you have to work as a team and that everyone is to be treated equally, with no exceptions. Be prepared to have a private discussion with repeat abusers if needed.

I've been promoted and now supervise two people, both are doing jobs that I know inside and out. I'm finding it hard to let go.

Don't stifle your staff. Tell them just the essentials of a project:

- ◆ What needs to be done. *I need a report showing this year's sales-to-date as compared to last year's.*

- ◆ When the deadline is. *The report will be handed out at the marketing meeting next Wednesday. I'd like to look it over on Tuesday.*

- ◆ Any unique formatting requirements. *You may want to take a look at what we did last month to give you an idea of the format.*

- ◆ Who provides input. *Lisa in accounting usually provides the figures.*

Then step back and let your employee do her job. It's fine to ask how the project is going, but resist the temptation to do your old job. You've moved beyond that position. It's somebody else's responsibility. You need to grow into your new job, just as your staff need to grow into theirs.

11-3

DEALING WITH UNCOOPERATIVE OR JEALOUS COWORKERS

Recently I received a promotion. A coworker who was friendly has now distanced herself. It's evident by her actions that she resents my new position. But I didn't do anything wrong. What should I do?

With promotions come new challenges, different hurdles to face. Continue to act in a professional manner and give her time to assess the situation. If she remains distant, it's really her problem and there is really nothing you can do. Face it—a true friend would be happy for you and supportive during your transition period.

I just received a promotion over another secretary who has been with the company longer. Some friends have told me that she's angry and is going to make trouble for me.

Although your friends may have meant well by warning you of possible retaliation, they have in fact added stress to your transition period. Unless the other secretary acts hostile or tries to undermine your position, do nothing. Their warning may be foundless. If the secretary does cause trouble, you'll have to assess the situation and form a plan to handle any problems.

It may be necessary for you to talk to her or, if the situation warrants it, to your boss.

Recently a secretary's position was split into two job functions. She kept one and I was promoted to the other. She is uncooperative and refuses to show me the ropes. Actually, by dividing up her job, her work load is lighter. I just don't understand her reaction.

Obviously she resents the fact that her job was split. She may have felt that management gave away the best part of her job. Unfortunately, she has chosen to take out her hostilities on you. It's a tough situation to be in. You can approach her and try to talk things out. A candid discussion may allow her the opportunity to vent her anger. If she continues to withhold information, you need to tell your boss, who can then decide what the next step will be.

11-4

HOW TO CONDUCT A GOOD INTERVIEW

I'm about to start interviewing people for a position in my department. I've never interviewed anyone before. What steps are involved?

In most cases, the interview process involves these steps:

1. Find out what company policy is regarding open positions. Some companies require posting internal positions for two weeks prior to going outside.

2. Give a job description and salary range to each potential candidate some time before the interview. Ask the candidates to get back to you if they are still interested in the position after reading the job description. Make yourself available to answer any questions regarding the job or the department.

3. Arrange for the first interview. Try to make yourself available at the candidate's convenience, either during work hours, lunch, or even after hours. Some candidates are reluctant to let their current bosses know they are interviewing for a job. Respect their right to confidentiality.

4. Have set questions to ask each candidate and take notes. Shorthand is a plus here to jot down anything that will help you remember a candidate's response. Key in on a phrase and write that phrase down.

5. As part of the interview, make sure you give the candidate an overview of company benefits and operations such as working hours, lunch hours, vacations, summer schedule, growth opportunities, continuing education policy and the general management style. Never assume that the person is aware of all company policies even though she might be an internal candidate.

6. Let people know what the interview process entails. This may be a two-step interview process, the first one with you and the second with your boss. Inform candidates that a second interview may be necessary. Let people know the timetable involved, whether a decision is expected in a week, two weeks, or whatever. Make it a point to personally notify each candidate of his or her status.

7. Once the interview is over, write down three or four observations. These might be at what level the individual's word-processing skills are (beginner, advanced, superior), what skills the person would bring into the job, and anything else during the interview that was noteworthy. This synopsis should be completed right after the interview, when impressions are the freshest. Sometimes it might take a week to interview all the candidates. Afterwards, you need only to look at your quick reference sheet to refresh your vision of the candidate.

8. Contact all the candidates and let them know what the final decision is. Be sure to talk to all of them on the same day. Don't let the grapevine tell potential candidates that they didn't get the job!

It is hard to get to know someone very well during a one-hour interview. Do you have any questions I might ask to help me get to know the candidates better?

Review the company's guidelines for interviewing candidates. Be sure you are aware of what questions may and may not be asked in order to remain in compliance with EEOC standards.

Have a current job description available to give to the candidates. Make a list of qualities you are looking for in candidates. Listed here are some questions you might wish to ask:

1. How would you define a job well done? Describe your work standards.

2. Do you have any problems working under pressure and meeting deadlines?

3. Have you attended any conferences or seminars related to job growth or improvement? What did you get out of them?

4. Have you ever misunderstood someone else's instructions, verbal or written? Why do you think that happened? How did you handle it?

5. How do you plan a week's activities? How do you set priorities? Describe a typical work week.

6. Do you enjoy composing correspondence?

7. What skills can you bring to the department?

Here are some additional questions that might be adapted to suit your department's needs:

1. How would you rate your overall word-processing skills? Are you familiar with certain features (which your department uses) such as macros, headers/footers, tables, equations, columns, or newsletter design? For those items you are not familiar with, do you have an interest in learning those features?

2. How well do you react to pressure?

3. On a scale of 1 to 10, with 10 being the best, rank your proofreading skills.

4. Flexibility is a key ingredient as you may often be asked to shift gears midstream. Describe a recent situation in which you did shift gears and how you handled it.

5. The team is only as good as the players. What makes you a good team player?

6. Have you devised any procedures, set up any systems that you are particularly proud of?

7. Have you been given the opportunity to attend continuing education seminars/classes? If so, what have you taken? If not, what would you like to take?

8. Some phone work is necessary to respond to members. How are your telephone skills?

9. How strong are your grammar skills?

10. Can you find what you've filed? How are your overall organization skills?

11. Do you learn new software applications easily?

12. How do you handle complex verbal instructions? Any tricks that you use to help you remember?

13. Occasionally a project may need extra effort in the form of either coming in early, staying late, or rearranging your lunch hour. Have you demonstrated this flexibility in your schedule in the past? If not, do you perceive any problems?

I've interviewed several internal candidates for an open position in my department. I wasn't really pleased with any of them. Now what? Can I expand the candidate search outside the company?

Once you have complied with company policy regarding open positions, you should be able to expand your job search. However, would you be interested in an internal candidate who didn't apply? If you have exhausted your search for internal candidates, then approach management to interview outside.

I was recently promoted to senior assistant. My first assignment is to interview for a junior assistant. I want to put the candidates at ease and get them to open up. How can I do this?

Try sitting next to potential candidates rather than across a desk. This approach is more friendly and less intimidating. Ask a few warm-up questions. "Did you have trouble locating our office?" "How was the drive?" For internal candidates, try asking "What made you apply for the position?"

As senior secretary, my job is to interview potential candidates for word-processing-positions. In recent months, one advertisement has generated a lot of resumes. How would I go about screening the applicants?

Read the resumes. The ones whose skills or experience did not match your requirements should be sent a rejection letter.

Rejection Letter

September 22, Year

Ms. Kathryn Prine
1022 Sunnyside Avenue
Libertyville, IL 60048

Dear Ms. Prine:

Thank you for your interest in our position of Secretary—Marketing Department. Unfortunately, your skills do not match those required for the position.

We wish you luck in your job search.

Sincerely,

Lynda R. Abegg
Senior Administrative Assistant

Other things to watch for on a resume are:

1. Incorrectly addressed cover letters or envelopes, with names misspelled, the wrong company name, incorrect street address, etc. If the applicant is unable to get the address correct, how do you know she even applied for the right job?

2. Not responding correctly to the advertisement. If salary history is requested, then salary history should be provided. It's as simple as following directions.

3. Typos in the resume itself. Again, if the applicant can't take the time to proofread her own documents, then how can you rely on her to proofread the company's documents?

4. Job hopping or employment gaps. Were the job changes made for bet-
    ter opportunity or does this applicant lack the ability to stay and grow
    with a position?

Look for a good cover letter that tells you, the prospective employer, why
the applicant would be perfect for the job. What skills does she need that
are necessary to perform well in the position. What additional skills must
she acquire to excel in that position.

**As administrative assistant/office manager for a small company, my duties
include hiring and firing people. So far, the last few new hires have turned
out to be disastrous. Their resumes looked fine and the interview process
went great. Once hired, though, the employee just didn't work out. How
can you tell if someone is going to work out?**

Before hiring someone, contact the references, both personal and professional. Verify that the educational information is accurate. Make sure everything checks out. Watch body language. Does the applicant avoid looking
at you when answering questions? Does the applicant adopt a hostile posture? Listen to your instincts. If something doesn't seem right, it probably
isn't. Don't be afraid to admit your hiring skills need fine-tuning. Attend a
seminar or two.

11-5

HIRING TEMPORARY WORKERS

**We have enough work right now for another secretary. However, six
months from now I don't know if we will have enough work. Just how
should I handle this?**

It sounds like a perfect opportunity to hire a temporary worker. Develop
clear responsibilities for each position. Check with Human Resources to see
if they have a pool of temporary workers from which you could draw. If
not, you can advertise for this position specifying that it is a temporary position and give an approximate length of time, perhaps three months with the
possibility of an extension to six months. Another option is to hire a secretary through a temporary agency.

A secretary in our office is pregnant and has already indicated she wants to take a leave of absence once the baby is born. I'm in charge of the secretaries and will need somebody in her position. Just how should I handle the situation?

Make sure each position you are responsible for has an up-to-date job description. Sit down with this secretary and go over her duties and responsibilities. Then decide how to fill the position. Does your company have a pool of temporary workers from which it hires? If not, you may wish to advertise or talk to a temporary agency. If possible, have the secretary train her replacement to ensure the transition is smooth.

I am in charge of hiring temporary word processors. When I ask these individuals what their skill level is, the standard answer is advanced. However, in reality, their skills sometimes miss the mark. Then I end up getting reprimanded for not screening the applicants properly. How can you determine a person's skill level?

Get specific information as to why the temporary worker was not acceptable. Was the temporary's work inaccurate? Was the job done inefficiently? Did the temporary follow instructions?

If the problem is related directly to word-processing skills, prepare a test. By testing the candidates, you will be able to assess their skills objectively.

If you want to create your own test, you can ask the candidates you're interviewing to type a document that is representative of the work level that will be expected. For example, you might ask for a complex document containing page numbers, italics, a date footer, some indented material, widow/orphan protection, justification left, and tables. For another level of experience you might ask the candidate to create a primary/secondary merge file, or a letter with a figure box inserted.

There are software packages specifically written for testing purposes. Some features measured are keystrokes, accuracy, efficiency, and elapsed time. Customization is also available with some of these packages.

It's harder to screen candidates if the problem masks itself as a word-processing problem when, in reality, it's a personality conflict. If it's a personality clash, meet with the dissatisfied manager to discuss exactly what she is looking for in a temporary worker.

If the temporary is from an agency, then a discussion of your requirements with your representative is needed. Be sure to explain exactly what you need and what was lacking in skills from their temporaries.

SOLVING COMMON SUPERVISORY PROBLEMS

One secretary in the word-processing pool has developed a bad attitude. She comes in late, leaves early, takes long lunches. She doesn't care if I know. I can't let this continue, but I don't know exactly what to do.

She's waiting for you to make a move. You need to talk to her *now*. Be sure you are armed with facts and not impressions. Know how many days off she's taken and have specific dates when she's arrived late and left early or taken extra time at lunch. Show her recent examples of her work efforts that have been less than adequate. Facts will demonstrate to her that you indeed have reason for concern. Explain to her what is expected and what cannot be tolerated. Ask if there is a reason for her behavior. Expect her to be defensive. Be firm. Let her know you expect an improvement in her work and in her attitude. Such behavior lowers morale and can be infectious.

Maybe I'm just getting old, but it seems to me the junior secretaries don't want to wait around for anything. If their career path doesn't show major upward strides in a few years, they're gone. I'm frustrated. I'm on an endless treadmill of hiring and training; hiring and training.

Be sure you are screening the candidates properly. Tell them that a career path at your firm may not have a quick path to senior levels, but it is a steady one. Security is an important benefit for many people.
Perform exit interviews with the secretaries who are leaving. Perhaps there is an ongoing problem you are unaware of that needs to be addressed.

One secretary whom I supervise has begun to make a lot of proofreading errors. When do I tell her?

Talk to her immediately. Show her recent examples of her work effort. Ask if there is anything wrong. If you fail to mention it to her, she may think her errors are no big deal and then her work will continue to slide. Encourage her to attend a proofreading seminar to refresh her skills.

It's evident one secretary feels that filing is beneath her. She lets it stack up and then asks for assistance when she finally tackles it because it has become such a huge project. How should I approach this situation?

Go over her job responsibilities. Point out that timely filing of company documents is part of her job description and an area in which she will be rated. Explain to her that it's best if filing is done daily. Ask her for any solutions to the problem. Perhaps she could set aside a certain time each day to file.

I have talked to an employee about her job performance, but it really doesn't seem to have done any good. Her work is still less than acceptable. What is the next appropriate step?

When talking doesn't work, the next step often is a written reprimand, one that will be placed in her personnel files. The memo is usually written to the employee and a copy is given to Human Resources. Be sure to discuss the situation with Human Resources before you proceed. They may want legal counsel to review the letter before it's given to the employee.

A written reprimand should outline the employee's responsibilities according to her job description. Included should be specific examples of her less-than-acceptable work. It should also outline a course of action as well as a time frame in which improvement is expected. It should also discuss the consequences if there is no improvement, which could range from a demotion to termination.

Once the letter is written and approved by the appropriate people, it should be given to the employee. Keep samples of her work during this time. After the probationary period is over, a decision needs to be made whether or not her work performance has improved. If so, a memo to that effect would be needed. Human Resources probably will want to review it before it is given to the employee. If she has shown little or no improvement by the end of review time, the solution will have been outlined in your original letter. Again discuss the situation with Human Resources. Legal counsel may also be sought.

One of the people I supervise has voluntarily entered an alcohol treatment program. It was obvious she had a serious drinking problem. I really don't know how long she'll be out and wonder if I can replace her?

Legal opinion regarding such employees and their status with the company should be received from professional counsel. Under ADA law, companies with 25 or more employees must consider drug or alcohol addiction physical handicaps. The length of time she may be out can vary. You cannot permanently replace her while she's in treatment.

Legal counsel may recommend spelling out the conditions under which the employee may continue her employment. The agreement signed by both parties also specifies consequences, including termination, if the employee violates the terms such as what happens should the employee show up at work under the influence of drugs or alcohol.

In the meantime, transfer someone to handle her work load or hire a temporary until she returns.

A few times I've asked one secretary to call some customers for me and give them a status report. A few days later I find out that she forgot to call. Her lack of follow-through is jeopardizing my job. How should I handle this?

Have a candid conversation with her. Ask her to analyze why the calls aren't being made. Does she trust the information to memory? Does she write it down, but loses the piece of paper? Does she procrastinate because she hates telephone work? The first reprimand can be verbal. However, warn the individual that a repeat performance will be dealt with more severely, which may include a written memo in her personnel file. Explain to her how important customer service is to your operation and that her inaction is damaging your company's reputation. A candid discussion may cause some creative solutions, such as using a steno notebook for writing down all assignments. No more lost pieces of paper or forgotten assignments. If phone skills need polishing, a seminar may be needed to brush up her skills. Maybe setting a time to make phone calls on a daily basis will solve the problem.

11-7
EVALUATING YOUR STAFF'S PERFORMANCE

I am now supervising two junior secretaries. I know how important job assessment can be for the future growth of the people who report to me. Do you have any suggestions for the best way to handle job assessment?

Make job assessment an ongoing project. Don't just think about it the week before it is due. Jot down brief notes on your calendar or daily reminder notepad when the person excelled or handled a particular project well. Also note any shortcomings. With your notes, you will be able to give concrete examples in your assessment. Some areas you may wish to consider are cooperation, accuracy, initiative, timeliness, communication skills, comprehension, and dependability.

As a new supervisor of the word-processing team, I must now review several secretaries. How do I go about that?

Make sure that you have a copy of each person's job description. If additional duties have been taken on, be sure it is reflected in the job description. Your company may have a standard form to perform job appraisals. If not, there are many books available to assist you with reviews. Some items you may wish to include are quality and quantity of work load, ability to meet deadlines, communication skills, computer literacy, and initiative. Be sure to give the individual a copy of her updated job description as well as the review. Include areas where growth is expected or desirable.

I supervise several secretaries, one of whom is ten minutes late three out of five mornings a week. Her review is coming up and I'm not sure how to handle it. We've already talked about it twice.

Put it in writing and include it in her annual review. If you have flex time, suggest she change her starting time. Explain that her tardiness impacts the other secretaries who are forced to do her job when she's not there.

It's review time and our company is on a strict budget. One secretary in particular has done a superb job. I wish there was more I could do for her, but basically raises are limited to a cost-of-living increase. Is there any way to soften the blow?

The best policy is to be straightforward. Find out from personnel if merit raises may be available in the future. Then tell her exactly what's going on. Be sure that her written review contains the fact that she has excelled in her position. It's always tough telling people that you can't give them what you'd like to, but if the information is presented in an honest manner, even if people don't necessarily agree with the reasoning behind company policy, they can understand. Encourage your superstar to continue her excellent work record. It might be, too, that next year the company may be in better financial shape, allowing for raises to be commensurate with work performance.

Check with Human Resources to see if you can give her a day off with pay —not all awards are monetary.

CHAPTER TWELVE

◆

ON-THE-JOB LEGAL ISSUES

Laws are made to protect us. There are literally millions of laws that affect the way we do business. Some determine whether a person or company needs a license to perform a particular job. Others explain what forms to fill out and when to pay taxes. Still other laws tell us how to behave in the work place, from what the wage guidelines are to what steps to take to protect the public and employees from hazardous products or waste. In other words, the law tells us the rules for fair play. This is a rather simplistic explanation of our complex legal system, but it is important to know and understand the law and how it protects you at work. Note: *This book is not designed to render legal advice or opinion. Such advice may be given only by a licensed practicing attorney. If you have a legal problem or question, contact an attorney.*

12-1

DON'T ABUSE COPYRIGHTS

I am typing a medical article for a doctor, and he is going to copyright it. Where do I put that little copyright symbol? Also, what is the proper way to type the symbol?

221

The copyright notice can be located anywhere on the document as long as it is not concealed from view. You can type the word "Copyright" (or the abbreviation "Copr.") on the front page of the article followed by the date. The size and style used to display it can be of any dimension as long as it is easily readable and is not blurred. The copyright symbol is the letter "C" enclosed in a circle. If your keyboard does not have this symbol, simply type the letter "C" and draw a circle around it. ©

What kind of material can be copyrighted?

In addition to written words such as books, articles, poems, and editorials, a wide variety of material may be copyrighted:

- Computer databases
- Software programs
- Newspapers
- Directories, catalogs
- Advertising text/jingles
- Comic strips, cartoons
- Works of art, sculpture
- Company logos
- Diaries, journals
- Photos
- Recordings, motion pictures

This is just a partial list of items that can be copyrighted. For a complete list and more comprehensive information on what can and cannot be copyrighted, go to the library and check the card catalog for information on copyrights.

My boss asked me to run copies of a magazine article and send it to the sales staff along with our new sales brochures and other reports. Since it was a rather large job, I took it to a local copy center and asked them to run the copies. The manager of the copy center told me they would not run the copy of the magazine article unless I had permission from the magazine because it was copyrighted. I have run copies of magazine articles

before and never asked for permission. I was under the impression that if you give full credit to the author, it was okay to copy an article. Has a new law been passed that I don't know about?

A copyright prohibits the unauthorized copying of original works of literature, art, music, sound recordings, and other creative works both published and unpublished. Giving credit to the author does not justify copying an entire document, or a significant portion of it. The person or company owning the copyright can demand payment from others who use, copy, or distribute material they have copyrighted. Congress recently amended the Copyright Law to include criminal as well as civil penalties for infringing a copyright. The manager of the copy center acted responsibly when refusing to make copies of a copyrighted article. Without permission from the owner of the copyright, the copy center could become liable.

I thought I did not need permission to make a copy of a copyrighted article since I work for a nonprofit corporation. I also thought schools were exempt if they were copying the article to use as a teaching tool. Isn't this right?

Material may be used without permission if it qualifies as "fair use." To be considered fair use, the material must be used for teaching purposes, news reporting, commentary, criticism, or research. In determining whether the use is fair, four specific criteria must be considered:

1. The purpose for which the material will be used, including whether such use is not-for-profit

2. Whether the material contains information essential to the public good, such as scientific or medical discoveries as opposed to material that is entertaining

3. The amount of the copyrighted work that is used. While a 100-word quotation may represent a small portion of a book, the same quotation could be considered a substantial portion when taken from a 500-word article. However, if even a small number of words are found to contain the "essence" of the copyrighted material, it may not be considered "fair" to use it without permission.

4. If your use of the material keeps the author from selling it. For instance, when you copy an article from a magazine, it prevents the magazine from selling more copies, or from selling copies or reprints of the article.

How can I get permission to copy an article?

Most publishers of books and articles have a "Permissions Department." Write a letter directed to them giving the name or title of the article and the purpose for which you will use it. Be sure to mention whether your corporation is a nonprofit organization or a teaching facility and the number of copies you need.

I was asked by someone in another department if I would give them a copy of my new computer program. They said the company paid for the program so it belonged to the company and the company could make as many copies as it wanted. Is this true?

Even though the company bought and paid for the software program, that does not give them the right to make unlimited copies and distribute them. The owner of a computer or software program is entitled to make a copy of it if it is used for archival purposes.

12-2

TRADEMARK GUIDELINES

What is a trademark and how are trademarks used?

A trademark is sometimes referred to as the "brand name" of a product. It is any word, name, or symbol used to identify or distinguish a particular product from those manufactured or sold by others. The owner of a trademark possesses the exclusive right to use it to identify particular products and to exclude others form using it. The symbol ® (the letter "R" enclosed in a circle) indicates a trademark has been federally registered by the U.S. Patent & Trademark Office. The abbreviation for this symbol is Reg. U.S. Pat. & Tm. Off. The symbol TM is used with a trademark that has not been federally registered.

I just began working for an advertising company with several large, well-known accounts. How should I refer to their products in letters? I know trademarks are supposed to be capitalized, but I suspect there is more to it than that. What are the rules for using trademarks in correspondence?

A trademark can be a word or several words, a name, a symbol, or even numbers. A trademark should always be written in a manner that will distinguish it from the surrounding words. Trademarks can be written in all caps or they can have initial caps but enclosed with quotation marks. The use of first initial caps is also acceptable.

>   SCOTCH brand transparent tape
>   "Scotch" brand transparent tape
>   Scotch brand transparent tape

A trademark is a proper adjective and should never be used as a descriptive adjective. This means that the common or generic word should follow the trademark.

REVLON	nail polish
HEINZ	ketchup
FRENCH'S	mustard
KODAK	camera

A trademark should not be used in the possessive form:

The aroma of OPEN PIT barbecue sauce wafted from the grill; not *OPEN PIT'S aroma wafted from the grill.*
The new PERT shampoo has an herbal scent; not *PERT'S new herbal scent shampoo.*
REVLON nail polish introduces five new fall shades; not *REVLON'S new fall shades.*

A trademark is not a noun and should not be used in the plural form. Just because it ends in an "s" does not mean it is plural: KEDS, PAMPERS, CHEERIOS.

Never use a trademark as a verb. Do not say, *Let me run a Xerox of that report,* or *I'll Xerox the report for you.* It is appropriate for you to say you will make copies on the XEROX copier or that you will make photocopies on the XEROX machine. Trademarks are very valuable and corporations do not want them to be used as the generic equivalent of the product. Once a trademark becomes generic, anyone can use it. The generic name is the common descriptive name of the product it identifies. PERT is the trademark for the generic word "shampoo." The word "aspirin" fell into general use and no longer distinguished itself as a particular brand but became the generic word for "headache pain relief." Cellophane is another trademark that through general use came to mean the product. If it becomes generally acceptable to say, *Let me get you a XEROX of the report,* it won't be long until XEROX will become the generic word for copy.

12-3
WHISTLE BLOWING

My boss is taking kick-backs from a contractor. I work in a development firm and the contractors make a cash payoff to him so they can get the jobs. Should I tell him I know? Should I tell his boss?

What your boss is doing is illegal. Accepting kickbacks can harm the company (and affect everyone's job) if they are not getting the best people at the best price to do the job. You need to decide how to proceed, whether or not to act. Get legal advice before accusing your boss of anything illegal. Proof will be required to back up any accusations.

I had to work last Saturday and saw one of our employees load up her trunk with the company's product and just drive off. I called the police and she was arrested. Instead of being a hero, I am called a "snitch" and hardly anyone at work will speak to me. My boss is mad and said I should have called him before I called the police. I am not the one caught stealing. Why am I being treated like this?

Your company was publicly embarrassed by the theft and the intervention of the police. While some companies would have been pleased with your action and even given you a reward, other companies prefer to handle employee theft and take disciplinary action on their own. You didn't give your company a chance to handle the problem internally. Your company's corporate culture is, obviously, not to air its dirty laundry publicly.

My boss steers company contracts to a firm he owns with two other partners. I don't think anyone at our company knows he is a partner in this firm. Should I mention it to the president of our company?

If he is steering company contracts to a firm in which he is a partner, it is a conflict of interest. It may be grounds for dismissal. Before you say anything, make sure you have the facts and data to back up your supposition. You can be sued for defamation of character if it is not true. If you decide to say something, seek legal counsel first and follow their advice on how to proceed.

I work in the office of a large printing company. We routinely dump some of our chemical waste illegally. I found out when I was reconciling some invoices from trucking firms. The barrels they removed contained toxic waste, but they were marked like regular waste and went to the local landfill. There was a story on the news about chemicals leaking into the water supply. I don't want to lose my job, but this is illegal. I am losing sleep trying to figure out what to do. Also, this was not just a mistake; management knows what is happening. Should I call the Environmental Protection Agency?

Once again, you must tread very carefully and make sure you have the documentation to back up your story. Seek legal counsel before you proceed. Certainly, you may contact the Environmental Protection Agency and talk to someone about the problem. Perhaps they can begin an investigation. Another route you can take is call an investigative reporter who works for a local newspaper. These investigative reporters will take your evidence and check everything out, and if the evidence is there, will expose the wrongdoing in the newspaper.

My boss was just arrested for awarding contracts on the basis of money and gifts he received from the bidders. I work for two other managers so when he told me not to bother keeping a chronological file of his letters, I was pleased not to have to do the extra work. He came in over the weekend and cleaned out his desk. I don't have any paperwork of his at all. Although I have been questioned, I really don't have any information. I'm frightened. Can I be arrested, too?

Unless your position is directly responsible for the awarding of contracts, you should be in the clear. Your boss is the one who made the decisions regarding the contracts, not you.

I know my boss was involved in illegal trading, but I never said anything because I didn't want to lose my job. Besides, he gave me some pretty big bonuses. He was arrested but since he did all the trading, he can't implicate me in any way, can he?

First of all, contact a lawyer to find out exactly where you stand, legally. Those big bonuses could be considered bribes, which would certainly imply you knew what was going on and were being paid well to keep quiet. Your silence could implicate you as an accomplice.

It is obvious to me and others that the guys in the mailroom are selling drugs. Why doesn't anyone else notice, like the supervisor of the mailroom? No one will say anything because we don't know exactly who is involved.

This is a classic communication gap. The employees suspect something illegal is going on but are afraid to tell management. The employees feel that the problem is so obvious management must know about it and, since no action is taken, must condone it. On the other hand, management feels that if there were a serious problem in their company, someone would bring it to their attention. Talk to your boss or to someone in your Human Resources area.

Someone is doing something illegal in my company, but I don't want to say anything publicly. I want to send an anonymous letter, but my friend says management doesn't take anonymous letters seriously and will just throw it away. Should I send it anyway?

Management reacts differently to anonymous letters. Because they are not signed, they are often not given much credibility. Many companies believe they are from an angry employee blowing off some steam for being reprimanded. However, it may make you feel as if you are at least taking some kind of action by alerting management of a serious problem or violation in your company. Your letter should be specific. Some companies do investigate the charges in anonymous letters because they feel if an employee feels that strongly and is too frightened to sign his or her name, there may be some merit to the allegations.

How do you know when you should blow the whistle and when you should simply ignore a problem?

After seeking legal counsel, you should speak out whenever you see or know of any wrongdoing. That does not mean you are encouraged to run out and blow the whistle on every situation you encounter. It does mean you should weigh the severity of the situation. If people are being hurt, physically, financially, or emotionally, you probably should speak out. You must also consider whether there is evidence or proof to back your claim. Will others stand with you or will they melt into the background once you have spoken? Are you tough enough to face the possible alienation of friends and coworkers? Do you wish to speak out publicly or anonymously? After carefully weighing all the options, take the route that is best for you.

How do you get people to listen to you when you are blowing the whistle on some wrongdoing?

First of all, make sure you have the evidence to back up your claim. Get advice from legal counsel before proceeding. Approach management with your concern and the evidence to support your claim (you can do this either face-to-face or anonymously). If management takes no action you should talk to your attorney, who may suggest you contact the local law enforcement agency or federal enforcement agency in your area. In some instances, it may be advisable to contact the local newspaper, specifically an investigative reporter, so the problem can be brought to the attention of the public.

12-4

DEALING WITH SALARY AND WORK ISSUES

I just found out that our company hired a male secretary at our branch office to do the same job I do, but he is being paid $3,000 more a year. Does the Equal Pay Act apply to my situation?

When Congress passed the Equal Pay Act of 1963 (also called equal pay for equal work) it meant that women who were doing the same work as men would be paid the same as men. In other words, you couldn't pay a female accountant less than you paid a male accountant. Find out exactly what your coworker's title and responsibilities are. Next, find out what kind of experience he has. Has he been a secretary for twenty years or two years? Finally, find out about his educational training. Did he attend a secretarial school? Does he have a college degree? If, after taking everything into account you believe you are being treated unfairly, talk to a Human Resources representative as a first step.

A new secretary was just hired to do the same job I'm doing, but at a higher salary. I've been with the company for five years and have always gotten excellent annual reviews. How should I handle this situation?

Ask Human Resources for a copy of the job description for the other job as well as your job so that you can compare them. Talk to your boss or someone in Human Resources about your concerns. Perhaps the other secretary has more experience or a higher skill level. Keep conversation regarding the two jobs to comparing duties, skills, and education. Usually, a comparison of this nature will allow a reasonable resolution of your concerns.

My boss asks me to run personal errands for him. He sent me to pick up his cleaning yesterday and today he asked me to type his son's college term paper. If I refuse to do his personal work, can I be fired?

Most companies do not want their employees performing personal errands on company time. Some of the larger corporations have hired people specifically to help employees with personal errands of this nature. Sometimes they are referred to as the "company concierge." Unless your job description states you are expected to handle personal errands of this nature, sit down and talk to your boss about it. Try not to get emotional, keep the conversation low-key: Your workload does not allow time to run personal errands. If your boss still insists, then talk to Human Resources.

Some companies don't mind personal errands (such as typing term papers) if you are compensated by your boss and the typing is done during nonworking hours. Some companies allow no personal work under any circumstances. What is your corporate culture? Questions of this nature are hard to address because of varying state laws and differing company policies. Try to straighten it out through negotiation before issuing ultimatums.

The Accounting Department's file room is a mess. Over the past year, three secretaries quit and two transferred to other departments so no one has even tried to keep up with the filing. Printouts are stacked in unmarked piles, they have duplicate files under different names, and supplies are scattered all over the room. People just keep stacking the stuff in corners. My boss told Accounting that I would organize their file room and put everything in order for them while he is on vacation next week. He gave me a patronizing speech about how well organized I am and what a good team player I am, ad nauseam. I don't want to do it and I don't think I should have to. If I refuse, can I be fired?

Whether or not you will be fired depends on many things, state law, federal law, corporate culture, the size of the company, whether refusal would be considered insubordination or not. While you may not want to clean out the Accounting Department's file room, try for a negotiated settlement.

1. Tell your boss, "fine, I'll clean out the file room, but I think for doing such duty, I deserve some kind of special reward." Maybe a day off

would be nice or perhaps lunch for you and a friend at a nice restaurant. You should be able to negotiate something of interest.

2. Do a first-class job. Don't go in with the attitude that you will do only what you have to do. If you do a first-class job you will earn the admiration of your boss, the Accounting Department, and any number of people in your company who may be looking for a team player.

12-5

HANDLING ISSUES OF RACE AND RELIGION

I recently quit my job because my boss and coworkers made me so miserable. If I was ten minutes late, I would be docked for it. Even though I was hired as a secretary, I was given only the filing to do. If I did something incorrectly, they would laugh and whisper but never offer to help. I am black, and everyone in my department is white. A friend told me I could sue the company even though I quit my job. Is this true?

Your friend was probably referring to *constructive discharge*. A person who quits his or her job because of intolerable working conditions can file a complaint of *discriminatory constructive discharge* with the EEOC; that is, of course, if you feel you were treated unfairly due to racial discrimination.

I have worked at XYZ Company for two years as a secretary. However, I have been going to school at night and just received my Certified Professional Secretary designation. When an executive secretarial job opened up, I applied for it but was told I did not have the qualifications. I am Laotian. They promoted a white woman into the position who typed only 45 words per minute (I type 65 words per minute) and who does not have a CPS. After I worked so hard to meet the requirements of the executive secretarial position, I felt angry and put down. Is this fair?

A lot of things in life aren't fair. A far better question would be "Is this legal?" If you feel you are being discriminated against because of your national origin, you should contact your local EEOC office for guidance.

I feel I am being discriminated against because of my religion. I am forced to take off Christian holidays, such as Christmas when our office is closed, but if I take off a non-Christian holiday, I am not paid. Can I work the Christian holiday and then take off on my religious holidays?

Most companies allow non-Christians to practice their religious faith and take off holidays, if requested. However, these holidays are usually considered unpaid leave unless the person wants to use accrued vacation time. (Some businesses offer a certain number of "personal" days that may be used for this purpose.) Most companies will not allow employees to "switch" holidays.

12-6

WHAT TO DO ABOUT AGE DISCRIMINATION

In 1967, the federal government passed the Age Discrimination in Employment Act (ADEA). The ADEA prohibits discrimination in employment based on a person's age unless there is a legitimate reason for the decision. Yet, age discrimination still occurs in hiring, firing, and promoting of employees.

My children are grown and my husband recently passed away. I decided to go back to work because I need the income. I had worked as a secretary for 15 years. I have kept up my typing speed, but offices have changed a lot, so I took a "refresher" secretarial course at our local college to bring me up to date. I have a lot to offer an employer, but no one wants to hire me. I think it is because I am 51 years old. A lot of employers feel secretaries should be young. Is there anything I can do to get someone to give me a chance?

There are a lot of secretaries in your position. Attending the refresher course to update your skills was a positive step. Next, check your resume to make sure there is no reference to your age. For instance, you do not need to put the year you graduated high school and/or college, merely that you *graduated XYZ School*. Don't discuss the ages of children and/or grandchildren during interviews. And, there is no need to list all your accomplishments; just go back 10 or 15 years.

A support group for older workers might help you deal with some of the issues you face. Almost every newspaper prints a list of support groups and when and where they meet. If you have trouble finding something in your area, contact AARP (The American Association of Retired Persons). Don't let the name fool you. They offer a variety of education programs for older workers. If you become a member, some of the resources they provide are:

- ◆ *Working Age*, A newsletter that highlights employment trends.
- ◆ NOWIS, a database of employment programs.
- ◆ Worker education materials and management guides.

AARP is located at 1909 K Street NW, Washington, DC 20049 if you wish to contact them for any materials or membership information.

You might want to sign up with a temporary agency to help you get your foot in the door and further improve your skills.

If the question of age does come up in an interview, what can one do? If you tell the person interviewing that it is discriminatory to ask a person's age, you probably won't get the job.

Don't apologize for your age. Use it to your advantage. You can say that your age is an asset, not a liability; experience has given you seasoning and judgment. You might also mention that studies have shown older workers to be more hardworking and dependable. You can always redirect the question by telling the interviewer what you accomplished and what you could accomplish if you were given the position. If the person interviewing you asks your age and you do not get the job, he is putting the company at risk. You may file a complaint with the EEOC if you feel you were not hired because of your age.

I am 45 years old and my boss tells me I do an excellent job. However, most of the secretaries I work with are in their twenties. They often get preferential treatment, especially when it comes to promotions. A job was posted that required shorthand. I applied for it and was turned down because I told them my shorthand was rusty and I would have to practice. I was told by Human Resources that this particular position demanded good shorthand skills and I would therefore, not be considered. However, I learned later that a much younger woman was hired who had no shorthand, but the company was sending her to school to learn it. This is not the first time something like this happened. How old do you have to be to file an age discrimination complaint?

The Age Discrimination in Employment Act prohibits discrimination against workers age 40 or older. It is administered through the EEOC. Document what happened and the reason you were given for not qualifying for the position. Talk to a representative in the Human Resources area in your company about what happened to you and how you feel. If there have been other instances of preferential treatment based on age, also document those. If the company does not respond, or responds inadequately, contact your local EEOC office to file a complaint.

I have been a secretary at XYZ Company for 22 years. During that time I have worked in almost every department and have kept up with the latest technology. I have a good overview of the company and work well with coworkers. However, some of the younger secretaries have made snide remarks that I should retire and let someone else take over. One person suggested that I am getting too old to handle the pressure and asked when I planned to retire. How should I respond to these remarks?

It sounds as if you may be a victim of age harassment. Don't let anyone pressure you into anything—you are obviously a valuable employee with lots to offer. It is illegal to force older workers into retirement. Tell anyone within earshot that you have no plans to retire.

I am a senior executive secretary for a manufacturing firm. We recently had a big layoff and I was laid off while secretaries who had been with the company a shorter time (and made less money) were allowed to stay. Is this fair?

According to law, layoffs should be based on seniority or merit. That means that the least senior person or the least productive person should be laid off before you. Your employer may have violated the Age Discrimination in Employment Act (ADEA). The ADEA was created primarily to promote employment of older persons based on their ability rather than on age, prohibit arbitrary age discrimination in employment, and to help employers and workers find ways of meeting problems arising from the impact of age on employment.

12-7

OVERCOMING DISCRIMINATION BASED ON A PHYSICAL DISABILITY

The Americans with Disabilities Act was passed to force employers to focus on a person's abilities, not their disabilities, when making hiring decisions.

Businesses with 25 or more employees must make reasonable accommodations for qualified disabled workers and job applicants.

A friend I went to high school with was in a car accident and is confined to a wheelchair. She has taken all kinds of computer courses. She gets so depressed because no one will give her a chance and hire her. She had an interview at my company, but was told there were no openings right now. I know they have two open secretarial positions and think they told her that only to spare her feelings. Is there any way you can force someone to at least give her a chance?

Businesses with 25 or more employees must make reasonable accommodations for qualified disabled workers and job applicants. For instance, companies should not run an ad for employment with only a telephone number to call; they would be discriminating against a deaf person. The Disabilities Act will ensure that people like your friend will be given a chance. Ask your friend to follow up with the Human Resources representative in your company. In a tight job market, persistence will often help land the position.

12-8

UNDERSTANDING AND COPING WITH SEXUAL HARASSMENT

Some women don't mind a pinch or a pat; others do. Some women don't mind off-color jokes or crude language; others do. When is it sexual harassment and when is it just "fun"? Sexual harassment (as defined by the EEOC) is the "deliberate and/or sexual or sex-based behavior that is not welcome nor asked for or returned." It could be crude comments or sexually explicit jokes. It could be touching. It is sometimes phrased as a joke or something "in fun" making you feel that you are not "one of the crowd" if you don't laugh and go along. Sexual harassment is any unwelcome verbal or physical advance made by someone in the work place that is offensive or objectionable and causes you discomfort, creates a hostile atmosphere, or interferes with your job performance. You do not have to be touched or propositioned to be harassed; obscene gestures, displays of nude or pornographic pictures, jokes with sexual overtones all contribute to a hostile work environment. If someone is doing something you find offensive, you must tell them to cease. If the conduct continues, then it becomes harassment.

If, after you have made it verbally clear that you do not care for a person's advances and/or comments, the next step is to put it in writing. Write the person a letter stating exactly what it is you find offensive. Often, that is enough to stop the harassment. If it continues beyond that point, send a copy of the letter to your Human Resources representative in your company and a copy to the harassing person's superior.

If the company takes no action or takes what you may consider inappropriate action, contact the EEOC office in your area. A sexual harassment claim must be in writing to be valid. It can be filed in person by going down to the EEOC office or by mail. You might also want to contact an attorney who handles discrimination cases.

I was sexually harassed last year by a manager who is no longer working in my department. Is it too late for me to file a claim?

There is a "statute of limitation" on filing a sexual harassment claim. In some states, it is 180 days from the date of the incident. In other states, it is 300 days from the incident. There is no penalty for filing early, but you will face serious problems if you file late. Therefore, the rule of thumb is that a claim must be filed, in writing, within 180 days of the incident unless you have (in writing) from the EEOC that you have been granted an extension.

If I file a sexual harassment claim, do I have to give my real name? I live in a small town and I want to protect my privacy.

The EEOC will allow another person or organization to file the claim on your behalf to keep your identity secret. This can be done by an attorney, a union, or a rights group (such as NOW, the National Organization of Women). The confidentiality rule encourages employees to file charges immediately after the sexual harassment has occurred and helps protect you from retaliation while the investigation is ongoing.

A few weeks ago I filed a claim with the EEOC and now I'm waiting for them to take action. What exactly will they do?

The EEOC will notify your employer and the person or persons charged in your complaint within ten days after you file it. The employer and person charged will then give their version of what happened. The EEOC will also interview witnesses to the events and can also subpoena files or documents.

If the EEOC feels there is reasonable cause, it will attempt to negotiate a settlement informally. If your employer rejects the settlement, then the EEOC will either file a lawsuit on your behalf or allow you to file it yourself.

If the EEOC believes you were not sexually harassed, they will issue a "no cause" letter. You have the right to appeal that decision. You also have the right to take the case to court yourself. However, your employer can use the evidence and the "no cause" letter from the EEOC to try to convince a judge or jury that you were not sexually harassed. You have 90 days from the date you receive the "no cause" letter, also called the right-to-sue letter, to file your lawsuit.

I would like to file a complaint, but I don't want it to drag on and on. How long will it take to settle the case?

You can request that the EEOC give you either a "no cause" ruling or a right-to-sue letter within 180 days after filing your claim. However, once the EEOC sends you a right-to-sue letter, it will usually stop its investigation and any benefit you would have gotten from further investigation will be lost. Also, once you receive the right-to-sue letter you have 90 days in which to file your lawsuit. Be sure you have already retained an attorney who is willing to move quickly on the case.

I just got a great promotion and a big increase in salary. My new boss made it quite clear that he hired me because he thinks I'm sexy (all his secretaries have been blondes with long hair who have been promoted to even higher positions in the company). He also made it quite clear that if I don't sleep with him, he will make the work so difficult that he will have to fire me. I need my job and I need this salary because I am a single mother. If I file a complaint it will take a long time to settle and my life will be miserable anyway. What should I do?

Submission to his demands as a condition of your employment and his threats to create a hostile and intimidating work environment are against the law. The company is liable for his behavior. What you are saying is that you will be miserable if you stay in this job, and you will be miserable if you do not. Furthermore, you will be miserable if you file a complaint with the EEOC. People remain silent because they are afraid—afraid of losing their job, afraid of retaliation, and afraid that nobody will believe them if they do speak up. You are the only person who can make the decision. Weigh your options carefully.

A friend of mine once filed a sexual harassment claim and no one in her office would speak to her, much less be seen eating lunch with her. She was only telling the truth, something some others did not have the guts to do. Many of these same people pushed her to file the claim—then refused to substantiate her claims or speak to her. Why are people so two-faced?

Because the motivation behind sexual harassment is power and control, the person filing a claim is immediately put on the defensive. It takes a lot of courage to file a discrimination charge. Few people have the strength to go against the power brokers in a company, especially when they know that everything they do and say will be dissected and examined, that they will be called liars and troublemakers. Friends will desert them. Emotions run high and the stress can seem unbearable. People are two-faced because they are afraid to stand up for their rights (or anyone else's). Ignoring the problem, however, won't make it go away. If people remain silent, sexual harassment will continue to be seen as a personal problem rather than as a social issue.

My boss constantly comes around my desk and leans over my shoulder to see what I am working on. He frequently puts his arm on my shoulder or brushes against me. I act as if I don't notice, but I do notice and it bothers me. I want to say something, but I am afraid he will be offended. Should I say something?

Your boss is not worried about offending you, yet you are worried about offending him. If it makes you uncomfortable, ask him to please not put his arm around you when you are discussing business. If he continues to do it, then it is harassment and you should report it to his superior or to your Human Resources department.

I'm a secretary for a group of five men who are in marketing. They are always teasing me and telling off-color jokes. It makes me uncomfortable, but I laugh and go along with it. I don't want to cause trouble, but I would feel better if they would stop. How can I make them stop without seeming like a party pooper?

Who cares if you seem like a party pooper—you're not having any fun at this party anyway. Learn to say "no" clearly. Do not give a giggly or laughing "no" but a clear concise "no."

"I don't like jokes that demean people."

"I really didn't think that was very funny; now, if you'll excuse me."

If they continue with their bad-boy behavior, document every incident in detail. Put it in writing. Inform your supervisor that you do not appreciate their comments and give him a copy of your notes. If he refuses to take action, inform the Human Resources department or determine if there are any union or company channels you can utilize. When all else fails, contact the EEOC office in your area.

My boss will call me into his office and start telling me about his arguments with his wife. I have always listened sympathetically. However, now he's started telling me she's frigid and I feel he's stepping over the boundary of just wanting someone to listen to his problems and is insinuating something else. If I tell him I'm not interested in hearing about his sex life, can he fire me?

Trust your instincts. When you feel your boss has stepped over the line, then he has. Tell him politely, but effectively, that you do not wish to discuss his personal life in the office.

One secretary in our office is sleeping with the boss and everyone knows it. She recently got a big promotion and salary increase while I did not get any increase because of a "supposed" salary freeze. The boss has never "come on" to me or anything, but if a person is passed over for a raise or promotion by someone who is sleeping with the boss, is that considered harassment?

Victims of indirect sexual harassment are those working in a sexually hostile work environment. The employer has been found liable when employees who do not submit to sexual favors (or are not requested to) have been passed over for promotions and salary increases. You may wish to discuss your situation with the Human Resources department in your company, the EEOC, or seek private legal counsel.

One guy in our office thinks he is a real Romeo and is always grabbing the young girls and kissing them and even pinching them occasionally. They laugh it off, but I can see it embarrasses them. I find his behavior intolerable. Can I complain about his behavior even though he is not doing these things to me?

Even if you are not the victim of the Romeo's advances, his actions create a hostile and degrading work environment. Yes, you can report his behavior to the Human Resources department in your company.

If I say I am being sexually harassed and my boss says I am making it up, it becomes his word against mine. What can I do to prove my credibility?

Keep a detailed diary or journal of all events, including the date, time, and any witnesses who may have been present. Describe how you feel—"My stomach turns sour when I go to work." Save any notes, cards, or materials sent to you. Talk to other employees who may have witnessed the incident or may know if anyone else has been harassed. Perhaps someone left the job because of harassing behavior. Witnesses and accurate documentation will help provide evidence of sexual harassment; otherwise, it may be your word against his.

I am a customer-service secretary and am being sexually harassed by a customer who wants to date me and threatens to cancel his account (it is a major one) if I won't go out with him. He says I am supposed to keep the customer happy. What can I do in a situation like this?

Even though the person is not an employee at your company, your employer may be liable if you have informed a supervisor or other manager of the incident and your employer has failed to take immediate and appropriate action. Employers have a duty to try to prevent sexual harassment. Also, perhaps this person's employer does not realize how the company is being represented and would appreciate being informed.

Can I be fired for filing a complaint with the EEOC?

A company cannot retaliate by firing you (or transferring you to a lower-paying job or bypassing you for promotion) if you file a complaint. Retaliation is a separate violation of the law and should be reported to the office or agency where you originally filed the complaint.

A lot of the men in my company complain that sexual harassment claims are unfair and that women are just waiting to haul men into jail for telling a dirty joke. Can women really do this?

Sexual harassment is repeated and unwanted harassment on the job. If a man were to make an insensitive comment or tell a dirty joke, no one is going to file a complaint *unless* it continues. No one should fear a harassment charge from an innocent mistake.

A woman in our company filed a sexual harassment charge against her boss because he demoted her. It was later found out that the woman was just

being vindictive and no harassment had taken place. What can you do if you are falsely accused?

Your best defense against a false sexual harassment accusation is who you are. If you have a reputation for being fair and no one can substantiate the claim or come forward with a similar accusation, you should be exonerated.

What can a person or a company do to prevent sexual harassment?

Employers should provide, publicize, and enforce a policy forbidding sexual harassment. The policy should be circulated to all employees and be included in the personnel manual. If the policy is to be effective, it should also contain a procedure for reporting harassment.

12-9

PREGNANCY AND YOUR JOB

Although pregnancy is natural, under the law it is treated as a "temporary medical disability" during the time a woman is physically unable to work because of her pregnancy or childbirth. Discrimination on the basis of pregnancy, childbirth, or related medical conditions constitutes unlawful sex discrimination.

I just started a new job. I also just found out I am pregnant. Can I be fired because I am pregnant?

An employer cannot fire or refuse to hire a pregnant woman if she can perform the major functions of the job. An employer also cannot fire or refuse to hire a pregnant woman because it may increase the cost of insurance benefits.

I am six months pregnant and I have a good job, but I am also having a difficult pregnancy and my doctor wants me to stay home until delivery. Will this affect my job?

A pregnant employee who is temporarily unable to work as a result of her pregnancy must be treated in the same manner as any employee with a temporary medical disability, which means modifying work tasks, offering alternative work assignments, or providing leave without pay if the employer does not have a paid, short-term disability policy.

Is it true that the company has to hold your job for you until you return from pregnancy leave?

An employer cannot prohibit a pregnant employee or an employee on short-term disability leave or family leave from returning to work when ready (provided the plan includes job protection). An employer may, however, require its employee to submit a doctor's statement concerning her ability or inability to work.

My boss wants me to return to work right away, but I want to spend a few more weeks with my new baby. Can he force me to return to work?

An employer cannot force an employee on short-term disability to return to work. Once again, the employer may require a doctor's statement concerning your ability or inability to return to work.

I know my boss is a little distressed because I am pregnant. She's worried I won't return after the baby is born. I need my job and do plan to return. What can I do to ease some of her concerns?

Discuss with your boss the amount of time you anticipate you will be off. Make it clear that you want to return to your present position. Write a short memo outlining what you discussed and ask your boss to let you know immediately whether she is in agreement. Keep a copy for your files.

Ever since I announced that I am pregnant, my boss has been avoiding talking to me about it. I have brought up the subject of my maternity leave and when I plan to return to work, but he is vague and uncomfortable. What can I do to get him to discuss this with me?

Since you can't get him to sit down and discuss your maternity leave and plans with him, write him a short memo outlining your expected time frame and state that you plan to return to your present position (or a comparable one) following your child-care leave. Ask if he is in agreement with your plans. Keep a copy for your file.

I was terminated shortly after my boss found out I was pregnant. Can I file a claim, and if so, where do I file it?

Pregnancy discrimination is also handled through the EEOC and should be filed within 180 days (in some cases, 300 days) of the alleged violation. Please contact your local office for details.

CHAPTER THIRTEEN

◆

BUSINESS ETIQUETTE

We are all aware of the basic rules of social etiquette—don't talk with food in your mouth; remember to say "please" and "thank you"; and always send a thank-you note when you receive a gift. But business etiquette is more than just good manners in the work place. It is a set of guidelines for behavior that will give you the professional edge—and the self-confidence—you need to handle a variety of business situations.

<hr>

13-1

TIPS FOR PROPER INTRODUCTIONS

I frequently meet people in the reception area for my boss. How should I introduce myself?

If there are several people waiting in the reception area and you are not sure which person is waiting to see your boss, say her name—"Ms. Johnson?" When that person stands or otherwise indicates she is Ms. Johnson, walk forward, shake hands, and say "I'm Linda Jones, Mr. Larsen's assistant. Mr. Larsen is in the conference room; please come with me."

When I have to introduce people to my boss, I get confused and tongue-tied. Just who is supposed to be introduced to whom?

There is one basic rule in business introductions—the more important person is introduced to the person of lesser importance. "Ms. Vice President of Marketing, I would like you to meet Mr. New Office Manager."

I prefer to greet some associates with a friendly kiss rather than a handshake. Recently, I was embarrassed when someone I gave a friendly peck on the cheek seemed to recoil and offered me a handshake instead. Was his action appropriate?

It depends on the setting and the people involved. Generally speaking, kisses are not exchanged at business meetings or in conference rooms or meetings in offices. Kissing should be avoided. A secretary or junior executive who kisses a senior executive seems to be seeking favor; on the other hand, a senior executive who greets a secretary with a friendly kiss may appear to be taking advantage of his position by making inappropriate advances and could find himself charged with sexual harassment. At business meetings that are more social in nature, such as banquets or conventions, a friendly peck on the cheek may be acceptable.

I was taught that women do not have to shake hands when they are introduced to someone and that it is the woman's option to extend her hand if she wants to shake hands. Is this still correct for women?

You are confusing social etiquette with business etiquette. When you are introduced to someone professionally, you should always offer your hand in a firm handshake (not one of those limp-wristed-let's-just-touch-fingertips); look them in the eye and say something like "pleased to meet you."

If I am seated at my desk when someone is introduced to me, should I stand or remain seated?

Always stand and give the person a firm handshake.

Several senators will be visiting our office next month. Do you address a senator as "Mr. Maxwell, senator from Illinois?"

Do not address a senator as "Mr." A senator should be addressed as "Senator, Senator Maxwell, or Senator Maxwell of Illinois." In making introductions, you should introduce your coworkers to the senator (following the more-important-person introduced to the less-important-person rule). "Senator Maxwell, I would like you to meet Joe Larsen, our vice president of marketing."

13-2
HOW TO ADDRESS YOUR SUPERIORS AND COWORKERS

I am starting a new job and don't know how to address my new coworkers. Should I call them by their first names or the more formal Mr. and/or Ms.?

It is always safe to use "Mr." or "Ms." until you are asked to use first names. Listen to how your new coworkers address one another and take your cue from them. Since most people spend eight hours a day working with one another (which is more waking hours than you spend at home) and since companies today have adopted a more relaxed attitude, it seems appropriate to address coworkers by their first names.

I'm not too sure how to address my boss and his associates.

Ask your boss how he would like to be addressed. He may say that a first-name basis is fine. However, even if on a first-name basis in private, addressing your boss as Mr. or Ms. is particularly effective when customers or outsiders are present. When on the phone, it sounds more professional to say, "I'll have Mr. Luczak return your call." Of course, if it is one of his friends or a frequent caller, then by all means say, "I'll have Gregory return your call when he returns to the office."

My boss said he does not want me to use his first name, but always to address him as Mr. Miller. Isn't this rather pompous?

Most companies today have a "team-building" first-name-basis environment. Since your boss obviously prefers to remain more formal, you could follow his lead and ask that he address you as Ms. Atcher.

13-3
SOCIALIZING WITH YOUR BOSS

My boss is really great and I enjoy working for him. Is it acceptable to invite him to lunch for his birthday?

No. You may invite a coworker or someone who works for you to lunch, but you should not invite your boss. Even if he has invited you to lunch on your birthday, this is one invitation that is not reciprocated.

Is it okay for a secretary to ask her boss to dance at an office party?

If other people are dancing, it is appropriate to ask your boss to dance. But it would not be appropriate to dance repeatedly with him.

My boss invited her staff and spouses to a barbecue at her house. Must I go?

A positive response will certainly be viewed more favorably than a negative one. Obviously it's important to your boss to get to know her staff outside of work. Consider it a positive networking opportunity and attend.

13-4

GIVING YOUR BOSS GIFTS

My boss always gives me really nice Christmas and birthday presents. Some of the secretaries give their bosses gifts, but I thought secretaries were not supposed to give bosses presents. Am I supposed to reciprocate? If so, what would be an appropriate gift?

It is not necessary to buy your boss gifts. However, if you have a close working relationship and would like to express your appreciation, a small gift would be appropriate—perhaps a book, a bottle of wine, a box of his favorite candy, something for his office, or a sports or hobby-related item (such as a box of golf balls). If you are talented, baked goods such as cakes, breads, cookies, or preserves are appropriate, as well as homemade gifts.

My boss will be 50 next month. His staff wants to have a little bash for him. What do you think?

For some milestone birthdays, more than a wish is needed. A cake and a card signed by the group would be fine. Keep it simple and sincere.

13-5

WHEN YOU'RE MEETING WITH YOUR BOSS AND THE PHONE RINGS

Several times I have been taking dictation in my boss's office when he gets a phone call. Should I stay or leave?

Since you have no way of knowing who is calling, the polite thing is to leave. If you stand and he waves you to stay, then you know he will only be a few minutes. If, however, he makes no indication, then you should step outside and busy yourself with mail or filing or even going over your shorthand or speedwriting notes until the call is completed.

My boss often comes to my work station to meet with me. I never know what to do when the telephone rings. Should I answer it and interrupt the meeting, or put the phone on voice mail?

Ask your boss what he would like you to do. Some people prefer that you only use voice mail in an emergency, while others prefer to have your undivided attention and don't mind using voice mail during a meeting. Ask your boss if he's expecting an important call; if so, using voice mail is probably not a good idea.

13-6

DEALING WITH GOSSIP

A new secretary has been telling everyone about my boss's escapades at the spring sales meeting. I know she's blown the situation way out of proportion as another associate has told me what really happened. How should I handle this?

The best way to deal with a gossip is to confront her. Tell her you know that she's been talking about your boss in an inappropriate manner. If she doesn't cease immediately, you will take whatever action is necessary to deal with the situation, including confronting her boss and your boss. The scare tactic usually works. Say it with enough conviction so she will know you mean business. A gossip really doesn't want to have a face to face with anyone. Her power is drawn from talking about the faceless enemy.

I just returned from lunch with a group of coworkers. Unfortunately, they decided to discuss another employee, someone with whom I am quite friendly. The conversation centered on the fact that she was having marital problems. However, they had a few of the facts wrong. I didn't know what to say, so I said nothing. Did I do the right thing?

You were right in not saying anything, even if some of the facts were wrong. The problem is, once others realize you have additional information, the questions would continue. You would find yourself explaining a lot more than you initially intended. By keeping quiet, no one can accuse you of leaking personal information. Don't add to what's already circulating in the grapevine.

13-7

WHEN YOU'RE ASKED TO DO YOUR BOSS'S PERSONAL SHOPPING

My boss often sends me on personal shopping expeditions, which I absolutely hate. I feel this is a waste of my time and my skills, but I am afraid to say anything.

The only way out of this situation is to find someone to replace you. Locate a personal shopper. Tell your boss that you don't feel competent to make personal shopping decisions for him. Then mention that "Ms. Shea is available as a personal shopping consultant. There is usually no charge for this service, personal shoppers are paid by the store they work for."

Or say "Are you aware that your favorite store has a personal shopping consultant available. I have spoken with the consultant, who seems to be very knowledgeable and had some great suggestions that I would not have thought of."

This type of behind-the-scenes maneuvering should get you out of the middle.

13-8
WHAT TO DO ABOUT OFFICE POOLS

Some friends in the office want to start up a weekly football pool. In my old company, nobody batted an eye over this type of gambling. Even the managers would get involved. However, I'm not too sure about my new company. How do I find out?

Some companies turn a blind eye to office pools, while others have a strict policy against gambling. Before getting involved in anything, check out the situation thoroughly. Ask your boss his opinion on the matter. Remember just saying you "didn't know it was against company policy" is not acceptable and could put your job in jeopardy.

13-9
REMOVING UNWANTED GUESTS FROM YOUR BOSS'S OFFICE

How can I remove unwanted guests from my boss's office, particularly when I know she has a report to finish?

Set up a system with your boss to remove those who have overstayed their welcome. If your boss has said to make sure her guests are gone by 3:00 P.M., walk into the room with a typewritten message. Hand it to your boss. Let her inform her guest that she has an important phone call waiting.

If a coworker is lingering too long, interrupt and remind your boss that she still needs to talk to Ms. Petri in New York.

Be sure to discuss these methods with your boss in advance. One boss would give his secretary two buzzes on the intercom, which meant, "Get them out of here!"

13-10
INTERRUPTING YOUR BOSS IN A MEETING

Just what is the best way to interrupt my boss in a meeting?

Type the message so it will be easy to read. Word the message so a "yes" or "no" response it all that is needed. "Ms. Judy Bluff is on the line with the information you requested. Would you like to take the call?"

13-11

WHAT TO DO ABOUT SERVING COFFEE TO YOUR BOSS

We're on the verge of the twenty-first century. Do secretaries really serve coffee?

Coffee is no longer an issue. In today's offices, most bosses get their own coffee. The only exception may be when guests are present. And remember, if you are going to the coffee machine, ask your boss if he would like a cup too. But no need to go out of your way to serve coffee.

One successful secretary gets her boss his first cup of coffee each morning. As she hands it to him, she goes over the day's schedule, reminding him of any important meetings or report deadlines. He gets his own coffee after that.

13-12

GUIDELINES FOR WORKING IN A CUBICLE

Should I knock before I enter a cubicle? I always feel as if I'm barging in.

Even though there's no door, knocking or a gentle tap on the cubicle wall is more polite and will get the person's attention, especially if she has her back to you. Even if she is on the phone and you just want to drop off some documents, it will alert her that she has what she needs. Or just stand in the doorway and say, "Knock, knock," and wait for her to invite you in.

Where I work, people shout over the cubicle walls to coworkers. This is distracting. What should I do?

Shout back. Say, "Hey, I'm on phone. Could you please keep it down!" Or put some sort of flag on the end of a pencil or ruler. When things get too noisy, wave it in the air as a reminder that you are on the phone or that others are working.

In the past, I've always sat by myself. Now with the addition of another manager, I'll be sharing my work space with another. Any do's and don'ts?

A few cubicle do's and don'ts are:

1. *Don't* eavesdrop on any of your coworker's conversations. That might sound trivial, but in a shared work environment, it will be hard not to. If you accidentally hear something, pretend you didn't. And don't repeat anything. The sure way to build hard feelings is to reveal items that weren't intended for your ears. Don't respond to questions directed to your coworker either. Unless you are asked a direct question, consider her conversations with coworkers private.

2. *Do* keep common work space areas in ready condition. First determine what area will be considered common work space and what will be private. Common work space may be a shared printer, file drawers, office supplies, etc. Ready condition means replenishing supplies whenever needed, replacing files whenever not in use, and refilling the paper tray when empty. Nothing is more aggravating than to find someone else's letterhead in the printer or that all the express-mail envelopes have been used.

    Lots of offices have a shared typewriter for typing express-mail forms, logging items on index cards, or even typing an occasional label or envelope. Don't leave paper in it all morning. Finish your job and leave the area open for your coworker to use.

3. *Don't* be tempted to rearrange or remove items from private work areas. One secretary was annoyed that her coworker always left a mess on her desk. She took it upon herself to straighten it one night. Was her coworker grateful? On the contrary, she was angry that anyone would be so brazen as to invade her work space. She spent hours looking for papers that had been moved.

4. *Do* be considerate of the other individual. Music may be fine for you but annoying to your coworker. Come to some sort of compromise. Maybe you'll only listen to it while she's at lunch or in the afternoons when the office is noisy anyway.

5. *Do* offer your assistance as needed. Remember you may need some help handling a mailing a few weeks from now.

6. *Do* take messages for each other. This may even be extended to each other's bosses. Ringing phones are a distraction. Common courtesy dictates answering calls and taking messages.

13-13
RULES OF THUMB FOR SMOKERS

I'm a smoker, but I don't have a private office. Can I smoke at my desk?

Most offices have adopted a clean-air policy, which means no smoking except in designated areas. In some large companies, for example, unless you have a private office, smoking is not permitted; in others smoking anywhere in the building is not allowed.

I am a smoker. I just landed a job at a nonsmoking building. How do I handle smoke breaks?

At one firm, employees receive one 15-minute break. Smokers usually use that break to go to a smoking area. For a lot of people, it means heading to a designated area in the cafeteria for smokers or going outside the building. Remember, in nonsmoking buildings, all common-access areas are off limits to smokers. Do not light up in hallways, elevators, or restrooms.

13-14
WHAT TO SAY WHEN YOUR BOSS ISN'T TAKING CALLS

My boss wants me to screen all his calls. Once I know who is on the line, is there any polite way to tell the caller your boss is unavailable and she'll call back?

To leave a more positive image, it's much easier to say "I'm sorry, but Ms. Patel is in a meeting right now (or will return shortly). If you leave your number, I'll have Ms. Patel return your call." Or "Who's calling please?"

"Ms. Takimota, I'm sorry, Ms. Patel is unavailable at the moment. May I have her return the call." Avoid saying, "I'll see if she's in for you," which implies she is selectively taking calls and can leave the caller with a negative image of the company and the individual.

I've heard you should never tell the caller if your boss is on vacation. Is this true? If so, what should you say?

Say "She's out of the office but calls frequently for messages. If you leave your name and number, she'll return your call." Burglars have been known to check on their intended victim's whereabouts. An unwary secretary mentioning that her boss is on vacation may be the information the thief is looking for.

Recently, an individual called for my boss when she was working at home. The caller wanted my boss's home phone number and I refused to give it out. Now I'm wondering if I did the right thing.

Never give out personal information to individuals you do not know. Take the caller's phone number and tell them you will have your boss return the call. You can always call your boss and ask if she wants to release her home number.

Close confidants are already likely to have her number. When in doubt, don't give out any personal information.

13-15

HANDLING BIRTHDAYS, MARRIAGES, BIRTHS, AND OTHER CELEBRATIONS

How do most companies handle employee events, such as birthdays, anniversaries, promotions?

At one firm, an envelope was passed, along with a note asking those who contributed to sign. Once collected, the money was used to purchase a cake. The names of the contributors were listed on the card.

At another company, individuals were responsible for gifts, but the company would purchase a cake. Those who felt obligated to give a personal gift could either buy one or share the cost by going in with friends on an item.

Sometimes a department may elect to buy a joint gift. As an example, in one company Accounting, which had five employees, pitched in $5 each toward a joint shower gift.

So you see, the gift giving is not uncommon. What is uncommon is how each company approaches the task.

Our office celebrates birthdays on a monthly basis by buying breakfast treats, such as sweet rolls and donuts. It's a very nice idea, but they're sabotaging my diet. Is there anything I can do?

Try to avoid the area in which the goodies are available. At one company, birthday treats were in the lunchroom on the first Monday of every month. One secretary wouldn't go near the area until after the treats disappeared. However, don't be afraid to ask for healthy breakfast treats, such as fresh fruit, muffins, or bagels. Chances are others at your company feel the same way.

It seems every week someone in the office is getting married, having a baby, or getting promoted out of the area. Envelopes are constantly being passed around for collecting money. I can't afford it. What should I do?

Stop feeling obligated to give to each and every gift. Be selective. If you're talented, you may wish to make your own gifts for those special people.

Our department celebrates birthdays by taking the individual out. This may have been fine when there were only a few of us, but now, with seven in the department, it's hard to get everyone to agree on a date.

Combine birthdays whenever possible to celebrate them once a month. In one office, three individuals had birthdays less than a month apart. One luncheon was arranged celebrating all three birthdays. The date was selected when the celebrants and the largest number of people were available. Catered-in lunches might be an option, such as pizzas, box lunches, or deli trays. Another suggestion is to eliminate the birthday luncheons entirely. Instead, buy breakfast treats for the party person.

In our office, a coworker brings in treats for the birthday person. Unfortunately, she forgot. A few weeks later, another coworker was given a cake. Of course, now there are hurt feelings. I can see that our current system is just not going to work.

At some companies, the birthday person brings her own treats.

In our office, birthdays are coordinated by 12 different teams, each in charge of a month's celebrations. The problem is, we're not consistent. Some popular people receive a luncheon, while other people are brought home-made cupcakes or store-bought donuts. This inconsistency is causing resentment. What can we do to solve the situation?

Have some general guidelines. Variety is nice, but inequity is inappropriate. Tell the teams that everybody is to have small treats, such as cupcakes, cookies, sweet rolls, etc. Luncheons, unless done for everybody, should be avoided.

Another secretary is getting married. We would like to give her a small shower. Is this appropriate?

Many companies have showers, either bridal or baby. In the absence of a formal company policy, each person is asked to bring a dish for the luncheon shower as well as a gift. Others just have cake and coffee. Often the fiance or spouse is invited as well. The shower can be a surprise, if desired. For bridal showers, a collection of favorite office recipes may be assembled as a gift to the couple, or each guest could be asked to bring a favorite spice.

Another manager just received a promotion. He will be leaving soon to work at another location. My boss wants me to arrange something for him, but what?

Promotions, anniversaries, even retirements can be handled alike. Check with Human Resources to see if there is a formal policy. The company may donate money toward a gift or cake, or even sponsor a luncheon. If not, ask your boss what the budget is, who should be invited, and when and where it should be held. If he has no preferences, then you have a few options. For large groups, breakfast treats or cake and coffee are always appreciated. Gifts are always nice remembrances. For small groups, an intimate luncheon and card and/or gift work well. Be sure to arrange for someone to take pictures. Before you set a date, though, check the honoree's availability with the person's secretary, especially if the event is to be a surprise.

13-16

HANDLING CONDOLENCES, ILLNESS, AND DIVORCE

Another secretary has had surgery for carpal tunnel syndrome. She'll be out for at least eight weeks. We'd like to show her we care and wish her a swift recovery. What type of gift would be appropriate?

Check to see if your company has a formal gift-giving policy for sick individuals. Some companies set aside $25 for such gifts, which usually are cut flowers or planters. In the absence of a formal company policy, send the same type of gift. Other suggestions are books or edibles, such as cookies, candy, or fudge. Some offices pass the hat and collect money from other well wishers.

Another secretary recently was divorced and has gone back to using her maiden name. Should we acknowledge the fact she's divorced?

Unless you know the person well or the topic comes up in conversation, the best policy is not to comment on her situation. Human Resources, however, may wish to issue a memo reflecting her name change, such as "Effective immediately, please note the following name change: Susan Montgomery is Susan Cooper. Her phone extension remains the same X3456."

My boss just lost her brother to a long-term illness. I know there are others in the company who would like to express their sympathy. How should I handle this?

Route or post an announcement mentioning that condolences may be sent. Include any information about visitation, if local, along with directions, services, whether flowers or donations are appreciated, as well as your boss's home address:

> Mr. and Mrs. Daniel Moore and Family
> 44 S. Blackhawk Drive
> Westchester, IL 60154

Notify Human Resources. The company may have a formal policy to send flowers or to make a donation when an employee loses a family member.

A friend was laid off and left the same day she was given the news. A few of us were pretty friendly with her and would like to say goodbye. We're not too sure how she'll react because we're all still employed. Should we call her?

If you're unsure how she'll react, send a card signed by the group and suggest that she call to arrange a date to meet for lunch. If she wants to meet with you, she will.

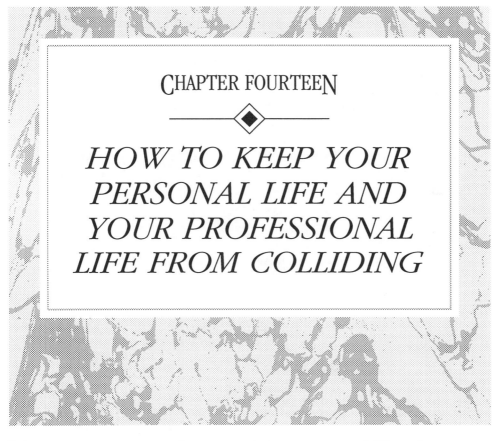

CHAPTER FOURTEEN

◆

HOW TO KEEP YOUR PERSONAL LIFE AND YOUR PROFESSIONAL LIFE FROM COLLIDING

It happens to everyone. At some point, your personal life and your professional life will collide head-on. You could be romantically involved with a coworker, have a sick child or parent who needs your attention, or you could find yourself in an uncomfortable position for any number of reasons while socializing with coworkers. No matter what the circumstances are, you must always remain professional as you find ways to deal with personal issues in the work place.

14-1

THE DO'S AND DON'TS OF SOCIALIZING WITH COWORKERS

Companies host parties or sponsor events to celebrate the holiday season, a company anniversary, or even just to say "thank you" for a very good year. These parties give coworkers a chance to interact in a social environment.

However, a company event is not the same as a social event shared with your friends. There are certain rules to be followed if you are to survive the corporate social scene.

I've been assigned to attend a meeting out of town commemorating a good sales year. This means travel and an overnight stay. I know I'll enjoy meeting the sales managers with whom I have spoken, yet never had the opportunity to meet. I also know my coworkers and the other sales managers plan to party to the wee hours. But after a busy day, I just want to go back to my hotel room and relax. Do I have to party?

Some people are beat after a full day on their feet. All they want to do is go back to their room and relax. Attend all the "official" scheduled functions and then, if that's what you feel like doing, do it. Tell your coworkers you're tired and want to relax with a good book.

Our company has an annual Christmas party for employees only. Attendance is mandatory, or so I'm told. Frankly, I'd rather pass on it as I don't really like to socializing with coworkers. However, it doesn't look as if any excuse will be acceptable. Just how do I get through it?

Smile and sip. Smile and mingle. Smile and nibble. Smile and slip out the door.

I'm really looking forward to our company's year-end party. I'd like to let my hair down, but my friends tell me not to drink too much. What should I do?

Don't threaten your career by trying to be the life of the party. Keep a low profile.

- ◆ Don't drink too much. You can disguise any beverage by adding a lemon or lime twist. This will keep people from offering to get you a drink.

- ◆ If you are able to have a few drinks and still act professionally, then by all means, do. But set a limit! If need be nurse one drink for the entire evening.

- ◆ Don't be goaded into drinking more than your limit. Be firm, but polite in your refusal. "No, I've already had my limit," should suffice.

- ◆ Leave before the party is over. You'll know the right time. Key executives will also be leaving.

♦ Remember to smile and mingle. Office parties are a great way to meet new employees or to reacquaint yourself with others you don't see too often. This is a good time to network. Broaden your horizons. Talk to people in other areas.

Our company traditionally hosts a holiday party and I'm on the planning committee this year. The company is worried about the amount of alcohol that might be consumed. What is the best way to handle this situation?

If an employee drinks too much and is involved in an accident, the company can be liable. Control the situation.
Consider:

♦ not serving alcohol. Have plenty of nonalcoholic beverages or designer bottled waters.

♦ use a quota system such as two tickets per employee. Stipulate that the bartenders will not accept cash.

♦ offer alcoholic drinks before dinner only at the cocktail reception. Serve only nonalcoholic drinks during and after dinner.

♦ avoid table wines, which encourage employees to drink until leaving the party.

♦ serve nonalcoholic punch. Most people can't really taste whether or not alcohol has been added anyway.

Each year our company hosts a cocktail reception for the new board members and their spouses. My boss is in charge of arrangements. As his assistant, I'm expected to attend. I don't do well in social business situations and am afraid I'll say or do something inappropriate. Of course, my colleagues are quick to inform me that my predecessor failed the acid test. How can I keep from doing something that night that might make me look foolish?

Your coworkers are really trying to warn you that what you say and do *does* make a difference. Since you are expected to attend in an official capacity, stick to nonalcoholic beverages. If asked, "Why aren't you drinking? Can I get you something?" A quick smile, followed by, "No thanks, I'm responsible for the setup," should suffice. No one could possibly question your wish to remain clear-headed and on top of things.

Plan a few safe topics to discuss if cornered. Sports are always a good topic. The weather—past, present or future—is fine. Steer clear of potentially controversial topics, such as politics, religion, or taxes. Ask people about their plans or whether they've taken any interesting trips lately. "I hear you visited Europe. What country was most enjoyable?" Or "Did you *really* see the pyramids? I'm fascinated by them. Please tell me all about them!"

14-2
KEEPING YOUR PERSONAL LIFE PERSONAL

Sometimes our lunch hour becomes a gossip session. As the newest one, I feel uncomfortable whenever the topics become too personal. I don't want to discuss my personal life, but I do want to develop friendships at work. How do I handle this situation?

Keep quiet. Don't be goaded into revealing personal information to lunchtime friends. Sometimes they will discuss personal items in order to find out information about you. Whenever you are in an uncomfortable situation, the best solution is to avoid responding with personal information. Say "My life is not that exciting" or "Nothing I do is as interesting as that." Try to bring up topics such as the latest movies or a trip you're planning as a way of changing the subject.

I had a bad experience at another company when a friend I confided in told everybody about my private life. I don't want that to happen again. How can I safeguard myself?

The simplest solution is to keep your private life removed from the office by not discussing it. Although that might seem a bit aloof, in the long run it's the only way to guarantee that your private life remains just that, private.

14-3
WHEN YOU'RE ROMANTICALLY INVOLVED
WITH A COWORKER

A coworker has asked me out. I am attracted to him, but don't want to jeopardize my job.

There's nothing wrong with an office romance. If handled properly, it shouldn't jeopardize your job. Watch out if you work in the same department or if one of you has control over the other's job. That could present legal and/or ethical problems. Keep a low profile—no holding hands or kissing behind the file cabinets! The fewer people that know you're dating, the better.

I have been seeing a really nice guy who works in accounting. He said we had to keep the fact that we were dating a secret because management frowns upon such activity. My friend said it's because he's probably married. What should I do?

Your friend is just trying to tell you to be cautious before becoming too involved. Keeping a low profile when dating coworkers is sensible. Even well-meaning friends interfere. In one office, it was only when Diana announced her engagement to Bob that the other employees found out they were dating.

I recently ended a two-year affair with a married manager. I realize it was a big mistake. Everybody seems to know about it. How do I clear my reputation?

Short of changing companies, there is no easy way to clear your reputation. Long after any affair has died, the gossips inform any new employee or unknowing manager of past indiscretions.

If you are unable or unwilling to change companies, then a personal overhaul is in order. Be sure your office image is professional in all aspects. Classic dresses or suits with low-heeled pumps are appropriate. A visit with a beauty consultant will make sure your makeup and hairdo have that professional polish.

Use the grapevine to your advantage. Admit that the affair is over, that it was a big mistake. Say you want to put it all behind you and begin a new life.

However, don't expect instant respect. There will be some who will watch you closely. Don't give anyone reason to expect you to be less than sincere.

14-4

MAKING SURE ALL PARTICIPANTS PAY THEIR SHARE AT LUNCH

Our department goes out frequently for lunch. Somehow, there never seems to be enough money to cover the bill, let alone leave a tip. Several people, or at least one person in particular, will pay her portion only, forgetting to add in a tip. Then, there's the one who orders the expensive meal or exotic drink and wants to split the bill evenly. These lunches are getting to be too much of a hassle. What can you do about lunchtime free loaders who spoil it for everyone else?

Take charge of the situation. Next time you go out, tell all parties beforehand that you plan to add gratuity and split the bill evenly, unless someone orders a particularly expensive entree, in which case that person will be asked to kick in more. It's as simple as that. By alerting everyone at the beginning, you're saving anyone the embarrassment of being singled out.

If you have a rough idea how much lunch will be, tell everyone. "Last time we went to Margarites, it ended up costing each person $8.50 with tip included." Tell everyone upfront this is what to expect. If they don't like it, tell them you are sorry that they won't be joining the group this time.

Another idea is to go to a buffet-style lunch where there are several choices for one price.

At a recent all-day seminar, a few of us went out for lunch. Several people left before the bill was presented. Although they left money on the table, somehow we came up short.

A rule of thumb: Don't let anyone leave before the bill is presented. If people are planning to leave early, tell the waitress so the check can be presented when the meal is served.

What can we do about people who never seem to leave the right amount or never have change?

Many luncheon parties end on a sour note because people don't leave the right amount. Of course, it is the remaining people who must bear the brunt of the expense.

Tell everyone to leave $10 and after the bill and tip have been figured, any amount left over will be divided among the participants. For those who never have change, tell them that the restaurant is fully capable of making change and have them ante up.

14-5

SUCCESSFULLY COMBINING PREGNANCY AND MOTHERHOOD WITH YOUR JOB

The working mother must juggle the many responsibilities of work and home without compromising either.

People keep asking me if I'm going to come back to work after the birth of my baby. I don't know if I'll return or not. How should I respond to my boss as well as to inquisitive coworkers?

The perfect response is "I *plan* to return." Practice saying it a few times. Do not feel obligated to reveal more than necessary until the child is born and you have made your final decision. It's always a good idea to keep all avenues open.

Don't let everyone know that you are vacillating between wanting to be a stay-at-home mom and a working mother. You may be viewed as a person unable to make decisions, and your boss and coworkers may feel you are less than a committed worker. Just that simple sentence, "I *plan* to return to work," will do nicely until you know for certain.

I'm a single woman expecting my first child. I made this decision consciously. It was not an "accident" as some people believe. How should I respond to such crude comments?

Don't feel obligated to respond. You don't owe anyone an explanation for your decision to have a child. "I'm looking forward to becoming a mother," should be enough of a response for anyone.

I'm 90 percent sure I won't be returning to work after the birth of my baby. How soon should I tell my boss?

Do your homework first. Find out what your company's policy is regarding maternity benefits. Does your company, for example, offer paid maternity leave? If you tell them upfront you are not coming back, will you lose any benefits? Remember, for companies with 50 employees or more, you can take a 12-week leave of absence per year under the new family-leave law. Some new mothers find that by taking a leave of absence rather than outright quitting gives them the breathing room they need to make a decision about working.

Once you have all the facts, you'll know the best way to proceed. The close relationship you have had in the past with your boss will give you the additional insight needed to decide if and when is the best time to tell him.

My pregnancy has been the pits. I start off tired in the morning and end the day with swollen feet and a bad attitude. My boss has begun to make comments about my tardiness and emotional outbursts. I know I'm out of whack and can't seem to get back on track. I really like my job and don't want to jeopardize it.

Pregnancy obviously affects your body. What people often don't realize is that pregnancy also affects your moods. Discuss the situation with your doctor. Perhaps a change in diet or vitamins may present the desired results. Perhaps a reduced work schedule would help. If ordered by your doctor, a reduced work schedule would be considered disability.

Perhaps working fewer hours per day or fewer days per week at your request would restore you to good mental and physical health. Time off requested by the employee is usually considered vacation time. You might be able to arrange to do some of your work at home. It all depends on company policy.

I work full-time now, but want to work only part time after our baby is born. Should I start looking for another job right after the birth of my child?

Why not start with your current company? Tell your boss you'd like to work part time. See what type of response you get. More and more companies are realizing the value of good employees, whether they are full time or part time.

Part-time work may be an option, with the salary negotiable. The down side is that a change in employment status may also reflect a loss in benefits such as retirement or medical. Vacation and sick leave may be pro-rated. The up side is that you have the freedom to spend more time with your child, yet still make a valuable contribution to the company as a trained employee.

Job sharing may be another option, where two people handle the responsibilities for one position. One may work Monday, Tuesday, and Wednesday morning, while the other works Wednesday afternoon, Thursday, and Friday. The end result is that both secretaries are able to work fewer hours and yet still remain with the company.

I plan to return to full-time work after the birth of my first child. When do I start looking for child care?

Since you've made your decision to return to work, you need to start laying the groundwork now. Check to see if on-site child care is available at your company. If so, consider yourself fortunate. On-site care greatly reduces the guilt and anxiety associated with being a new mother. Inspect the center. Find out if space is available to accommodate your child. If not, you may have to put your child on a waiting list. Some centers have age restrictions, such as accepting children two and over. Request an information packet, which will show you what forms need to be filled out as well as what type of medical information is required.

If on-site care is not available, ask your coworkers for suggestions. Find out what arrangements other people have made. Would they recommend their sitter or center to you? Would their arrangements suit your needs?

A few questions to ask yourself if on-site care is not available are:

1. Do I want in-house care or outside care?

2. If outside care is okay, do I want a daycare center or a private home?

3. If using in-house care or a private home, does my sitter have a back-up for emergencies, vacations, etc.?

4. If using a daycare, what arrangements can I make for sick days? Remember, if a fever is detected, you will be called to pick up your child.

5. Have I interviewed future caregivers, visited the facility, checked on their references, called local family services agencies to find out if any complaints have been lodged?

6. Have I found out the proper way to handle unscheduled time off, if necessary.

I am sure I will be returning to work after the birth of my first child. I am not sure, however, if I want in-house or out-of-house care. I know if I make the wrong decision, it will affect my work performance. What are some of the issues I should consider before I make up my mind?

Bear in mind that the only right answer is the one that fits *your* needs, not your coworker's or a close friend's needs. And you are right in realizing that child-care problems can and often do impact on an individual's work performance. The right care will allow you the freedom to perform your job without worrying whether your child is being cared for properly.

Generally in-house care is easier on the parent. No bundling the child up for transportation to and from the sitter. With a private sitter or even daycare, travel to and from must be taken into consideration, and whatever time you think you need, allow more. For example, even if the sitter is only 10 minutes from your home, the trip may add an additional 30 minutes to your commute to work, with traffic, weather conditions, and whether your child is having a good day or a bad day.

You must also consider cost when making your decision. Usually, out-of-house care is less expensive than having a caregiver come to your home.

Our new working mother seems to have lost enthusiasm for her job. She calls in sick often or leaves early, and generally does not seem happy. Meanwhile her work is being farmed out to us and frankly I'm tired of handling her overflow. What can I say so it won't look as if I'm not a team player?

Sometimes an adjustment period is needed for the new mom and patience is required. However, if you feel it has gone on longer than necessary and resentment is building, then a discussion is needed. Discuss the situation with your boss. Be sure you can back up any comments with specific examples, such as dates, times, etc. Let the boss decide the best way to handle it.

I have a chronically sick child and sometimes I need to take an occasional day off to take care of him. My boss seems to resent this. Since I have no control over the situation, how can I keep his resentment to a minimum?

Designate a coworker as your backup. Make sure she knows where you keep your files in your cabinets as well as on your computer system. Try to finish every project daily whenever possible. Don't think "I'll handle that tomorrow" since tomorrow may be the day you need to take off for your sick child. Be sure to extend the same courtesy to your backup as well. This is one place where team work really helps.

My boss is losing patience with me. My children are home alone during the summer and call constantly. I know this can be a nuisance, but I need to know if they're okay. What's the solution?

A phone call or two certainly isn't a nuisance. What is distracting is constant calls from children fighting with their sibling and asking for intervention. Set some basic ground rules about when they should call. Be firm.

Unoccupied children are more apt to be creative on their own—and sometimes this creativity is channeled in a negative fashion. Assign them tasks. Encourage them to pursue a hobby or read. Make sure they know what their limits are.

One creative mother motivated her children to behave when alone with a promise of ordering pizza on Fridays after work. This kept calls and sibling fighting to a minimum.

Invite your children to visit the office, see your work area, meet your boss, and have lunch with you. They will realize how very important your job is not only to you but to the whole family. Stress that phone interruptions are fine, but they need to be tempered with good judgment.

14-6

FATHERHOOD

My wife and I are expecting our first child. We both work at the same company. Can we each take off 12-weeks unpaid leave?

Since you both work at the same company, only one can take the 12-weeks unpaid leave.

I'm a single parent. What makes me different is that I'm a male secretary. Right now my son is undergoing a battery of tests. Depending on the diagnosis, I might need to take some time off. Can I?

The family-leave law protects you. As long as your company has 50 employees or more, you are allowed to take up to 12-weeks unpaid leave per year to care for a seriously ill family member. Discuss the situation with your boss and Human Resources.

I'm a divorced male secretary. My children (10 and 12) will be spending the summer with me. I'm worried about their impact on my job. Since my boss is in charge of customer service, personal phone calls are frowned upon.

Just as you plan your day, plan your children's. Sign them up for a sports or summer activity camp. Or hire a high school- or college-age sitter to take them places, such as to the local pool or parks. Is summer school offered? What about swim or tennis lessons? Ask coworkers for suggestions on what their children do. Take charge of the situation by planning activities.

14-7

CARING FOR A SICK PARENT OR SPOUSE

My widowed mother just had a stroke. She's been recovering at my house and the extra work is wearing me out. By the time I come to work I'm exhausted. I've been calling in sick when it absolutely gets to be too much, but I can see that this situation will probably go on a lot longer than I originally thought.

Talk the situation over with your boss. It may be that a leave of absence could be arranged or a flexible work schedule agreed to until your mom gets back on her feet.

For companies with 50 or more employees, the new family-leave law allows 12-weeks leave of absence per year for individuals to take time off for the birth or adoption of children or to care for seriously ill family members. The number of weeks is reduced by time already taken off, such as vacation, sick, or personal days. Once you've discussed the situation with your boss, talk to Human Resources.

My father broke his shoulder. He lives out of state and needs someone to care for him for a few weeks. Although I'm sharing the responsibility with my sisters, I will still need to take a week or two off. Should I ask for a leave of absence?

Discuss the situation with your boss. Explain what happened, what is anticipated, and how you would like to handle the situation. See if the boss has any suggestions. For a few weeks off, you may want just to use vacation time. If you think you might be off longer, find out what your other options are. You may want to take advantage of the family-leave law.

My father is seriously ill. The hospital has called me a few times to rush over. The stress is getting to me. I'm really having a hard time concentrating on my job.

Talk to your boss. You may need to take some time off. Your company may allow you to use sick or vacation time, or to take an unpaid leave of absence.

14-8

HANDLING AN UNEXPECTED PERSONAL CRISIS

My spouse left me. There are so many things to worry about at home that I cannot concentrate while I'm at work. I don't know what to do.

Try to decide what would help the situation. For example, do you need a week off to get things in order? Would working part time help out tremendously right now? Now that you have a possible way to handle the problem, talk with your boss. She may be able to offer additional options or agree that you need to take some time off. In any event, don't wait until your boss wants to discuss your poor work performance. Teams work more efficiently with communication. Explain the situation.

I found another secretary crying at her desk. Apparently she's in a serious relationship that's going nowhere. She's been making a lot of mistakes. Should I tell her boss why?

Tell her you're available for lunch if she'd like to talk to somebody. You might be able to offer some positive suggestions. However, if it appears that a solution is nowhere in sight, encourage her to talk candidly with her boss, who may have some stronger thoughts in the matter if her performance is slipping. Be careful if asked to help with her work, even on a temporary basis. As long as the work is getting done, she's not forced to face that the relationship is jeopardizing her job.

CHAPTER FIFTEEN

◆

CONTROLLING JOB-RELATED HEALTH PROBLEMS

In order to do a job well, you must be healthy, both physically and mentally. If you understand your body and listen when it sends you signals, you can eliminate many health problems and prevent minor illnesses from developing into major ones. Most health-related problems found in an office are not gender-specific; however, since the majority of secretarial positions are held by women, we have focused on women's health concerns. Note: *This book is not designed to render medical advice or opinion. Such advice may be given only by a licensed, practicing physician. You should always discuss any health-related problems with your physician.*

15-1

CONTROLLING JOB-RELATED STRESS

Stress has become part of life for most office workers. Juggling careers, children, spouses, bosses, and parents can become an overwhelming burden.

For women, who still carry the lion's share of the housework and family responsibilities, it can be almost impossible to meet the demands of juggling both family and career commitments.

What is stress?

Any factor in your life that causes mental or emotional strain or tension can result in stress. Frustration in your job or repressed anger at a boss or coworker are the primary causes of stress in an office.

What are some of the things that can cause stress in an office?

Stress can be caused by many things. What is stressful to you may not be stressful to others. Stress is often a matter of perception:

- Stress is pressure from others who are waiting for a project and want you to work faster, more accurately.

- Stress is doing two things at once.

- Stress is guilt because you have to work late and will miss dinner with your family.

- Stress is working for more than person.

- Stress is coping with change.

- Stress is when you don't know something you should know.

- Stress is when you have no control over your job.

- Stress is every day for most secretaries.

What are some of the specific symptoms I should watch out for?

Some of the symptoms of stress are:

- Nervousness—the faster you type the more errors you make, compounding the stress.

- Hyperventilation—you feel as if you can't breathe and find yourself gasping for air (it is better to try to take several very deep long breaths when this happens).

- Exhaustion—you always feel tired.

- Upset stomach or headaches.

- ◆ Difficulty sleeping; insomnia.

- ◆ Chronic stress may contribute to hypertension and depression.

I work for eight people in a sales department. It's always busy—I arrange all their travel, set up meetings, type reports, and answer constantly ringing telephones. I'm beginning to have trouble coping with this stress day after day. I see no way out. Is there anything I can do?

Recognize what causes stress in you and how you personally react to it. When things get hectic and you feel a headache coming on (or that feeling of not being able to breathe), take a short break, drink a glass of water. Sometimes, massaging the temples works wonders to relieve tension headaches.

- ◆ Try to stay calm. You can do only one thing at a time. Pick up the first page of the project to be typed and begin. Go slowly. Force yourself to concentrate by working slowly and precisely until you begin to relax. You will then automatically fall into your typing rhythm.

- ◆ While you are on your break, you can mentally organize your projects; for instance, say to yourself, "When I get back, I will first type the letter for Dan, then return the phone calls from the field reps. All filing I will put in a drawer until I can get to it."

- ◆ The fact that you feel you are not in control (you can see "no way out") contributes to your stress level. Try to get into control by getting organized and assigning priorities to projects. See if you can't forward your phones for an hour or so each day so you can have uninterrupted time to accomplish specific work.

I work for several people in the communications department. We are always trying to meet deadlines for this publication or that annual report. People know when the items are due for publication, but wait until the last minute to put it on my desk for typing. I end up working through my lunch hour to keystroke the project. Then come the revisions. I am completely exhausted at the end of the day. When I complain, everybody just says "it goes with the territory." Is there anything I can do to relieve the deadline pressure?

Here are a few tips you might find helpful:

- ◆ If the project is due on the tenth, state in your memo it is due on the eighth. This gives you some extra time to meet the real deadline.

- When you get a request for a project, highlight the due date on the letter before it goes into your boss's office.

- Mark the due date on your calendar in red for "hot."

- Give your supervisors little reminder notes that "such and such project is due on June 8th."

- About ten days before the due date, ask if there are any preliminary notes or information you can enter into the computer.

- In other words, become a real nag.

I have worked at the same company for eight years. I always liked my job and the people I worked with. Our company was recently sold to another, larger company. A lot of the people I worked with were either terminated due to downsizing or left for other jobs. I find I hate going to work. It's not any one person, it's the whole place. I would like to quit but am afraid I won't be able to find a comparable job. What can I do?

Recognize that you are under a lot of stress. Change induces stress. Your company has changed, the people you work with have changed, but you have not changed. During periods of rapid change, the number of employees who quit their jobs goes up. Change is something you have to "choose" to do. Feeling confused and frightened is normal, but if you bail-out prematurely by quitting, you may miss a great opportunity.

If you quit your job and start a new job, you would still have to cope with change. You would have to make adjustments to the new company, new ways of doing things, maybe even learn new software. Yet, you would work really hard to fit into your new company and job. You would take these changes in stride. Think of your present job as a new job with a new company. Change is a transition—it bridges the gap between the old and the new.

People keep complaining about stress and I complain about as much as anybody, but I actually work much better under stress. At the end of a stressful day, I feel exhausted but I also feel good, as if I had really accomplished something. I also get a lot of compliments such as "I knew I could depend on you" or "You're great; you came through again." A friend told me I have some sort of masochistic desire to please. Is this true?

No. Not all stress is bad. Stress in our everyday lives can be beneficial. Finishing something we have been putting off (just before it is due) gives a feeling of accomplishment. Stress can perk you up, get the blood flowing, put some zing in your day, and then you get all those great compliments and feel like the hero who saved the day (and you very probably did). It can be an adrenaline rush. It's when we have to operate under continuous stress with little or no control over our jobs that it can become a danger to our health.

What can I do on a daily basis to relieve the stress and tension from my job?

There are several things you can do to help relieve stress:

- Get organized. Good organization of projects and work-related tasks helps to reduce tension.

- After a tension-filled morning, splash some cold water on your face.

- Take a walk at lunch (if it is winter and cold, bundle up and walk briskly; if it is summer, make the walk more leisurely). Walking is a great stress reliever because of its rhythmic, repetitive action. It also tones the muscles of the legs, hips, and buttocks.

- Exercise is a great tension reliever—do some simple stretching exercises at your desk or aerobics after work.

- Eat smart—avoid coffee, tea, and soda. The caffeine will only make you more uptight. Drink herbal teas or decaffeinated beverages. Mineral waters are both soothing to the stomach and relaxing to the mind.

- Eat light—a cup of soup with crackers or a turkey or tuna sandwich. Stay away from greasy foods; that hamburger will feel like a block of cement when you get back to the office.

- Avoid alcoholic beverages. Some people feel a little drink at lunch will help them relax or a few drinks after work will relieve the tension they've been under. One drink can easily escalate to two or more. Alcohol will not relieve your tension and it won't solve your problems, but it will escalate mood swings.

- Take time to do something you enjoy, whether it is more time with your children, reading a good book, playing with your cat, or a long leisurely soak in the tub.

Are there any stress-reducing exercises I can do at my desk?

Simple stretching exercises such as head and neck rolls will help relieve tension. Roll your head from left to right slowly about five times, the repeat from right to left. Some other exercises you can do at your desk:

- Roll your shoulders back slowly for a count of ten, then release. Repeat this maneuver several times.

- Roll your shoulders in a circle from back to front, then repeat from front to back.

- Squeeze a golf ball, first with the right hand, then with the left. This can be a great tension-reliever when you're on the telephone. Put the golf ball or a tennis ball between your knees and squeeze, then relax; squeeze, then relax.

- Do leg raises while seated at your desk.

- Lay your head on your desk, pull in your stomach muscles, stretch your arms out straight. Alternate deep slow breaths while tightening, then releasing the stomach muscles.

- Sit up straight with both feet on the floor. Lay hands in your lap, relaxed. Close your eyes. Take ten very deep breaths; slowly release. Meditate or contemplate something pleasant and relaxing while you do this.

- Take a brisk walk around the office. Splash cold water on your face or the back of your neck. Do some stretching exercises, reach for the ceiling then slowly bend to the right and left from the waist while holding your hands over your head.

What kinds of foods can I eat at my desk that will help reduce stress?

There is no particular food that will reduce stress. However, a diet based on the following food groups will keep you healthier:

- Grains, such as pasta, cereal, bread, and rice. Avoid sauces that may be high in fat.

- Fruits, such as apples, bananas, oranges, and peaches. Try some of the fruits you may not eat very often such as mangos and kiwi.

- Vegetables such as broccoli, spinach, carrots, and cabbage. Most veggies can be eaten raw and are easily transported to work.

◆ Eat moderate amounts of lean meat and low-fat dairy products. Avoid caffeine, high-fat cheeses, sweets, salty snacks, and butter.

DESKTOP EATING
Light Lunches

◆ Cereal with skim milk and fruit

◆ Yogurt, which can be mixed with cereal or fruit

◆ Sandwiches made with whole-grain breads and "low-fat" lunch meat

◆ Toss a salad in a plastic bag. Buy a single serving low-cal salad dressing and don't put the dressing on until you're ready to eat.

◆ Raw fresh veggies with low-fat cheese

◆ If your company has a microwave:

   Baked potato topped with low-fat cheese

   Low-cal, low-fat frozen dinners

◆ Small can of tuna (in water) with low-fat crackers

Snacks

◆ Low-salt pretzels

◆ Popcorn (plain). If you insist on butter and salt, at least use the "lite" version.

◆ Fresh or dried fruit (prunes, apricots, apples)

◆ Cut-up veggies

◆ Breakfast cereals which are low in sugar and salt

◆ Check your grocer's shelves; lots of new healthy, tasty snacks are now on the market.

Beverages

◆ Mineral waters

◆ Herb teas (hot or cold)

◆ Plain old water

15-2

COPING WITH BURNOUT

I'm a secretary for a financial analyst. It's a very busy office. He does a radio show on investing every morning, and the phones ring like crazy. He has admitted this is a problem. His secretaries burn out and quit in about six months to a year because of all the telephone work. Of course, each caller wants to talk to him personally and doesn't want to tell a secretary his or her financial background. It is very frustrating. I end up giving my boss phone messages that say John Smith called with a phone number. How can I solve this problem?

You have two problems. The first is how to deal with the constantly ringing telephones and the second is how to get the callers to leave more complete messages.

Some suggestions for handling the constantly ringing phones:

♦ Hire temporary workers for the peak telephone periods. This will free the secretary to work uninterruptedly.

♦ Try job sharing. With two people handling the phones, one in the afternoon and one in the morning (or on rotating days), there is less likelihood of burnout.

♦ Offer an incentive to the secretary and/or telephone personnel for each new client they can bring in (this would have to be set up in an equitable fashion). Perhaps a day off for each ten new clients or a cash award or a savings bond. The office personnel would look forward to taking those telephone calls.

♦ With another person (or persons) to help handle the telephones, the secretary is able to perform her duties with minimal interruption. Because it is more expensive to train people, your boss will save money in the long run. There is always a window of lost opportunity during the learning curve for the new person or during a transitional phase.

You now have time to solve the second problem, getting callers to leave more complete messages:

♦ If the caller wants only to leave a name and phone number, have the telephone secretary ask for an address so that she can send out a packet of information. She can say, "We like all potential clients to receive our informational package so that they are aware of our full range of services."

◆ The secretary should return the calls of the people who would leave only a name and a number and identify herself as Mr. Newman's assistant. Say "Mr. Newman receives so many calls, it would be helpful if I could give him more complete information; that way, he can assemble the material or provide the answer when he returns your call." Stress the fact that you frequently handle highly confidential material for Mr. Newman.

15-3

WHAT TO DO ABOUT SECONDHAND SMOKE

We have a designated smoking area in our office. However, the ventilation system must pull it down the hall because I can often smell it. I am allergic to cigarette smoke and around midmorning my eyes start getting itchy and I start coughing. Is there anything I can do to relieve my symptoms?

Call the building manager and see if something can be done either to redirect the smoke or to vent it in another direction. Secondary smoke can cause damage to your heart, lungs, and respiratory system. Purchase a small desk-size air purifier. They work very well and it should offer you some relief.

I am a smoker. I have smoked for over ten years. I have no intention of quitting. People in my office who never minded cigarette smoke before are suddenly annoyed by it. Since I work in a smoke-free building, I go outside to smoke. All I want is a little peace and quiet to enjoy my cigarette. I am tired of the rude comments of passersby and my coworkers. How can I tell them my cigarette smoking is none of their business?

People today feel that cigarette smoking is their business. The smoke from other people's cigarettes pollutes the air they breathe. Secondary or passive smoke that is inhaled can be just as dangerous as smoking the cigarette. Medical evidence has confirmed that smoking cigarettes can cause several types of cancer as well as heart attacks.

On the other hand, as long as you follow the rules and don't smoke where smoking is not permitted, coworkers have no right to be rude.

Perhaps, they feel they're doing a good deed and can "kid" you into stopping. Try ignoring them or gently telling them that, for now, you'll continue smoking.

We are supposed to have a smoke-free environment in our office. My boss is a senior vice president and he smokes a pipe. He closes the door to his office so he can smoke. Because he is a senior vice president, no one will say anything. When I go into his office to discuss the day's events or file, I cough and choke. He ignores me. I just found out I am pregnant and the slightest whiff of his pipe smoke makes me ill. I am also worried about my unborn child because I have heard that secondary smoke can damage a fetus. Is this true?

Research indicates that the risk is real for you as well as your unborn child. Tell your boss you cannot tolerate his pipe smoking in the office. If he refuses to quit smoking in his office, see a Human Resources representative. You are entitled to a safe, smoke-free environment.

15-4
PREVENTING AND TREATING CARPAL TUNNEL SYNDROME

Carpal tunnel syndrome is an inflammation of the tissues surrounding the nerve that connects the hand to the brain. This nerve passes through a tunnel in the wrist bones or carpals. Any swelling of the tissues causes the nerve to become pinched. This condition can affect one hand or both. It is caused by repetitive stress, such as that of typing continuously on a keyboard. It was also found in people who worked on assembly lines doing repetitive tasks with their hands. Some people feel pain in the pad of the hand or even in the fingers. A persistent tingling or numbness of the hand is another symptom.

I spend most of my time at work typing on the computer. Is there anything I can do to prevent carpal tunnel syndrome?

You can prevent repetitive stress injuries by changing the way you do your job. Here are a few suggestions:

- Sometimes all you need to do is adjust the computer and/or the chair you are using to find relief. When you are at your computer, watch your posture. Don't cross your legs or slouch. Sit up straight with both feet flat on the floor. Use a small pillow at the back of your chair for lower-back support.

◆ Wrists should be level with the keyboard so you don't have to arch them up or down. Use a wrist rest. One secretary uses a rolled-up towel to keep her hands at the proper level without cramping. Keep your hands and fingers limber by grasping and pressing a rubber ball or sponge. Also note that long fingernails force you to extend your fingers to press the keys.

◆ Take frequent rest periods when sitting at your computer for long periods of time. A ten- or fifteen-minute break every two hours will help relieve the stress in your arms, wrist, neck, and back.

◆ Position your monitor so that you are looking straight ahead. Looking down at your monitor can cause eye strain and puts pressure on the neck. Looking up at your monitor places stress on the neck and shoulders.

◆ Products are available such as ergonometric chairs and even hinged keyboards that put less stress on the wrists and arms.

I have been getting pains in my hands lately and sometimes I get neck pain. Should I see a doctor? Is there a specialist I can go to for computer-related health problems?

If you believe you are suffering from computer-related pain, seek treatment as soon as possible. There are preventive measures you can take before your problem becomes chronic or disabling. See your regular medical doctor first. General practitioners are trained to screen for all types of problems. Your medical practitioner may refer you to a physical therapist, an orthopedist or a neurologist. Chiropractors have been trained in the treatment of problems with the hands, wrists, back, and neck. Acupressure and acupuncture have also been used to treat pain associated with repetitive stress injuries. As with all health issues, ask questions. If you feel your needs are not being met, go elsewhere.

Is there a cure or treatment for carpal tunnel syndrome?

Depending on the severity of the case, pain from carpal tunnel syndrome can sometimes be alleviated by a splint. A diuretic may be prescribed to eliminate fluid buildup in the area. Steroids may also be injected to reduce the inflammation. Sometimes surgery is necessary to free the pinched nerve by opening up the "tunnel."

15-5
_____

VDTS AND EMFS

No, it's not a "social" disease. VDT is an acronym for *Visual Display Terminal*, also called a computer monitor. EMF is an acronym for *Electromagnetic field* and there is currently a concern that EMFs emanating from VDTs create a risk to the user. Electromagnetic fields are all around us and have been linked to leukemia, brain tumors, breast and skin cancer, reproductive problems, and even mood disorders like depression. They are silent, invisible waves that weaken as they travel further from their source. In an effort to lessen our exposure to EMFs and VDTs, it is necessary to determine the sources of these electrical waves in the office.

Is it true that radiation from the monitor on my computer can give me cancer?

There is no question that computer terminals and monitors emit low-level electromagnetic fields. There is a dispute over whether these EMFs pose any risk. Until scientists can determine whether or not electromagnetic fields are dangerous, it would be wise to use common sense. Since EMFs weaken as they travel from their source, don't sit close to the monitor (just as you shouldn't sit close to the television). Try to put about an arm's length between you and your computer screen. If sitting away from your computer screen makes it difficult to read, there are software packages that will display larger characters. Monochrome monitors have lower emissions than color monitors.

♦ A number of companies are now marketing a low-emission CRT (cathode ray tube).

♦ You can switch to a laptop or notebook computer with a liquid crystal display. Liquid crystal display monitors emit less magnetic radiation than do standard CRTs (cathode ray tubes).

♦ When you are not using your computer or monitor, turn it off. Electrical fields are created anytime an appliance is plugged in but *magnetic* fields occur only when the appliance is running.

15-6
_____

MINIMIZING COMPUTER-RELATED EYE STRAIN

Can looking at a computer monitor all day ruin your eyes?

Computer-related eye problems can be experienced by anyone who has demanding visual needs. While computers do not generally cause eye problems, they can bring latent eye problems to the surface.

What are symptoms of eye problems?

Symptoms are eyes that feel itchy and dry. Blurred vision is also a common eye problem or squinting to make out a word or symbol. Frequently losing your place on the screen is another symptom of eye problems. Headaches are sometimes caused from poor vision or eye problems.

Eye problems can also cause a person to lean forward to read the screen better or sit too far back from screen, which can cause problems in the neck, shoulders, and back.

My eyes bother me a lot because I am constantly reading my computer screen. The fluorescent lights in our office also bother my eyes. Since I know the company is not about to change its lighting just for me, is there anything I can do?

Proper lighting is very important in any work area. Lighting should be indirect and even. Light should never be pointed directly at the document you are working on because of the resulting glare. You should also avoid looking directly at a light source. Make sure you are not facing a window or other light source.

The brightness of your monitor should be set at about the same level as the lighting around you. A tiltable monitor stand will allow you to position your monitor at a 90-degree angle to windows and other direct sources of light.

I wear sunglasses in the office to reduce the glare from my monitor. It seems to reduce eye strain. Are the sunglasses really beneficial or is it just a way to attract attention (as one of my coworkers recently stated)?

Sunglasses do prevent glare and so would reduce the amount of glare reflecting off your monitor. Actually, you are not the first person to wear your sunglasses while reading your monitor. There are also special tints available for eyeglasses that will help reduce glare. Discuss options with your optometrist or opthalmologist. She may even tell you to keep wearing your sunglasses.

One of the simplest and most effective ways to minimize glare is to use drapes or blinds to control the light coming in the windows. Antiglare screens are available for monitors. Check to make sure it does not darken your screen or cause the images to blur and make them even harder to read.

15-7

WHAT TO DO ABOUT SICK-BUILDING SYNDROME

I have been working for my company for about a year, and I love my job. We are in a high-rise building, and the windows are sealed shut. It seems everyone here is always sick with colds and flu. I have always been healthy but I have had the flu twice this year and at least three nasty colds. I believe we have a very high absenteeism rate. I think this building is making me and others sick. This is a good job and I don't want to upset my boss. What should I do?

Your building could have a ventilation problem. Ask someone in Human Resources to give you absenteeism data, especially the number of absences due to upper respiratory problems. Approach your boss in a nonconfrontational way. You could say, "Because of the number of absences due to upper respiratory problems, I believe we may have a ventilation problem. I've done some research and thought you might want to review it" and give the report to your boss. You should be able to reassure him that the cause in most cases is due to careless operation of ventilation systems and that the solution is not always costly.

I think management in our company knows that the ventilation in our building is inadequate but they won't give out any absenteeism information and refuse to admit we even have a problem. I'm tired of sneezing, wheezing, and feeling generally miserable. If management refuses to address the problem is there anything anyone else can do?

You can contact the National Institute of Occupational Safety and Health at 1-800-356-4674, but before you do, arm yourself with as much data as possible.

I spent two days in the copy room running copies for a huge project. On the second day I started getting a sore throat, began coughing and experiencing other sort of flulike symptoms. Do you think being closed in the copy room could have made me sick or was it really a case of the flu?

Copiers contain many different chemicals and give off fumes that can irritate the eyes, nose, and throat and cause coughing spells. Limit the time you spend in the copy area by taking frequent breaks. Copiers should be located in open, well-ventilated places away from workers.

Laser printers and fax machines have similar chemicals and should be used with the same precautions. Other toxic office supplies that should be used with care are permanent ink markers and correction fluid.

I believe I am allergic to the plants on my desk. A floral company puts a new plant on all our desks each month. Some don't bother me, but others cause sneezing and wheezing. Could my plant be making me sick?

Plants contain microorganisms that breed in the dirt. Watering causes these organisms to multiply, and they can become airborne when the heating and cooling fans come on. Misting and overwatering plants creates a growing ground for mold and mildew, which can trigger allergies. Pesticides that are not completely washed off plants can cause headaches and skin rashes. Ask the floral company to put your plant somewhere else.

The marketing department keeps stacking old newspapers in the back of the file room. I think they emit a "stale" odor and make me feel ill when I have to spend a lot of time retrieving files. My boss said I just don't like being cooped up in there. Do you think those old newspapers can be making me ill?

Stacks of newspapers can emit odors and also provide a breeding place for organisms. The problem can be worse if the newspapers are damp or stacked near an air register. The newspapers should be recycled or tossed regularly.

In our company we usually eat at our desks, and people routinely toss their wet garbage in the can under their desk. Is this a health risk? My boss and coworkers laugh at me, but I am genuinely concerned.

If the cans are emptied regularly, it should not be a problem. Trash cans are another breeding place for all kinds of organisms and are also an open invitation to roaches. It would be better if diners disposed of food in a separate container located away from their desks.

15-8

COPING WITH PMS AT WORK

Women are unique. They have special needs. Women in the work force face special problems that men do not. Every month many women ride an emotional roller-coaster that makes it difficult to cope even with simple stress. PMS can cause emotional distress as well as physical problems. PMS is more severe in some women than in others and, for them, it is important to learn when to expect it and what to do to lessen the discomfort so it does not interfere with their ability to do their jobs.

I think I have PMS, but I'm not sure. What are some of the emotional and physical symptoms?

The amount of discomfort women experience from PMS varies. The symptoms may be mild enough not to interfere with your job. However, some women with PMS find that it does interfere with their ability to function normally. Some of the emotional symptoms of PMS are:

- Irritability—overreacting to things, blowing things out of proportion
- Mood swings—feeling okay one minute and suddenly becoming irritable or hostile
- Depression—feeling miserable and unhappy for no apparent reason
- Hostility—feeling angry at everyone: your husband, your boss, your best friend, the checker at the grocery store, the woman in the restaurant
- Crying spells
- Difficulty sleeping
- Tension

  Some of the physical symptoms of PMS are:

- Breast tenderness or swelling
- Bloating
- Constipation
- Migraine headaches
- Dizziness or fainting, in some cases.

I get terrible cramps with my period. I can't work until they pass. Aspirin doesn't help relieve the pain. Is this from PMS?

Cramps are not a physical complaint of PMS; however many women do experience cramps when they get their period. If you suffer from severe uterine cramping it may not be a symptom of PMS but *dysmenorrhea*, a condition that may require special treatment. If you feel your cramps are more severe than you think they should be, contact your doctor.

I get very irritable with coworkers. I know I am being unreasonable, but I am just out of control. Is there anything I can do to relieve some of the irritability I experience?

Simple changes in your lifestyle can greatly reduce some of the symptoms of PMS. Don't smoke or drink alcohol. Nicotine and alcohol are mood-altering drugs that seem to encourage emotional swings. Cut out caffeine. Coffee, tea, cola, and chocolate should be avoided because they seem to increase both physical and emotional symptoms. Watch your salt intake. Salty snacks contribute to swelling and bloating. Exercise regularly to work off tension and control anxiety.

I can always tell when it's PMS time. I find myself eating candy bars and potato chips at my desk, even though I normally do not eat these items. We are not supposed to eat at our desks but I sneak candy bars. I just can't help it. I smeared chocolate on a document I had been working on for several days. Why do I have these cravings?

Many women crave sweets or other foods at this time. Since you are aware of these cravings, try not to give in to them. Drink lots of water. Substitute fruit for something sweet. Salt, in particular, contributes to swelling and bloating of the breasts and abdomen and should be avoided. Some doctors think the cravings are caused by a hormone imbalance.

One of my coworkers said exercise will help control cramps and PMS. Is this true?

Exercise is a great way to work off some tension and give you a general feeling of well being. You don't have to join an expensive health club—walking is one of the safest and simplest ways to exercise. Walking does not require special training or expensive equipment, just a comfortable pair of walking shoes. Walking tones the muscles of the legs, hips, and buttocks and builds up the muscles that support the arches of your feet. It is a weight-bearing exercise that increases bone density. Walking is a great stress reliever because of its rhythmic, repetitive motion.

I am really miserable once a month. It is starting to affect my job performance, and I think my boss believes I am faking it just to stay home. Is there a medication or pill that will "cure" PMS?

There is no magic pill available yet to "cure" PMS, but there are medications you can obtain over the counter or from your doctor to help curb the more severe symptoms. However, many of these medications have the potential for side effects and you need to discuss their use with your doctor to determine if the benefits outweigh the risks.

- ◆ Diuretics or "water pills" will reduce the swelling and bloating but overuse can rob your body of vitamins and minerals.

- ◆ Vitamin B6 may relieve some of the symptoms but it is important that your doctor select the right dosage for you.

- ◆ Anti-inflammatory drugs or analgesics (over-the-counter pain medications) are frequently recommended to control menstrual cramps and can also ease breast tenderness. Once again, it is a good idea to talk to your doctor about which ones are right for you. She may prescribe a stronger dosage than is available over the counter.

- ◆ Progesterone is a hormone sometimes prescribed for the more severe cases of PMS. It is usually given in the form of a vaginal or rectal suppository.

15-9

DEALING WITH MENOPAUSE

Menopause is that time in a woman's life when her menstrual cycle ceases, her body stops producing estrogen, and she is no longer able to have children. Instead of raging hormones, they have aging hormones. Some women dread menopause because they feel it means they are useless and old. However, some think of it as a new beginning, a time in life in which women experience greater freedom.

I take pride in my good health. I have not been absent from work due to illness for the last five years. I take vitamins and exercise. However, I am

approaching 50 and dread facing menopause. What can I do to prevent the problems associated with menopause?

Talk to your doctor, who may suggest you increase your calcium intake. Women should be taking 1,200 to 1,500 milligrams of calcium each day. Foods rich in calcium include dairy products, salmon, sardines and leafy green vegetables. Your doctor may recommend a calcium supplement.

- ◆ Vitamin D helps in the absorption of calcium. However, too much Vitamin D can produce side effects, so check with your doctor to be sure you get the appropriate dosage.

- ◆ Exercise, especially walking, will help keep your body fit. Brisk walking helps increase bone density. Before exercising remember to take the time to do some stretching and warm-up movements. Dress appropriately for the weather. As a guideline, you should exercise three times a week for at least 30 minutes.

- ◆ Estrogen therapy has been proven to minimize hot flashes, slow osteoporosis, and ease vaginal dryness. Your physician can prescribe estrogen treatment and discuss any possible side effects with you.

At what age do most women go through the "change"? I am having trouble sleeping and wake up frequently during the night. Sometimes I am too warm, other times I am cold. I just drag through the day and it is starting to affect my work. One of the other women in the office said I could be starting menopause, but I just turned 40.

The age can vary from 35 to 55, but menopause occurs in most women at about the age of 50. However, if you are having difficulty sleeping and it has begun to affect your work, see your doctor for a good physical.

A woman I work with is constantly complaining; she is either too hot or too cold. She calls the maintenance people to adjust the thermostat. Then the rest of us either get too hot or too cold. I think she must be starting to go through the "change" or menopause; she's beginning to drive us all crazy. Are there any other symptoms besides "hot flashes"? Should I tell her what I suspect?

The most common signals and symptoms of menopause are:

- ◆ Hot flashes. While harmless, they are uncomfortable and upsetting. A hot flash is a sudden "hot" feeling that spreads through your body, usually from the face to chest and lasts from 15 seconds to a few minutes. Many women complain they awake in the middle of the night, drenched in sweat.

♦ Vaginal dryness occurs because the vagina loses elasticity and the tissues become thin and dry. The result can be pain during intercourse.

♦ There may be some pain when urinating and you may have the feeling to urinate frequently (especially at night). Some women complain of feeling the need to urinate even when the bladder is empty.

♦ Osteoporosis is the result of calcium loss in the bones. Following the onset of menopause, a woman can lose up to 20 percent of her bone mass. Once lost, bone mass cannot be replaced, resulting in a condition known as "dowager's hump." Because the bones are so brittle, a fall can result in a broken bone. One theory is that estrogen helps absorb calcium into the bone.

Because of the danger of osteoporosis, you should tell your coworker what you suspect. However, you should do this as delicately as possible because this is probably not news that your coworker wants to hear. Free pamphlets are available at pharmacies and women's organizations. You could ask your coworker if she has read the latest medical information on menopause and leave her the pamphlet or article on the subject of menopause.

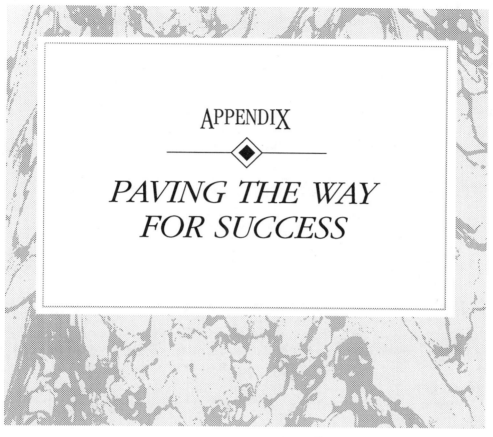

APPENDIX

◆

PAVING THE WAY FOR SUCCESS

Some good news from the U.S. Department of Labor—425,000 new secretarial positions will be added to the work force between 1986 and 2000. More good news! The January 26, 1993 "Odds and Ends" column reported a survey conducted by the Executive Resource Group. "The firm polled executive secretaries at 63 *Fortune* 500 companies and found that chief executives' secretaries had average pay of $53,600. Salaries for secretaries of the six other top officers were in the same range." Reprinted by permission of *The Wall Street Journal*, © 1993 Dow Jones & Company, Inc. All right reserved worldwide, *Wall Street Journal*. Competition is tough for those top jobs. Melba Duncan, president of a New York recruiting firm, said, "We're seeing competition from men for these jobs. She "has placed executive assistants in jobs paying as much as $75,000." (Christopher Conte, October 20, 1992, *Wall Street Journal*. Reprinted by permission of *The Wall Street Journal* © 1992 Dow Jones & Company, Inc. All right reserved worldwide.) While there is no sure path for success, there are some things you can do to increase your chances.

A-1

DEVELOP YOUR CORPORATE IMAGE

First impressions are important. People tend to make judgments based on what they see. The way you dress in the office determines how you will be perceived by management. Dress for the job you want, not for the job you have.

Your wardrobe should include:

- Classic suits and dresses. Avoid trendy styles that might look very chic for a year, but outdated in two.

- Mix-and-match separates, such as skirts, blouses, and blazers.

- Basic-colored pumps.

- Accessories such as scarves, belts, or jewelry.

Of course, if your office has casual day on Friday in the summer, join in and wear the team uniform. However, let common sense prevail. Remember that business is still being conducted and that outside guests may be present.

Along with the proper dress comes the winning attitude. Stay on the right path by:

- Coming in on time. Develop a reputation for being dependable.

- Producing error-free work.

- Paying attention to detail. Don't let little things become big problems.

- Cooperating with coworkers.

- Helping others when you are not busy. Be a team player.

- Projecting the confidence that you can get things done.

- Become a problem solver—not a problem maker. Problems are challenges or tests. As you pass the challenge or test, you will advance to the next recognition level.

- Reading everything that crosses your desk. Know the business you are in and what factors affect it.

- Developing mutual trust between you and your boss. If he believes in your skills as a top-notch administrative assistant, he'll let you take on projects or items that fall within your expertise.

- Making opportunities. Advancement is not an accident.

- Joining a professional organization. Don't underestimate the power of networking with all levels of people.

Keep up with the industry. Don't say, "When we get the new computer system in, I'll learn it." Take the initiative. If you wait, it may be too late. By then the company may have decided to hire somebody who *already* knows the new computer system.

When the typewriter was first introduced, there were many companies that manufactured them, such as Royal, Underwood, Olivetti, Smith-Corona, Remington. So what has happened? Manual typewriters were replaced with electric ones, which are being replaced with computers. And where are all those typewriter manufacturers? Well, there are only a few left, and secretaries who can use only typewriters have a hard time finding jobs.

Secretaries who break out of their traditional roles as support persons are able to move into management positions by taking the initiative. How do they do this?

- Jannell worked in purchasing. She always asked questions about the bidding process, how vendors were selected to bid, what makes for a good contract, etc. When the position of office equipment buyer opened up, she was a natural. Currently, Jannell is a key buyer for a government defense facility.

- Mary worked as a secretary in engineering, handling the payroll for that department. As the company grew, so did the payroll and her boss's responsibilities for maintaining it. He needed a trusted assistant to help him process the paperwork each month. Mary eagerly took on that assignment. As her boss was promoted, so was she. Today Mary is director of human resources.

- Ellen was secretary to the controller at a manufacturing facility. She was highly accurate and efficient. When a position opened up in accounting, she was given her chance. She spent several years keeping track of the inventory at the various distributors. Unfortunately, there was a downturn in this particular manufacturing environment and her position was eliminated. However, Ellen never was pushed out the door. Her secretarial skills again proved invaluable and she was kept on as senior secretary to the CFO. When things pick up for her company, Ellen knows she'll move up again.

- Laura started out as a secretary in the accounting department and soon graduated to accounting analyst. When the time came to look for another position, Laura realized that her accounting skills were highly specialized for the environment she was in and not easily transferrable. She reverted to her secretarial skills to ease the transition and landed a job as administrative support for a financial investor. A few years later, Laura applied for the job as administrative assistant/office manager for a small media firm. She was hired and is now second in command.

A-2

GETTING THE SKILLS AND QUALIFICATIONS YOU NEED TO MOVE UP

To get that better job, you need better skills. While there is no clear-cut path to the top, there are some things you can do to improve your chances for success.

- Utilize mentoring and networking techniques. Positive office politics can work for you.

- Anticipate job needs by looking to the future. Is your company becoming more automated? Look into courses on office technology. If the sales department has been expanding and you are interested in that field, ask if you can attend some of their sales meetings or conferences. Take the initiative in order to move forward.

- Your work effort is your resume. Is it something to be proud of? Is it something you would stand behind?

- Treat everyone equally. The manager of marketing now, may be a vice president in the future. You never know whom you will be working for, now or five years from now.

- Follow through and follow up. Don't let anything slip through the cracks.

Success requires hard work. Use your secretarial expertise to open the door to opportunity. Define your goals. Determine the type of career you want. See if your current qualifications match. Or ask people whom you trust for advice. Interview people who are already in the field you would like to pursue to see what qualifications are necessary.

Analyze any obstacles:

- Realistically weigh the career path and its potential for growth.

- Does it require travel? People sometimes want a specific job but forget to take into consideration that the position requires travel or that it may require you to work on weekends and/or holidays.

- Will the job require relocation? If so, are you able to move?

- What is the education or technical level of the job?

  Is a degree required?

  Are additional software classes needed?

- Do you need a license and/or certification?

  People in the real estate or insurance business usually need a license.

  Other positions require certification, such as a buyer or leasing agent.

- What are your resources?

  Do you have enough time to devote to the program?

  What will the classes cost? Don't forget to measure intangible cost, such as the loss of free time, as well as tangible cost—the dollars.

  Does your company have tuition reimbursement if you successfully complete the program?

- Are there any personal obstacles?

  Will your family give you the necessary support?

  Will your spouse help with the household chores?

Is there a person who can babysit while you attend classes?

Are you willing to give up your free time for studying and/or home-work?

Are you the main caregiver for an aging parent or disabled child? Is there anyone else who can help you?

Write a plan to achieve your goals. Identify the major steps necessary and how you will achieve them.

For instance, to become purchasing agent:

- Take purchasing courses at local college; first class: Buyers and Buying, Tuesday evenings

- Arrange for a babysitter on Tuesday nights

- Reduce leisure activities to accommodate study time needed

Benefits

- If I pass with an "A," company will reimburse.

- I will be considered for next open purchasing position if I successfully complete the first three courses in the purchasing program.

- Increased salary

- Knowledge that I can accomplish my goals

You indeed hold the key to your future. It's within your reach. Use your secretarial talents as a springboard to survival and success.

A-3
PREPARING YOURSELF FOR INTERNATIONAL BUSINESS

The U.S. economy is going global. Even if your company is not actively involved in international business now, there is a good chance it will be in the future. Position yourself to take advantage of the opportunities international business can bring.

- Learn a foreign language. Bilingual secretaries or translators are assets. Here's one skill that can put you ahead of the competition.

If your company already has a division in Quebec for example, French would be a plus. Try to choose a language that will be helpful to you or one in which you have a desire to learn. Look at the want ads. See what type of bilingual secretaries are in demand.

- Learn the culture and be sensitive to others' way of thinking and doing business. Research the libraries for information on how one is expected to dress or behave in a foreign country. Be knowledgeable on:

    what kind of food should be served and what should be avoided

    how to greet foreign guests

    how to avoid accidentally insulting foreign visitors

For those managers traveling overseas a lot, you will need to do some planning.

- Make sure your boss's passport is current.
- Determine whether a visa is needed as well.
- Check to see if any special shots or immunizations are required.
- List the address and phone number of the closest American consulate or embassy on her itinerary.
- Hotel information should include a map (frequently found in the hotel brochure), along with the telephone and fax numbers, including country and city codes.
- Make sure your boss knows the U.S. country code to make it easy for him to call the office.
- Make a list of cultural differences, local customs, dress code, and dining and   social etiquette.
- Specify any attire that would be considered inappropriate by local standards.
- Enclose a book of commonly used foreign phrases.
- Find out the exchange rate. Many travelers find it advantageous to buy traveler's checks in the foreign currency because the exchange rate is better.
- In the event your boss will be in a risky area where personal safety may be at stake, advise him of any precautions he should take. Designate a person to be contacted in case of trouble.

Since each foreign country is unique in its local customs, business etiquette, appropriate dress, and negotiating tips, you may want to refer to a book specifically written on this subject. You could also check out your library for additional information. The country's local embassy may be able to provide additional do's and don'ts.

Gift giving is an art, especially in foreign countries. Showing respect for the different cultural, religious, or philosophical needs is important if you want to be successful.

◆ Gift wrap, particularly in Asian countries, needs to be chosen with care. In China, for example, red paper is preferred because it symbolizes good luck and happiness.

◆ In some countries, the recipient may not open the gift in front of the giver as this is considered materialistic and greedy.

◆ Avoid expensive gifts. Useful items with the company logo such as pens, paperweights, name plaques, and pocket calculators are usually acceptable.

◆ Bilingual business cards are a business and social must.

◆ Many countries and religions impose dietary restrictions.

A-4

TIPS FOR PREPARING A FIRST-RATE RÉSUMÉ

Your résumé introduces you to prospective employers. Your résumé has to smile, shake hands, and inform:

◆ A good résumé should be one page and never more than two pages. The purpose of the résumé is to highlight your achievements and capabilities. Remember, companies can receive hundreds of résumés from an ad. If your résumé is too long, it may be tossed aside. Recruiters like to read the first few paragraphs to see if the person matches the job. Don't make recruiters hunt for the information they need.

◆ Prepare several versions of your résumé. For instance, if you are currently a legal secretary with a heavy legal background and you are looking for another legal position, your résumé should reflect this. If, however, you also think you could handle a job as an administrative assistant that you saw advertised, gear your résumé to that particular job, stressing your administrative skills.

♦ Résumés are a way of getting attention. While gimmicks don't always work, in a tough job market the person who is creative and aggressive will certainly be noticed.

♦ First, make sure your capabilities and experience meet the requirements for the job. If you don't have the skills and experience the company needs, nothing you can do will get your résumé, or you, noticed.

♦ Print your résumé on colored paper—light green or a gray-blue. It will be easy to spot on the recruiter's desk and will stand out from the others.

♦ One woman enclosed some playing cards (another, a lottery ticket) with her résumé and her cover letter asked, Why gamble when you can hire a proven performer?

♦ A legal secretary printed her résumé on legal paper using legal terminology (WHEREAS, I do hereby certify that I have the legal expertise to . . .) and she even notarized it.

♦ A medical secretary enclosed some candy pills and stated she had the right prescription to cure office ills.

♦ Once you have mailed your résumé, it is appropriate to call the company to inquire whether your résumé was received. This demonstrates good follow-up skills. Establish a personal contact with the person who is doing the hiring. Even if nothing is available at the moment, when a position does open up the recruiter may remember the person who called. If the recruiter is not available, leave a message with his secretary. She will see he gets the message and can become your ally. Don't keep calling and insisting on speaking directly with the recruiter. You want to demonstrate your interest in the position without becoming a pest.

We have prepared two sample résumés for your review. The first résumé is for a midlevel secretarial position. It is complete on one page. The second résumé is for an administrative assistant to a CEO. Even though this is a two-page résumé, note that all the pertinent information is contained on the first page. The second page shows actual office experience. Use the style that works best for you, or even a combination of styles.

Résumé—Minimal Experience

Maria Gonzales
252 W. Webster
Phoenix, AZ 85000
(303) 555-7003

I am seeking a position with a stimulating work environment where I can utilize my office skills while learning and growing professionally.

Office Experience:

- ◆ Word Perfect
- ◆ Lotus 1-2-3
- ◆ Wheelwriter 6 Printer
- ◆ Multiline telephone system
- ◆ Calculator
- ◆ Typing speed 60 wpm

Work Experience

Manufacturing Source, Inc.
200 W. Washington Ave.
Phoenix, AZ 85002

Secretary/Customer Service Representative   June 1993 to Present

Provide secretarial support for eight customer-service representatives. Answer phones and schedule meetings. Maintain department files. Type general correspondence and purchase orders. Purchase supplies for department. Prepare and monitor overnight mail packages.

Preschool Childcare Co.
9292 Greenville Road
Phoenix, AZ 86004

Secretary/Receptionist   January 1991 to June 1993

Typed correspondence, prepared mail and bulk mailings. Organized board luncheons and scheduled meetings with parents. Monitored budget and expenses. Posted receivables and disbursements.

Education

Graduated North High School
Completed college-level English and typing refresher course at Harper Junior College.

Hobbies

I enjoy biking, swimming, music, and reading.

Résumé—Extensive Experience

Nancy J. Gregory
817 Lorna Lane
Chicago, IL 60193
(312) 555-5000 (Office)
(312) 555-9070 (Home)

Experience

1987 to Present   Real Estate Development Co., 55 Commerce Lane, Chicago, IL 60606
Administrative Assistant to CEO

- Prepares correspondence for CEO's signature; prepares and/or edits speeches written by communications department.
- Supervises and coordinates secretarial staff, receptionist, and facilities personnel.
- Coordinates Board meetings, staff meetings, and outside business meetings to prevent scheduling conflicts.
- Arranges business travel, off-site meetings; makes scheduling decisions; prepares travel expense reports.
- Works independently with little supervision; frequently handles special projects.
- Prioritizes and monitors multiple tasks.
- Maintains confidential files and information.
- Handles telephone inquiries, screens calls.
- Establishes good rapport with customers and executives.
- Dresses in a professional manner; maintains a courteous, professional attitude.

Skills

Typing - 90 words per minute   IBM PC
Shorthand - 100 words per minute   Microsoft Word and Lotus 1-2-3

1983–1987   International Manufacturing Corp., 8700 W. Moore Dr.,Chicago, IL 60617
Senior Executive Secretary to CFO

- Prepared a travel policy for manufacturing divisions; monitored budgets, expense reports
- Planned meetings and business travel, domestic and international.
- Prepared correspondence, coordinated manufacturing reports as well as monthly Finance Department meetings.
- Handled confidential files and correspondence.

1977–1983   Construction Equipment Company, Chicago, IL 60676
Executive Secretary to Vice President, Finance

- Coordinated business travel, domestic and international

Résumé—Extensive Experience (continued)

Nancy J. Gregory   Page 2

- ◆ Responsible for approving all overseas travel for division.
- ◆ Maintained Finance Department budgets.
- ◆ Handled confidential correspondence.
- ◆ Prioritized workloads.
- ◆ Prepared spreadsheets on Lotus 1-2-3.

Professional Associations

Officer of Business and Professional Women's Club
Member of Executive Secretaries Association

Education

DePaul University–Bachelor of Arts
Moser Secretarial School–Executive Secretarial Degree

A-5

TRIED-AND-TRUE INTERVIEW TECHNIQUES

The personal interview gives you only one chance to make a good impression. Take advantage of the opportunity by persuading the interviewer that you are the best candidate for the position. It is not necessary to sit quietly and simply answer the questions asked. What if the interviewer is not very good and doesn't ask the right questions? After a few minutes if it appears the interviewer isn't going to ask relevant questions, volunteer the information. Tell the interviewer:

- What skills and experience you can bring to the job.

- What you have accomplished in your present position.

- How you established a good rapport with clients/customers.

Presentation is important during an interview. Be prepared to answer questions in a self-assured, confident manner.

- Dress appropriately for the interview.

- Be prepared with extra copies of your resume and letters of reference.

- Answer all questions truthfully.

A-6
HOW TO PREPARE FOR THE INTERVIEW

- Before the interview get together an "interview file," which should contain:

    Samples of your work or samples of specific projects you worked on

    Extra copies of your resume

    Letters of recommendation from former employers or letters of commendation for special achievements

- Gather all the information needed to fill out the employment application:

    Dates of previous employment

    Addresses and telephone numbers of former employers

    Personal references

    Social Security number

    Birth certificate

- Know where the office is and how long it will take you to get there. Leave one half hour earlier to allow extra time for any unforeseen occurrences. It is more acceptable to arrive early for an interview than late.

◆ Dress appropriately for the interview.

> Wear a nice suit or dress. A dark suit with a white blouse is still the best. Avoid brightly colored or floral dresses and clothes that are too short or too tight.

> Accessorize with care. Small button-type earrings are better than overly large or dangly ones.

> Don't carry an oversized stuffed purse. Use a briefcase for your files and information.

> Prepare the clothes you will wear the night before. There is nothing worse than discovering a spot on the suit or blouse you had planned to wear.

◆ Review any material you have obtained regarding the company, what services they perform or what product they manufacture. If nothing is readily available, go to the library and research the information:

> "I am familiar with ABC Corporation's products, I have shopped at your specialty stores many times and recently took advantage of your 'no fee' credit card offer."

> "I understand ABC Corporation was the first to introduce the new laser printer to the general public."

> "I saw an article in last Sunday's business section detailing your new division and expansion plans."

◆ Be enthusiastic. This does not mean to jump up and down like a cheerleader, but it does mean to let the interviewer know you are interested in the position.

> "I have always been interested in being a part of a large conglomerate, to understand how all the departments and divisions interact with one another."

> Know the qualifications for the position and be ready to discuss why you feel you are the best candidate to perform the functions they need.

> "I really enjoy finance (or marketing or communications) and know I could learn a lot working with you and your staff."

"I worked for a small company before and look forward to the opportunities available in such a large corporation" or "I worked for a large company before and look forward to working in a less bureaucratic atmosphere."

◆ Practice how to present your best qualities.

◆ Practice responses to possible questions.

◆ Get a good night's sleep.

A-7
SAMPLE INTERVIEW QUESTIONS AND ANSWERS

Since the interview will determine whether you will get the job and if you are worth the salary level at the beginning, middle, or the top of the range, be prepared to put your best foot forward. Practice your presentation, avoid nervous hand movement, and don't speak in a dull monotone. The following answers are merely suggested responses. Each person will have to determine the answer according to circumstances or job experience. Pencil in your own answers.

Why did you leave your last job? or *Why are you changing jobs?*
Be honest, but avoid criticizing your former employer. "The job was not challenging enough or did not offer enough responsibility." "A new assignment was needed in order to broaden my exposure as a corporate secretary." Or perhaps your position was eliminated due to "downsizing." Tell the interviewer that ABC Corporation eliminated several positions due to their financial crisis and, while you are sorry to leave such a fine company where you have been employed for several years, you are hoping to find a new and challenging opportunity.

Why do you want a position with our company?
"Because it offers the challenge I am seeking" or "because it is an area in which I have always been interested." A frequent error during interviews is to state that you want "more" than just a secretarial position. The interviewer then becomes afraid you will become bored with the position and

will either quit or ask to be transferred if another position opens up. Interview for the job that's available.

Why did you choose a career as a secretary?

Some possible answers would be, "secretarial work is what I have been trained to do, it is what I do best and what I enjoy most." "Secretarial work offers a variety of duties and challenges; the opportunity of working with a large group of people; the ability to work independently."

What are your greatest strengths?

Each of us have different strengths we bring to a job. Because secretarial work is so varied, the type of strengths needed for each job can be quite different. Perhaps a person with strong communications skills will be needed for one job while a person who has advanced figure aptitude will be needed for another. Assess your strengths. Some sample strengths employers often look for:

- enjoys working with people

- figure-oriented

- can handle pressure

- assertive

- able to work independently

- excellent communicator

- great organizer

- cares about the job

What are your weaknesses?

Employers know that most people have some weaknesses. Nobody is perfect. Employers look for the person who can recognize a weakness and take steps to remedy it. Stay away from personal weaknesses, try to focus on a business-related weakness that can be helped or improved. Sample responses:

- "I feel I am weak in the area of preparing spreadsheets and would like to take a computer class to improve my ability and efficiency."

- "I have such a large volume of work that I sometimes worry that I won't be able to keep up with all the phone calls and correspondence, and something important will be missed. I sometimes come in early for some 'quiet' time so I can catch up."

- "I put filing and ironing in the same category. I hate them both but manage to get them done."

What subjects did you like best in school? Least?

Did you like English and hate math or vice versa? Please don't say recess and lunch—they've been overworked. If you say you liked history or chemistry, be prepared to say why you liked them:

- "History gives one a basis for making decisions. When you are able to study what happened in the past, it helps you decide what might work best in the present."

- "Chemistry gave me analytical strengths and the ability to formulate answers based on scientific study."

- "English and literature opened up a world of ideas and thoughts and gave me the ability to express my own ideas and thoughts."

What are your goals? What do you expect to be doing in five years?

Well, what are your goals? Where would you like to see yourself in five years? Would you like to attend evening classes to further your education? Have you always wanted to work in sales? If you haven't formulated any goals, now is a good time to think about your future. Goals should be realistic with a plan for achieving them within a particular time frame.

What accomplishments have given you the greatest satisfaction?

Always assume the interviewer is discussing work-related achievements, not personal. Many women will respond with "the birth of my child," and while that may be your greatest personal achievement, it is not a professional accomplishment.

- Prepared a marketing presentation with little or no assistance.

- Coordinated a large out-of-town meeting for 150 attendees.

- Initiated a new process for handling invoices.

◆ Prepared a procedures manual for the field offices.

What can you contribute to our company?
"As an experienced secretary, I can save you time. An executive's most important commodity is time and with my skills and experience I can prioritize your mail, answer correspondence, screen your calls, coordinate meetings and schedules, and streamline routine tasks."
"Other contributions I can make to your company:

◆ I am honest and trustworthy,

◆ I have a good track record for getting the job done,

◆ I am enthusiastic and have a high energy level,

◆ I look forward to new challenges and the chance to learn and grow."

How do you think your bosses would describe you?
"I know exactly how they would describe me from my performance reviews. They would say my performance is very good to excellent in all areas and that I am particularly good at organizing and communicating. They also like my enthusiasm and the ability to meet deadlines."

What are your hobbies? What do you like to do for relaxation?
Don't list everything you have ever tried. Two, or maybe three interests are usually sufficient as most companies feel that a well-rounded person will have some outside interests. "Needlepoint, swimming, and golf." Try to have a mix of interests—not all active, but not all passive, either.

What are your salary requirements?
"I want to make a job change so that I can move up, so I don't want to make less than I do now. The position you have described sounds challenging, and I would appreciate the chance to discuss the salary when you make a firm job offer."

Do you have any questions about the position or the company?
◆ Ask questions about the company, its history or background. Where the company is headed—new products? New ideas?

- Ask about the people/department with whom you would be working. Is this a newly established department? Do the people work independently on projects or is it more of a team effort?

- Ask about your specific responsibilities and whether a position description is available. (If not, make a mental note to write one if accepted for the position.)

A-8

WHAT TO DO AFTER THE INTERVIEW

There are two important things you can do *after* the interview.

1. First, thank the person who took the time to interview you.

2. Second, *write* a thank-you note.

      It should be handwritten on personal stationery.

      If you can include something personal or something you discussed in the interview, please do:

          "I hope your daughter's dance recital was a success."

          "I hope the Human Resources department wins the softball trophy."

          "I saw the walk-a-thon on television and looked for the Wonderful Enterprises T-shirts. You must all be very proud of the (money raised, what you accomplished, etc.)."

If it comes down to you and another individual with basically the same skills and education, the "thank you for taking the time to see me" could be the tie breaker. Use this "thank you" note as a tool to sell yourself, express again why you think you are the best candidate for the job. It's always nice if you can mention something that happened during the interview, like, "I was impressed when you told me you were the largest real estate developer in our area."

Sample Thank You Letter

Dear Ms Jones:

I certainly enjoyed meeting with you yesterday to discuss the opportunity Wonderful Enterprises currently has available.

I feel my skills and experience qualify me for this position and look forward to hearing from you soon.

Thank you for your consideration.

Sincerely,

A-9

DO'S AND DON'TS OF INTERVIEWS

Do's

Do be prompt.

Do show interest and enthusiasm.

Do look the interviewer in the eye.

Do dress appropriately for an interview.

Do be prepared to take a typing and/or steno test. Some offices require aptitude or proofreading tests as well.

Do be prepared to take a drug test (more and more companies are requiring drug tests prior to employment).

Do ask questions:

about the company

about your specific responsibilities

about the people/department with whom you'll be working

Do respond to all questions, but don't tell the interviewer more than he or she needs to know.

Do send a "thank you" note.

Don'ts

Don't be late.

Don't gaze out the window or let your attention wander.

Don't chew gum.

Don't criticize your former employer.

<hr>

A-10

WHAT EMPLOYERS AND RECRUITERS LOOK FOR IN A CANDIDATE

It is the recruiter's job to find the best person for the job. The recruiter must run the ad to attract appropriate candidates, then review them to see whether they would be a good "fit" in the organization. It is up to the recruiter to verify the information contained in your resume. Finally, after screening, the recruiter will recommend three or four candidates to interview with the person they would be working with. Some top secretarial recruiters shared some of the items they look for in a resume and the candidate:

What Bosses and Recruiters Like and Dislike

- "First of all, I make sure their skills match the job requirements. So many people think they have skills they simply don't possess. Our executive secretarial positions require a typing speed of 70 to 75 words per minute. After testing, I find they type 50 to 55 words per minute. I tell them to take a keyboarding class to get their skill level up. I can't consider them until they meet the requirements."

- "If I get a resume that contains typos, I simply toss it. Errors reflect poor typing ability as well as a lack of proofreading skills."

- "Poorly written cover letters turn me off when one of the candidate's main responsibilities is to compose correspondence."

- "A candidate who uses slang. If a secretarial candidate cannot speak correct English or mispronounces words during an interview, I probably won't consider that candidate. On the other hand, if the person has an accent from another country but has a good command of English, I won't disqualify that candidate."

♦ "I like a candidate who has some goals, who is not just coasting through life but has a definite game plan."

♦ "I look for a candidate who seems motivated and has a desire to learn."

♦ "I am influenced by many things during the interview, how the person is dressed, the way the person expresses herself or himself, and I try to visualize that person in the job."

♦ "I like the candidate to look at me when he or she talks (instead of gazing out the window or looking at a spot behind me on the wall)."

♦ "Most people are a little nervous during an interview, so you have to get beyond that. One person I interviewed had a habit of twisting her neck after answering a question, but once I got beyond that, I found she was a perfect candidate (and once she got over her nervousness, she was fine)."

♦ "By the time you have a final interview, we have determined you are qualified for the position. I need to ascertain a final degree of comfort —mine. Will you work well with the team already in place? Are you open to new ideas?"

♦ "My job as a recruiter is at stake every time I recommend someone, so I want to make sure that person can do the job and work well within the organization."

♦ "By the time a candidate gets to me, it means he or she has already proven to have the skills and experience necessary to do the job. Basically, I try to determine which candidate would work best with my people, what kind of personality does the candidate have?"

♦ "I try to determine if the person is reliable—will he or she be here every day? Can I depend on the person to handle things in my absence?"

♦ "I look for someone with a good phone personality. We get a lot of phone calls, and I want someone who can talk to customers."

♦ "I want someone who really wants the job, someone who will enjoy the job."

◆ "I want a team player. Everybody in my department is important and each one has his or her own field of expertise. I like for my department to work together, sharing their knowledge and helping each other."

What Bosses and Recruiters Hate:

◆ "Candidates who don't seem to know the simplest etiquette; for instance, when I extend my hand for a handshake in greeting and they don't know what to do or give a limp or half-hearted handshake."

◆ "When a candidate comes in for an interview in tight-fitting clothes or miniskirts."

◆ "When people are told a particular job requires overtime but then balk when asked to come in on a Saturday."

◆ "Breach of confidentiality. I need to know I can trust my secretary."

◆ "When candidates say they know a particular software program (thinking they can bluff their way until they learn it), and then we end up having to send them to school to learn it."

◆ "Secretaries who spend too much time on the phone with personal calls."

◆ "Secretaries who call in sick on Mondays because they have been partying all weekend."

◆ "The secretary who shows up for work in miniskirts or casual clothes."

◆ "A person who makes a mistake, then tries to cover it up instead of saying, 'Sorry, look what I've done, what can I do to make it right?'"

◆ "Sloppy phone messages with incomplete information."

◆ "Misspelled names."

◆ "A secretary who is always scrambling around trying to find a file or letter."

◆ "After a secretary is here a while, she (or he) begins to let things slide, expense reports are late, correspondence is not answered as promptly as it once was, things like that. I don't want to have to continually remind my secretary to do something or find out in a meeting that something I assumed was being handled was not."

EVALUATE THE JOB OFFER

Is it better to work for a small company or a large one? That depends on you. Some people function well in a large, impersonal environment, while others prefer the family atmosphere in a small company.

- Large corporations offer more opportunities for advancement. However, your capabilities may be more readily noticed in a small company.

- In a large company, you may not meet many of the top executives. In a small company, you may work directly with the owner.

- Small companies may seem more like a family. In a large corporation, while you may not have a one-on-one relationship with top executives, a close-knit department in which you work can also become family.

- Large companies often have a mail person to pick up and deliver your mail. Office supplies are centrally ordered. Small companies offer you more hands-on experiences. You may run the postal meter yourself and deal directly with office-supply stores.

- In small companies, family members may be promoted over you. In large companies, several people may be applying for the same open position.

- Large companies usually have better benefits packages, such as health insurance, tuition reimbursement, vacation and sick-leave policy. However, small companies may be more lenient and understanding if you need personal time off or need flexible hours.

- In both work environments, you may meet a variety of people and can expand your personal and professional relationships.

Whether you decide to take the position with a large or a small company, do your best and learn as much as you can. Both offer opportunities, and it is up to you to define those opportunities.

How to Choose Between Two Jobs
In large corporations you may interview in several departments simultaneously or you may have interviewed at different companies and receive an offer from each. If you receive two job offers ask yourself these questions to help you choose the right opportunity for you.

- Did you feel more comfortable in one company or department than in the other?

- Did one opportunity seem to offer more challenge or be more interesting to you?

- Were the offices and equipment comparable, or did one seem more technologically advanced?

- Where would you learn the most? Which one would make you stretch a little?

- How do the two positions stack up on an organization chart? Are the positions of equal importance or is one at a higher level than the other?

- Compare the benefits. Benefits may be the determining factor.

A-12

HOW TO PLAN YOUR FIRST DAY, YOUR FIRST WEEK, YOUR FIRST MONTH

You got the job! What you do now can and will affect your future advancement.

First Day

- Normally, someone (your boss or designated coworker) will offer to take you to lunch on the first day, but not always. You could be starting at a busy time. It would be a good idea to make a light lunch, preferably something that would keep. If your boss asks you to lunch, accept the invitation and save your prepared lunch for the next day. If a coworker asks you to lunch, tell her you brought your lunch and ask if she would like to join you.

- First days vary from company to company. The first day you are usually introduced to coworkers, given a tour of the offices, shown where the copier and fax machines are and where other office equipment is located.

- Take inventory of your desk. Make sure you have the items necessary to do your job. Some of the basics needed are a stapler and staples, staple remover, paper clips, pens and pencils, telephone message pad, tape dispenser and tape, and scissors. A Rolodex® is helpful. Check your stationery supplies to make sure you have the appropriate letterhead. Order any supplies you need.

The First Week

♦ Familiarize yourself with the company and its product or the type of services it offers. Nothing impresses the boss more than an employee being knowledgeable about the company.

♦ Get an organization chart and study it so you will understand who reports to whom and exactly what the corporate chain of command is.

♦ Learn where the conference rooms are located, who reserves them, and how many can be seated comfortably.

♦ Make a list of phone numbers of the individuals who can answer your questions, such as who troubleshoots computer problems, who handles replacement light bulbs, etc.

♦ Find out how entry or exit from the building is handled before or after normal working hours. Are building passes needed and for what items?

♦ Inventory your files so you will know how to locate items. Also read the files to get a feel for the way your boss handles business matters, to familiarize yourself with key words and phrases he uses.

♦ Familiarize yourself with names of people on the Rolodex®. If the carbon copy style of telephone message pads is used, read the old ones. You can learn who the callers are and what requests were made.

♦ Is a company newsletter available? If so, skim as many issues as you can. This will give you insight into the philosophy of the company, what direction it's taking, what it values in its employees—such as supporting company sporting groups or a summer outing—what type of awards are given to employees and what they are for.

♦ Familiarize yourself with your hardware (computer and printer) and the software (programs) that are available. Take inventory of documents already stored on your system. Remember you may have to edit a report created by your predecessor. Your boss will expect you to find the document and handle corrections quickly. Locate the manual for your word processing software.

- If the hard drive is used to store documents, create your own directory. That way you'll know any documents you keyed in are stored in your directory. If diskettes are used, start a brand-new one for your files. Remember that directories or diskettes are like file drawers. Use as many as you need to keep your computer files in order. Use a C, D, or E hard drive? These are like file cabinets. Always make sure documents on the hard drive are stored in the right file cabinet and the right file drawer.

The First Month

By now you should have a pretty good feel for what is going on, who is who, and where to find what. You can begin to make changes.

- Update the Rolodex®. Consider utilizing subject classifications for telephone numbers. Under *office supplies* list the number of the individual to call to place an order or under *repairs* the name of the individual who handles replacing burnt-out bulbs.

- Do you think a different filing system would be more efficient? Present your suggestion to your boss.

- If you haven't already done so, begin answering some of your boss's correspondence. Even if she makes changes, you will only have to edit the letter or memo and you will learn how she responds to certain correspondence or situations.

- Do you think you have a more efficient way of sorting the mail, ordering supplies, paying invoices? Let your new boss know.

- Take the initiative. Introduce yourself to people in other departments. Get to know who your coworkers are and what they do.

- Make yourself visible. Sign *your* name to notes and memos to others. Do not refer to yourself as Ms. West's secretary, say "I'm Eileen Murray in Finance."

- When people call and ask for assistance, identify yourself by giving your full name and say you will check it out or find the answer for them. If you refer someone to another department or person, say

"Please call me, Eileen Murray, if Accounting is unable to handle your problem or answer your question."

A-13
_____

A PROFESSIONAL DESIGNATION ENHANCES YOUR PROSPECTS

The CPS® designation sets professional standards for secretaries and measures secretarial proficiency. Certified Professional Secretary® is the registered service mark for the rating.

In order to get the CPS® designation you must first verify educational and secretarial employment experience requirements, then pass a six-part, two-day examination administered biannually in May and November by the Institute for Certifying Secretaries, a department of Professional Secretaries International.

The CPS® examination requires proficiency in six categories:

1. *Behavioral Science in Business.* Basically, this is the study of human relations and organizational techniques utilized in the work place. It focuses on motivation, solving, conflicts, and problem-solving techniques. The essentials of supervision, communication, and leadership styles are also studied.

2. *Business Law.* The secretary needs a basic knowledge of business law as well as the effect of governmental controls on business. How governmental controls and laws developed is emphasized over memorizing names and dates.

3. *Economics and Management.* Emphasis is placed on understanding the basic concepts of business operations. Economic and management principles and how they are affected by governmental regulations are studied.

4. *Accounting.* Study of the principles associated with accounting and finance operations. The ability to analyze financial statements and perform mathematics computations as well as the ability to summarize and interpret financial data.

5. *Secretarial Skill and Decision Making.* Office communication and administration unique to the secretarial position measures proficiency in office and records management. There is 50 percent office administration and 50 percent written business communication, editing, abstracting, and preparing communications in the final format.

6. *Office Technology.* Data processing, advanced communication applications, and records management created by technological advancements in computers and software systems are studied.

Qualifications for taking the CPS® examination include a combination of education and verified secretarial work experience. Full-time employed secretaries, experienced secretaries, college/university students, and business educators are eligible to take the CPS® examination. Membership in Professional Secretaries International® is required while the candidate is pursuing certification.

Many colleges and universities grant credit hours for the CPS® rating to those enrolled in degree programs. While credit hours may vary, the American Council on Education recommends 32 semester hours of academic credit. A directory of institutions granting credit for the CPS® rating is available from Professional Secretaries International.®

The examination is given the first Friday and Saturday in May and the first Thursday and Friday in November. Examination centers are located throughout the United States, Canada, Puerto Rico, and the Virgin Islands. To take CPS® courses, contact the local educational facility in your area. Generally, the courses are offered in junior colleges—many of which also offer an associates degree in Secretarial Sciences.

A-14
JOINING A PROFESSIONAL ORGANIZATION

Professional organizations keep you informed of the latest developments affecting secretaries and women in the work force. Listed here are some of the organizations you might wish to consider joining, depending on which industry you are in. Contact them directly for more information. The largest of these organizations is Professional Secretaries International® with over 44,000 members.

American Association of Medical Assistants (AAMA)
20 N. Wacker Drive, Suite 1575
Chicago, IL 60606
(312) 899-1500
Approximate membership 13,000
Publishes *Professional Medical Assistant* bimonthly

National Association of Executive Secretaries (NAES)
900 S. Washington Street, No. G-13
Falls Church, VA 22046
(703) 237-8616
Approximate membership 2,500
Publishes *Exec-U-Tary* monthly

National Association of Legal Secretaries (International) (NALS)
2250 E. 73rd Street, Suite 550
Tulsa, OK 74136
(918) 493-3540
Approximate membership 17,000
Publishes *Docket* bimonthly

National Association of Secretarial Services (NASS)
3637 4th Street, N., Suite 330
St. Petersburg, FL 33704-1336
(813) 823-3646
Approximate membership 1,800
Publishes *NASS Newsletter* monthly

National Association of Rehabilitation Secretaries (NARS)
c/o National Rehabilitation Association
1910 Association Drive, Suite 205
Reston, VA 22091
(703) 715-9090
Approximate membership 1,349
Publishes *Newsletter* quarterly

9 to 5, National Association of Working Women
614 Superior Avenue, NW., Room 852
Cleveland, OH 44113
(216) 566-9308
Approximate membership 13,000
Publishes: *9 to 5 Newsletter,* 5/year

Professional Secretaries International (PSI)®
10502 NW Ambassador Drive
PO Box 20404
Kansas City, MO 64195-0404
(816) 891-6600
Approximate membership 44,000
Publishes *The Secretary Magazine* 9/year

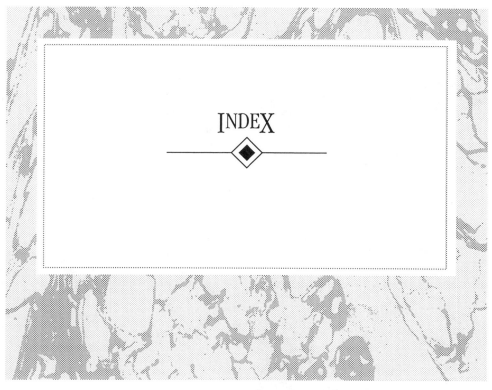

INDEX

A

Accept/except, 189
Adjectives, 179
Adverbs, 179
    conjunctive, 180
Affect/effect, 186
Age discrimination, 232-33
Age Discrimination in Employment
    Act (ADEA), 232, 234
Alcohol abuse, 54-55
All right/alright, 187
American Association of Retired
    Persons (AARP), 233
Americans with Disabilities Act (ADA),
    55, 234-35
Among/between, 187

Anonymous letters to management,
    228
Apology memo, 51-52
Apostrophe mark, 184
Applicants, screening, 212-14
Appointment calendar, 123
Approval requests, 21
Assessment, job, 218-19
Authority, communicating, 33-36

B

Bar-coded labels, 141
Bar coding, 144, 148
Behavior change, boss, 13-14
Binder labels, 147
Binders, 140

Stress, 271-77
  causes of, 272
  defined, 272
  relieving, 8-9, 275-76
    foods for, 276-77
  symptoms of, 272-73
Strikeout/redlining, 143-44, 160
Supervisory problems, solving,
  216-18
Symbols:
  foreign currency, 202-3
  proofreading, 163
  registered trademarks, 224

T

Takeovers, coping with, 102-6
Telephone communication, 26-32
  bugged telephone, 63
  coworker answers your phone, 31
  interrupting the boss for a call,
    30-31
  log, 26
  problem callers, 27-30
  voice mail problems, minimizing,
    31-32
Temper, boss, coping with, 96
Temporary workers:
  asking for, 148-49
  hiring, 214-15
3.5" diskettes, write-protect tab, 174
Three-folder system, 108
Three-hole punch, 140, 141
Three-hole punch paper, 141
Three-ring binders, 110-11
Tickler files, 12-13

letter marked for, 13
"Ticklish" situations, managing,
  53-54
Time management, 142-44
  in boss's absence, 150-51
To-do list, 121, 145, 146
Trademarks, 224-26
Transmittal reminder, 176
Travel, 133-37
  hotel reservations, confirming,
    135
  itineraries, 133-34
  mail, organizing for boss, 136-37
  meeting material, sending ahead,
    135-36
  organizing boss's paperwork for,
    133
  preparation for, 137-38
  Saturday-night stays, 135
  ticket errors, 135
  travel agency, use of, 133
Two-tiered mailbox, 25, 199

U

Uncooperative coworkers, dealing
  with, 208-9
Undeleting computer files, 171-72,
  174
"Under the gun" stress, relieving, 8-9
Unexpected personal crisis, 268-69
Unwanted guests, removing from
  boss's office, 249
Upper management, presenting an
  idea to, 23-24